Healthy
Indulgences

HEALTHY

INDULGENCES

Enjoy the Good Life
and Good Food with the
Low-Cholesterol Gourmet

Lynn Fischer

Hearst Books / New York

It is the policy of William Morrow and Company, Inc., and its imprints and affiliates, recognizing the importance of preserving what has been written, to print the books we publish on acid-free paper, and we exert our best efforts to that end.

Library of Congress Cataloging-in-Publication Data

Fischer, Lynn.
   Healthy indulgences / Lynn Fischer.
     p.   cm.
   Includes index.
   ISBN 0-688-13119-0
   1. Low-fat diet—Recipes.   I. Title.
RM237.7.F55   1995
641.5'638—dc20   94-31393
                                       CIP

Printed in the United States of America

First Edition

1 2 3 4 5 6 7 8 9 10

PRODUCED BY K&N BOOKWORKS

BOOK DESIGN BY RICHARD ORIOLO

To Virginia Von Fremd,
Manuel Trujillo, and Nina Miller,
who made major differences
in my life.

Acknowledgments

Much of the inspiration for my recipes and cookbooks comes from the fan letters I receive each week. Along with recipe requests, many are sweet handwritten notes from happy television viewers or readers of my cookbooks who tell me I have helped them improve their health, lose weight, lower their cholesterol, and remain enthusiastic about their successes. In addition, there are many people who helped me.

My personal aide is Andrea Goodman. We sit in a small office, side by side, every day, and no one could be easier to be with or more efficient. Unfortunately, I just promoted her to associate producer of the television show, *Lynn Fischer's Healthy Indulgences*. Another big thank-you for the depth and breadth of this book goes to Rita Calvert, of Calvert Street Gourmet Specialty Food Products, who began working with me a few years ago as our first television show's food stylist and art director. When you do five thirty-minute television shows a day you need someone with Rita's ability, taste, talent, stamina, and teamwork. We had a happy set and Rita, Leela Berman and Mark White, the director, contributed greatly to that.

Rita was the director of three weeks of marathon testing for the recipes in this book. To make certain the recipes were clear, I hired neophyte cooks who prepared every recipe, some many times. My testers were Joe Klein (model), Barbara Samaris (actress), Marty Kaplan (photographer), Alicia Billings (television director and cameraperson), Rhonda Robinett (owner of a discount bridal service), Catherine Clark (editor and caterer), Carol Alley (flight attendant), Susan O'Keefe (researcher), Chris Hall (student), Candice Powell (food buyer and marketing analyst), and Abigail

Gullo (student and actress who began as a show intern and graduated to working part time).

My Discovery Channel television series partner and executive producer was Arna Vodenos. She and I completed some two hundred half-hour *Low-Cholesterol Gourmet* shows, and I thank her. Arna is also producing my new show, *Lynn Fischer's Healthy Indulgences,* offered to public broadcasting by Maryland Public Television with MPT Producer John Potthast and Assistant Producer Melissa Martin. I thank Chuck Gingold, at The Discovery Channel, who aired our original shows that broke ground in low-cholesterol low-fat network television cooking programs.

Family is very important to me, I'd like to thank my brothers and sisters and their families, including my sister Ann and her husband, Bill; my brother Tom, his wife, Mary, and their two sons, Matt and Scot; brother Bob; and my brother Jim, wife, Trudy, and his kids, Annie and Jimmie. I thank my athletic dad, who still roller-blades with me at age eighty-eight (say "Hi Addie" if you see him blading or sitting on the dock at sunset in old Naples, Florida), and my late mother, Mary Connor, who was a world-ranked athlete winning the U.S. Open in badminton. I thank my niece Susie Fischer McGarry and her husband, Mark and their baby, Patrick. I especially thank my two grown kids, creative and beloved daughter, Lisa Bialac Jehle, and her son, Wolf, whom I miss, and my musically gifted, thoughtful son, Cary Warren Bialac.

I am very fortunate to have special friends who keep me enthusiastic about my work. They are Kathy Mclean, Lillian Smith, Dan Forth, Frank Smith, Ed Felshow, Susie Wydler, Terri and Bob McKenzie, Beth Mendelson, Linda Ringe, Bob Franken, Andrea and Marty Kalin, Pat Mahoney, Andrea Fleischer, and Joy Roller. I especially thank my attorney, literary agent, and friend Gail Ross, who has kept me headed in the right direction for eight years now.

I thank the Borden company for testing a dozen low-fat recipes for the book. (I take no payment from any brand or company mentioned in this book, including Borden.) I do have a free catalog with several hard-to-find fat-lowering items, which you can get by calling 1-800-8-FLAVOR.

And I thank Chris Loudon, a consummate professional and registered dietitian, who did the nutritional analyses, which was no small feat.

Contents

Introduction

The only thing more challenging than making low-fat dishes that taste good is convincing skeptics that low-fat food tastes good. The recipes in this book are low in fat, easy to prepare, and delicious. Your family and guests will enjoy the tremendous variety of foods and will leave the table with energy to burn rather than the all-too-familiar lethargic feeling that comes after a heavy meal.

The American Heart Association, one of many groups concerned with the health of our citizens, has come out with guidelines suggesting that we consume less than 30 percent of our total calories from fat. Americans typically eat 38 percent of their calories in fat each day. The recipes in *Healthy Indulgences* are nearly all far less than 30 percent of calories from fat.

If you're one of the many people who would like to learn how to change your eating habits but are baffled as to how to go about it, then *Healthy Indulgences* is for you. If you've already made the switch to a healthier way of eating but are looking for exciting new recipes, *Healthy Indulgences* is for you as well.

For those of you who are just starting to change your diet, it is important to keep in mind that altering your lifestyle from eating a whopping 38 percent (or more) of daily calories in fat to 25 percent a day does not happen overnight. It is usually a slow process of making small changes over a period of time. You will eliminate a substantial amount of fat from your diet just by replacing high-fat ingredients with low-fat substitutes when cooking. You can actually increase the volume of food you can eat *and* the variety.

Healthy Indulgences includes low-fat versions of macaroni and cheese, meatloaf with gravy, lasagna, fettuccine Alfredo, spaghetti with meatballs, Indonesian chicken, German potato salad, and huevos rancheros.

All the recipes in this book were tested and tasted several times by average cooks, many of whom weren't familiar with low-fat cooking. With two assistants and eleven testers, I tested and retested the recipes until they were user-friendly and delicious. Changing your diet is hard enough without having to wade through complicated multistep recipes. If we couldn't make a recipe simple to prepare and good to eat, then you won't find it here.

▪▪ Ingredients ▪▪

Although trips to ethnic food stores and gourmet specialty shops are adventures I enjoy, I realize that not everyone does. With that in mind, almost all of the ingredients used can be found in supermarkets.

Some low-fat and nonfat ingredients may not be available in certain areas, so I have suggested substitutions whenever possible. The best way to get your grocery store to stock a product is to ask the store manager to stock it. Then it's up to you to buy it regularly, so the store continues to carry it. Some seasonal fruits, vegetables, and herbs may not be available at all times. Here, too, I've given options.

▪▪ Fats and Oils ▪▪

All animal fats, such as lard, chicken fat, and butter, are very high in saturated fats. Butter has slightly less total fat and fewer calories than margarine, but butter does have 100 percent more saturated fat, tablespoon for tablespoon, than margarine. So I most often use liquid or diet margarine, which usually contains less fat and saturated fat than even regular margarine. When buying margarine, read the label carefully to avoid any that contain tallow (beef fat), coconut oil, and/or lard, which are sky-high in saturated fat.

All oil is 100 percent pure fat and all oils, whether canola, olive, lard, or coconut, have the same calorie content. What separates one oil from another (besides taste and flavor) is the amount of saturated fat, monounsaturated fat, and polyunsaturated fat in each. Since saturated fat is the culprit fat and most affects the level of cholesterol in the body (more than any other fat), I cook with oils that are lowest in saturated fat.

Canola oil, sometimes called rapeseed oil, is my first choice for cooking. (Safflower runs a close second.) Canola has approximately 4 grams of saturated fat in ¼ cup, or 1 gram per tablespoon. On the other hand, ¼ cup of coconut oil contains 47 grams of saturated fat. Although they both have the same total fat and calorie content, the difference in the amount of saturated fat is remarkable, and saturated fat is what to look out for. Peanut oil has 9 grams of saturated fat for ¼ cup.

Safflower, sunflower, walnut, and olive are the other oils I use. They are also lower in saturated fat, between 5 and 7 grams per ¼ cup. Aromatic, intensely flavored olive oil is a bit higher in saturated fat than is canola, but I feel it's worth it if used sparingly. It is the same as corn oil in saturated fat.

With the current food labeling laws, all foods must, among other things, indicate their saturated fat content. If you are in doubt about the saturated fat content of the oil you are buying, read the label. If it contains 2 grams or fewer of saturated fat per tablespoon, then feel free to use it in small quantities. But fat is fat.

Vegetable oil spray or olive oil spray appears frequently in my ingredients lists. Spraying oil instead of pouring it into a pan is one of my favorite low-fat cooking techniques as it dramatically reduces the amount of oil used. These cooking sprays are available in five different varieties— canola oil, vegetable oil, olive oil (which is made by several companies now, including olive oil importers), butter-flavored vegetable oil, and oil with flour (Baker's Joy), which is used for preparing baking pans instead of the traditional greasing with butter and dusting with flour. I often use a spritz of olive oil and a half cup of water to saute. The water evaporates and the olive oil flavor stays.

▓ Other Ingredients and Flavor Boosters ▓

Salt is listed in the ingredients but it is *always* optional, so be alert if you are on a sodium-restricted diet. I've listed salt because most dishes taste better with it, so add it to taste but be aware the nutrient values do *not* include any added salt.

Freshly ground black pepper is listed because it is so much more pungent when ground as needed. The ground pepper sold in spice tins and bottles can be up to two years old and its best flavor might have long disappeared.

Nutmeg is best when freshly ground, too. If you don't have a nutmeg grinder, it's worth the investment. The rich and lively sweet flavor of the fresh ground spice can't be matched by the store-bought ground version.

Zest, the grated rind (not the white pith) of citrus, appears in many of my recipes. The name comes from exactly what it lends to a dish. Whether you use a vegetable peeler, a grater, or a zester, the size of the zested orange peel or lemon peel will differ but in most cases won't matter. This is one ingredient I recommend you never omit (but wash the citrus first).

▪▪ Recipe Terms and Techniques ▪▪

A basic knowledge of cooking techniques is all you need to succeed with this book. Here, with explanation are a few terms and techniques I use.

Chopped means to cut the ingredient into ¼- to ½-inch pieces. This can be done with a knife or in a food processor or minichopper.

Coarsely chopped means cut into large shreds or dice into approximately ½-inch to 1-inch pieces using a knife or large or minifood processor.

Finely chopped means cut into ⅛- to ¼-inch diced pieces. A food processor or minichopper can finely chop, especially when pulsed. Be careful not to puree.

Defatted is the term I use to describe a soup, stock, or other dish that has had all its fat removed. You can chill the soup and scrape the congealed fat off with a spoon or pour the fatty stock into a defatting cup. The defatting cup is faster and easier. It has a low spout and the fat rises to the top and you pour off the nonfat flavorful liquid. See page 48 for a detailed description of the process.

Defatted meat and poultry means that every bit of visible fat and skin has been removed from the outside of red meat and from between the muscles and on the edges of the chicken, turkey, or duck. See page 234 for the technique.

Lean in this book doesn't mean nearly lean beef, pork, bacon, ham, or lamb but *completely* lean with no visible intramuscle fat and all white edge fat removed.

Julienne, or matchstick, means to cut the ingredient into narrow ⅛- to ¼-inch-thick sticks that are about 2 or 3 inches long. Use a knife or the julienne disk of a food processor.

Seeds reserved means just what you might think: Save the seeds from the bell pepper or the pumpkin and add them to the finished dish. Seeds add sweetness, texture, and dietary fiber. Like other seeds, grains, cornmeal, and nuts, their flavor improves when toasted in a 350°F. oven for 10 minutes as well.

▪▪ Nutritional Analyses ▪▪

READING LABELS Let's make this easy. I think you only need to look at the saturated fat content on every label. If it is under 2 grams per serving, no other ingredient number is important (unless you have a specific need to reduce salt or sugar), including calories, total fat, or percent of fat. If the saturated fat is low, probably the total fat and calories will be low, too. And the percent of calories from fat is important only if you look at a week's or a month's worth of food, not any individual item. Look for the words "low fat" as the Food and Drug Administration's definition means that it contains under 3 grams of total fat per serving. Be wary of words like "margarine" or "vegetable oil" on ingredient labels. They can be codes for foods you don't want, as margarine can legally contain tallow, coconut oil, suet, and lard. Vegetable oil can mean palm oil, palm kernel oil, and coconut oil. You want margarines that contain liquid (partially hydrogenated) canola, corn, safflower, or soybean oils. Cholesterol is only one fourth as important as saturated fat in lowering your cholesterol.

My motto is "Any small change you can make to improve your health improves your quality of life." Even if it's just walking more by taking the parking space far away from the store to defatting all your meat-based soups. It's a payoff you and your body feel almost immediately. Remember, after the fell swoops of eliminating most yolks, high-fat cheese, and dairy and butter, changes in lowering fat usually come from many, many small incremental reductions that add up.

All recipes have their nutrient values listed at the end. These list the saturated fat, total fat, cholesterol, sodium, and calories, with the first and most important number that of saturated fat. For some people it may be sodium, for others calories, but for heart and artery health, dietary saturated fat is the single most relevant and cholesterol-plaque-producing element.

Nutrient values are given for one 3½-ounce portion of cooked food unless otherwise noted (for instance, sauces are given in ¼ cup). Some recipes say "Serves 8." In a cake, for example, the ingredients are divided by 8 (which may be slightly more or less than 3½ ounces each). The nutritional analysis does include any ingredients listed as "optional."

Different nutritionists and dietitians calculate recipes differently because it depends on their information base. That base depends upon whether the calculations were made on, if the recipe contains chicken, for example; whether the chicken was male or female, old or young, free range or roaster. The same is true for beef and pork—even vegetables to a much lesser extent (some varieties of carrots and onions are sweeter than others). Understand that nutritional analysis figures are not absolute. Laboratories, testing facilities, nutritional experts, and USDA figures differ slightly but these differences are usually minor.

Information is rounded off. If, for example, the saturated fat content of a serving is 2.6 grams, it is listed as 3 grams. If it was 2.4 grams, we listed it as 2 grams. If the amount is less than 0.5 gram, it is listed as trace, which means barely calculable. If the amount is 0.5 but less than 1, we rounded it off.

Saturated fat   Make your goal to eat no more than 10 to 20 grams of saturated fat a day and you will thereby reduce total fat as well—10 grams if you're 100 pounds, 20 if you're 200 pounds, plus or minus.

Total fat   should not amount to more than 30 percent of your daily or weekly calorie intake. I like 15 percent better. If you are eating more than this amount, then the total fat analyses in these recipes will help you learn how to change from high-fat to reduced-fat eating without sacrificing taste or variety.

Cholesterol   Many experts feel we need no added cholesterol, that we make enough in our own bodies already. Remember, if you are eating it, there is no good cholesterol. Your body makes a good cholesterol (HDL and VHDL), however. Amounts of cholesterol are low here because my meat servings are 3½ ounces and my recipes use no yolks (except for two cheesecake recipes). Dietary cholesterol is one fourth as important to your health as is dietary saturated fat, however. If one takes aim at reducing the saturated fats, chances are your cholesterol count will go down as saturated fat is the major culprit.

The **sodium** analyses help those on sodium-restricted diets and help all of us keep our intake to under 2,400 milligrams a day. We do need salt, but there is plenty of salt naturally occurring in almost every vegetable and fruit. Adding copious amounts of table salt to our diets has become an unhealthy practice. Small amounts of salt bring out the flavor in our food and drastic sodium reduction is needed by only a small percentage of us.

If you are on a low-sodium diet, carefully read the labels of nonfat products. The salt contents in nonfat mayonnaise (and often sour cream and cream cheese) are about 50 percent higher than they are in low-fat mayonnaise, sour cream, and cream cheese. If you are on a salt-restricted diet, you may wish to use low-fat rather than nonfat to reduce your sodium intake.

Another way to get a salt taste using less salt is to mix Worcestershire and low-sodium soy sauce. Regular soy sauce has 1,028 milligrams of sodium per tablespoon; low sodium has about half that, or 599 milligrams, which is still fairly high. Worcestershire, however, isn't nearly as high at 167 milligrams. Mixing Worcestershire and low-sodium soy sauce, as we have occasionally done, will greatly reduce the salt yet have a similar taste.

Calories are not as important to count as are fat grams. One hundred calories of pure fat more or less sit in your arteries while 100 calories of complex carbohydrates, such as from a high-fiber pear or other fruit, burn as pure energy and part is eliminated from the body. Since nearly 38 percent of the typical American's total daily calorie count comes from fat, a reduction in fat calories (especially saturated fat calories) will mostly result in general reduction in calories all around.

■ Equipment ■

Well-made equipment and utensils and some simple labor-saving gadgets are essential. I assume you have many basic tools in your kitchen, but there are some items I find invaluable for healthy low-fat cooking.

Blender Countertop or hand-held or immersion blender is used for pureeing soups and sauces, and whipping skim milk, etc.

Defatting cups (Glass over plastic), large and small. It has a spout on the bottom perfect for no-fat gravy, soups, and sauces.

Electric steamer Ideal for cooking rice, seafood, poultry, couscous, and vegetables.

Fat-away pan A double meatloaf pan with holes in the inner pan so the fat drips into the other.

Food processor Full size for chopping and slicing and miniprocessor or minichopper for pureeing nonfat cottage or ricotta cheese, chopping nuts and herbs, and making herbed bread crumbs. (Packaged bread crumbs can have a lot of fat.)

Kitchen shears I keep two dishwasher-safe pairs on hand for trimming fat off meat, snipping herbs, cutting thin-crust pizzas into wedges, and cutting Phyllo dough.

Nonstick cookware Buy top-quality skillets, saucepans, and pots. The thin expensive ones get very hot and burn off cooking liquid (as well as the nonstick coating) faster than the heavier pans.

Peppermill Keep several mills filled with different kinds of whole peppercorns for freshly ground black pepper or sea salt (which doesn't contain starches but does contain more sodium).

Slotted spoons I prefer the large ones for straining food, small ones for wide-mouth olive cans and jars and many other uses.

Whisk They are necessary when cooking low fat as you use more cornstarch, flour, pureed mashed potatoes, etc.) They take the lumps out of most everything.

Low-Fat Alternatives

Choose:

milk, nonfat (skim)★

chocolate milk, skim
cottage cheese, nonfat★
ricotta cheese, nonfat
ice cream, nonfat
yogurt, nonfat
frozen yogurt, nonfat
sour cream, nonfat
margarine, diet or reduced fat
canola or safflower oil
salad dressings with some olive oil
    or nonfat
mayonnaise, nonfat
egg substitutes
scrambled egg substitutes with
    toast
chicken and beef stock, defatted
broiled skinless chicken
chicken, skinned and grilled
fast food single burger with
    double trimmings
London broil or any lean beef
    grilled, 3½ ounces, medium or
    well done
ham hock soup base, defatted
pork, lean, tenderloin 3½ ounces
Canadian bacon
bacon, defatted
fish, broiled or grilled
pasta marinara
pasta and clam sauce
shrimp, 4 large
lobster with cocktail sauce or on a
    salad

Instead of:

milk, whole, 1, 2, 3, or ½
    percent
chocolate milk, whole
cottage cheese, whole
ricotta cheese, whole
ice cream
yogurt
frozen yogurt
sour cream
butter
corn oil or peanut oil
salad dressings with cheese

mayonnaise
eggs
poached eggs on toast

chicken and beef stock
fried chicken
chicken, roasted
fast food fried fish sandwich with
    tartar sauce
sirloin, T-bone, Delmonico, etc.,
    steak, grilled, 3½ ounces, rare

ham hock soup base
pork, ribs, or chops 3½ ounces
bacon
bacon
fish, batter fried or butter sautéed
fettuccine Alfredo
pasta and cheese sauce
shrimp, ½ dozen batter fried
lobster with clarified butter or in
    a cream sauce

vegetable, rice, or pasta main dish	meat, chicken, or cheese main dish
tacos with beans	tacos with meat, chicken, and cheese
baked potatoes with nonfat sour cream and broccoli	scalloped potatoes with sour cream and cheese
won ton or vegetable soup	bisque or creamed soups
Western (oven) fries	french fries or deep-fat fries
eggplant in garlic sauce	eggplant Parmesan
pizza with vegetables	pizza with sausage and cheese
focaccia	pizza with pepperoni and cheese
bagel	doughnut
English muffin	bear claw or Danish
popcorn, light or air-popped	potato chips, regular
walnuts, pecans, or chestnuts†	peanuts, macadamia nuts, or cashews
pretzels	cheese puffs
bread sticks	cheese bread
potato chips with 40 percent less fat	potato chips
corn chips with 40 percent less fat	corn chips
cake, angel food	cake, pound or layer
fig Newtons	pastry
dried apricots, raisins, cranberries, cherries, or hard candy or jelly beans	candy bar

*Nonfat milk contains some fat.
†Less saturated fat.

Changing the Way You Eat

For those starting out on a new and healthful eating lifestyle, keep these tips in mind:

1. Say yes to healthy indulgences and no to moderation. I have seen too many people practice so-called moderation by leaving half their baked potato (with butter and sour cream), half their rare roast beef, some of their asparagus spears dripping with Hollandaise, and a chunk of their apple pie à la mode on their plates. By practicing moderation, they have consumed 1,000 calories and close to 24 grams of saturated fat, and they are understandably still hungry.

   The healthy and indulgent thing to do is eat the whole potato topped with a puree of nonfat ricotta cheese and chives (or in a restaurant, get rice or pasta). Have eight spears of asparagus with low-fat Hollandaise Sauce (page 293) margarine, or olive oil, and 3½ ounces of lean top round hamburger combined with lots of onions, celery, and bread crumbs and grilled. Top it with a zesty Spicy Chili and Steak Relish (page 286) and end with Mary's Old-fashioned Apple Pie (page 308) and a scoop of 3-percent nonfat ice cream, or, if at a restaurant, sorbet. All of this for about half the calories and just 7 grams of saturated fat and you sure aren't hungry.

2. Shop with zeal, and when hungry, buying foods that are both good tasting and good for you. Try new things and read the fat content in labels, choosing foods with the lowest saturated fat or under 2 grams per serving. You'll do it better when you're hungry.

3. Listen carefully to your body. Eat only when you are hungry. It makes eating more fun. And push the food away as soon as you feel full. Push it far away or you'll sit there and nibble. Eating when you're hungry helps regulate your body. If you've had a big dinner the night before and aren't hungry at breakfast, listen to yourself and just have juice and toast.

APPETIZERS

In Ben Jonson's sixteenth-century poem "Inviting a Friend to Supper," the Renaissance poet and gourmand promises a would-be guest, ". . . you shall have, to rectifie your pallate, an olive, capers or some better sallade . . ."

Ever since civilized people began to sit down to meals, and certainly since the French invented the Western style of eating in courses, appetizers have been valued for their ability to awaken the taste buds and enliven the palate. Any small savory—even Ben Jonson's caper or olive—can do it. So can a sweet; in Colonial America, special dinner guests were offered rare, costly pineapple as a sign of welcome before the meal (which is why pineapples are used on welcome mats, flags, balustrades, and finials).

Many cuisines enjoy this tradition. *Antipasto* is Italian for "before the meal." In Greece, the word is *mezedaki*. The Spaniards call appetizers *entremeses;* the Mexicans *antojitos;* and the Germans *Vorspeise.*

Americans, however, have elevated appetizers from a supporting role to the star of the party. We are less inclined to host elaborate five-course dinner parties, but we do relish inviting people in for informal food and friendship, often consisting of appetizers and drinks. Cocktail parties and buffets are so popular that I receive more requests for low-fat and nonfat appetizer recipes than anything else. And no wonder—party givers traditionally relied on appetizers such as cheese, chicken wings, Chinese-style ribs, bacon-wrapped chicken livers, Swedish meatballs, all of which are crammed with saturated fats.

My healthful appetizers make a party buffet as beautiful and scrumptious as the high-fat variety yet both you and your guests will end the evening feeling indulged, satisfied, and energetic. Included here are dips like hummus, guacamole (fat is okay), clam, and black bean, which are convenient and easy to prepare.

Hearty hot appetizers can be served as starters or as an entire meal and include many of my favorites: baked stuffed phyllo packets, crisp won tons, savory pissaladière on polenta crust, and a rich potato tart. The lighter appetizers, usually served cold or at room temperature, include a delicious mock caviar, deviled eggs, and caponata.

▪ Healthy Indulgences Party Secrets ▪

The secret to quick and easy low-fat party food is to use readily available low-fat products such as ratatouille, low-fat patés of onion, mushrooms, carrots, and more. Also use tapenade, plus tins of mussels, clams, and oysters in water for stuffing or flavor.

Substitute nonfat or low-fat dairy products such as cream cheese and sour creams when preparing dips, spreads, and fillings. Nonfat cottage cheese tastes as good and is as creamy as the high-fat, medium-fat, and 1-percent versions.

Nonfat sour cream, depending on the brand, is nearly impossible to tell from the traditional high-fat variety.

Nonfat cream cheese tastes best when pureed with a small amount (3 to 1) of the high-fat version or with nonfat cottage cheese or ricotta.

Nonfat mayonnaise brands vary in taste, from the sweet and vinegary midwestern-style to the smooth and more delicate in flavor. Some are made with tofu, some with egg with no fat, some with fat with no egg, so take your pick.

Nonfat cheeses don't stand on their own in taste or texture, but producers are constantly trying to improve. They are best when shredded and sprinkled on salads, chiles, and bean dips or used as garnishes.

Vegetable purees of cooked onions, garlic, broccoli, carrots, pimentos squash, parsnip, potatoes, or red or green bell peppers are excellent when appropriately seasoned with sun-dried tomatoes or chopped fresh tomatoes, vinegar, herbs, and spices to taste for spreads and dips.

Nonfat ricotta has good flavor but the texture is thin when used alone. Puree it with (2 to 1 or half and half) nonfat cottage cheese, cream cheese, farmer cheese, or tofu, if you like that taste. There is also nonfat Parmesan cheese.

Tofu is made from soy milk, which is a liquid extracted from ground soybeans. It has a pleasant yet bland taste that allows it to take on the flavors of whatever it is mixed with while adding texture. The silky style has the least fat, there is some nonfat, but even the fat in the firm style is mostly unsaturated. Use tofu sparingly as the slightly chalky taste is off-putting to some.

Party Hearty in Healthy Style

If you are invited to a cocktail party or buffet dinner, here are some tips to help you resist temptation when you step up to the beautifully arranged buffet table.

1. Fill your plate with the fruit and vegetable garnishes. By all means, eat those radish roses, carrot curls, and cherry tomatoes decorating the platters. Grapes, kiwis, kumquats, star fruit, and those ever-present melon balls are good eating.
2. For veggies, take just a small amount of the cream-laden dip instead of the usual big scoop.
3. Bread, toast, bread sticks, pretzels, and popcorn are safe bets, too.
4. Grilled or boiled skewers of lean chicken, meat, or seafood are fine. Avoid the wings, poultry with skin, and anything breaded and fried, including meatballs.
5. Although shrimp has no fat, it does contain cholesterol. Enjoy up to four jumbos with lots of cocktail sauce (which also has no fat).
6. Tempted by deviled eggs? Unobtrusively squeeze out the filling into your paper napkin and eat the whites, which have no fat or cholesterol.
7. Eat the hummus, salsa, duck sauce, or guacamole. Guacamole is mainly monounsaturated fat, mainly a pass-through, and the fat isn't all that high.

Black Bean Dip

I like a thick and chunky dip, so I mash some of the beans and puree the rest. An immersion or hand blender makes it even easier.

2 15-ounce cans black beans, drained

½ cup nonfat sour cream or nonfat yogurt cheese

½ onion, chopped

1 to 1½ tablespoons fresh lemon or lime juice

½ teaspoon chili powder

¼ teaspoon salt (optional)

¼ teaspoon Tabasco

½ lime cut into wedges

1 tablespoon chopped cilantro, for garnish

1 tablespoon nonfat sour cream, for garnish

In a food processor, puree beans, sour cream, onion, lemon juice, chili powder, salt, if using, and Tabasco. (This may also be done in a large bowl, using an immersion blender.) Serve at room temperature with lime wedges and top with the garnishes of your choice. Serve cold.

PER ¼ CUP: Saturated Fat: 0 gm   Total Fat: Trace
Cholesterol: 0 mg   Sodium: 147 mg   Calories: 86

Hunky Caponata

Caponata, the Italian version of ratatouille, can be used as a filling for hard-cooked egg whites, served hot over pasta or rice, or as a dip with Pesto Pita Triangles (page 33). This caponata is also used as a filling for Potato Galette (page 38).

Olive oil spray
1 medium eggplant (about 1 pound), cubed
1⅓ cups chopped celery (about 4 stalks)
1 large onion, chopped
1 green bell pepper, chopped
2 small tomatoes, chopped

¼ cup red wine vinegar
2 teaspoons sugar
½ teaspoon salt (optional)
¼ teaspoon freshly ground black pepper
¼ cup chopped parsley
¼ cup pitted chopped green olives
Black pitted olives for garnish

Lightly spray a large nonstick skillet with olive oil and place over medium-high heat. Cook the eggplant, lightly spraying them with additional oil, and brown on all sides; add water by the tablespoon as needed to prevent sticking. Add the celery, onion, and green pepper and cook until crisp-tender, about 4 minutes, adding spoonfuls of water as needed to keep the mixture moist. Remove the vegetables to a bowl and set aside.

In the same skillet, combine the tomatoes, vinegar, sugar, salt, pepper, and parsley and cook until slightly mushy, about 10 minutes. Add the reserved vegetables and the green olives, and simmer, covered, for 10 minutes. Spoon the mixture into a bowl, cover, and refrigerate a few hours or overnight. Serve chilled or at room temperature, and garnish with black olives.

PER ½ CUP: Saturated Fat: 0 gm   Total Fat: 0.5 gm
Cholesterol: 0 mg   Sodium: 73 mg   Calories: 29

Eggplant Caviar

This Middle Eastern-inspired dip is best served very cold with vegetables, corn chips, pitas, or thin crackers or flat breads such as lavash. All the raw vegetables can be chopped in a food processor, but be careful not to puree them. Mince the garlic separately, so you will not be tempted to overprocess the other vegetables. You can adjust the amount of lemon, sugar, and vinegar to your taste. Preparation takes about 45 minutes, including chilling time. This dip will jell if chilled overnight, and makes a fine mold.

1 large (about 1 pound) eggplant, unpeeled

2 medium onions, 1 unpeeled, 1 peeled and quartered

3 cloves garlic

1 medium carrot, cut into 4 pieces

1 green bell pepper, seeded and cut into eighths

1 large tomato, quartered

6 green pimento-stuffed olives

2 to 3 tablespoons red wine vinegar

Juice of 1 lemon

¼ to ½ teaspoon Tabasco or harissa

½ teaspoon salt (optional)

Pinch sugar (optional)

3 tablespoons small capers, drained (optional)

Black olives, ¼ cup chopped parsley or watercress, or lemon slices, for garnish

Pierce the skin of the eggplant and 1 unpeeled onion several times with a fork or knife. Cook the eggplant and the onion in a microwave oven at high for 7 minutes. Turn them over and cook for another 4 minutes. When cool enough to handle, peel the onion.

In a food processor, mince garlic. Add the cooked eggplant, peeled cooked onion, raw onion, carrot, pepper, tomato, olives, vinegar, lemon juice, Tabasco, salt, and sugar, if using, and pulse 3 or 4 times until coarsely chopped. Do not puree the mixture as it should be chunky. Remove mixture to a bowl, cover, and refrigerate several hours. Just before serving, stir in the capers. Garnish with olives, parsley, and lemon slices as desired and serve cold.

■■ PER ½ CUP: Saturated Fat: 0 gm   Total Fat: Trace ■■
Cholesterol: 0 mg   Sodium: 48 mg   Calories: 31

Clam Dip

■■ *Makes 2½ cups* ■■

Chock-full of clams, this dip usually disappears quickly.

8 ounces nonfat cottage cheese
2 tablespoons nonfat cream cheese
3 teaspoons fresh lemon juice
6 to 10 drops Tabasco
½ teaspoon prepared mustard
2 to 4 tablespoons good white
  wine

2 6½-ounce cans minced clams,
  drained
2 tablespoons chopped parsley
2 tablespoons chopped scallions or
  shallots
2 sprigs fresh watercress (optional)

In a food processor or blender, puree cottage cheese, cream cheese, lemon juice, Tabasco, mustard, and 2 tablespoons wine for at least 4 minutes, adding the remaining wine as needed. The dip should be thick and smooth. Remove to a bowl. Stir in the clams, parsley, and scallions, and mix well. Cover and refrigerate at least 2 hours. Garnish with watercress sprigs just before serving.

■■ PER ¼ CUP: Saturated Fat: 0 gm   Total Fat: Trace ■■
Cholesterol: 13 mg   Sodium: 142 mg   Calories: 47

Guacamole

"Guacamole" is an Aztec word and it's made almost the same today as it was two thousand years ago. The addition of citrus and tomatoes is new. Avocado is 8 percent fat if Hass but most is the far less threatening monounsaturated fat, so enjoy them in moderation. This dip is good with raw vegetables and low-fat (40 percent less fat) corn chips. Serve with a selection of garnishes, salsa, a dollop of nonfat sour cream, diced fresh tomatoes, chopped onions, or chopped black olives. (An avocado pit in the dip will not prohibit discoloration. Oxygen causes that.)

2 ripe avocados, peeled, 1 pureed,
1 diced
1 medium tomato, diced
1 small onion, coarsely chopped
(about 4 to 5 tablespoons)
1 to 4 tablespoons fresh lemon or
lime juice

¼ to ½ teaspoon minced, seeded
jalapeño or several drops
Tabasco
¼ to 1 teaspoon chopped cilantro
Salt (optional)

In a large bowl, combine the avocado, tomato, onion, lemon juice, lime juice, jalapeño, cilantro, and salt, if using, and mash lightly with a fork until the mixture is thick and chunky. Adjust the seasonings. To make a few hours ahead, sprinkle the guacamole with an additional teaspoon lemon juice, cover with plastic wrap sitting directly on the surface of the guacamole. Refrigerate and stir to mix in the added lemon juice just before serving. Serve with the chips, vegetables, and other garnishes.

PER ¼ CUP: Saturated Fat: 1 gm   Total Fat: 5 gm
Cholesterol: 0 mg   Sodium: 4 mg   Calories: 59

Hot Maryland Crab Dip

Makes 2½ cups

Although crabmeat is high in cholesterol, it has a negligible amount of fat, which makes this dip a healthy indulgence (as dietary cholesterol isn't nearly as important as saturated fat). It can be assembled the day ahead, covered, and refrigerated, then reheated for 5 minutes. Serve with Scandinavian crisp bread, such as Wasa or Finn Crisp. When thinned with ¼ cup nonfat milk, this dip becomes enough sauce for four servings of pasta.

1 8-ounce container fresh lump crabmeat	1 to 2 teaspoons fresh lemon juice
½ cup nonfat cottage cheese	2 tablespoons Calvados (apple brandy) or other white wine (optional)
¼ cup nonfat cream cheese or farmer cheese	2 tablespoons finely chopped onion
1 tablespoon horseradish	2 tablespoons finely chopped celery
1 teaspoon Dijon mustard	Several shakes cayenne or paprika
1 tablespoon nonfat milk	2 tablespoons chopped parsley

Preheat the oven to 350°F.

If the crabmeat is frozen, drain it well in a sieve, pushing on the solids with paper towel to remove all the moisture. Fresh or frozen, pick over to remove any bits of cartilage and set aside. In a food processor, puree cottage cheese, cream cheese, horseradish, mustard, milk, lemon juice, and Calvados 3 to 4 minutes.

In a small bowl, combine the cottage cheese mixture (which should be very smooth), the crabmeat, onion, and celery, and stir until well blended. Spoon the mixture into an ovenproof dish and bake for 25 to 30 minutes, until bubbly and lightly golden on top. Sprinkle with cayenne or paprika and parsley, for garnish.

Serve hot with the crisp bread.

PER ¼ CUP: Saturated Fat: 0 gm   Total Fat: Trace
Cholesterol: 25 mg   Sodium: 189 mg   Calories: 49

Hummus

I like to serve this tasty Middle Eastern dip with spiced pita triangles, but it is also good with raw vegetables, lavash, bread sticks, or as a filling for hard-cooked egg whites. Rather than adding olive oil to the mix, I spray a little on top of the dip just before serving. If you can't live without more than a spray, drizzle some good quality olive oil on the hummus before serving.

1 15-ounce can garbanzo beans
(chickpeas), drained
¼ cup tahini (sesame seed paste),
drained
½ cup fresh lemon juice
¼ cup fresh lime juice (optional)
4 to 6 cloves garlic

¼ to ½ teaspoon salt
Olive oil spray
¼ cup chopped parsley, for
garnish
Lemon slices, for garnish

In a food processor or blender, puree garbanzo beans, tahini, lemon juice, lime juice, if using, garlic, and salt, if using. Remove the mixture to a small bowl, cover, and refrigerate 1 hour. To serve, spray lightly with oil, and garnish with the chopped parsley and lemon slices.

PER ¼ CUP: Saturated Fat: 0.5 gm   Total Fat: 5 gm
Cholesterol: 0 mg   Sodium: 98 mg   Calories: 113

Salmon and Red Caviar Dip

Serve with toast points, unsalted bread sticks, or melba rounds. This dip can also be spooned into endive spears, celery ribs, or hard-cooked egg whites and garnished with a sprig of parsley. The red caviar can be added only at the last minute as it "bleeds" color.

½ cup nonfat cottage cheese	Few drops Tabasco
½ cup nonfat cream cheese	1 small onion, quartered
½ teaspoon fresh lemon juice	1 4-inch piece celery
¾ cup cooked (or canned) salmon, lightly chopped	3 ounces red caviar
	Several sprigs parsley

In a food processor or blender, puree the cottage cheese, cream cheese, lemon juice, salmon, and Tabasco 3 to 4 minutes. Add the onion and celery, and pulse 2 or 3 times to coarsely chop the vegetables. (You can also chop the vegetables separately and stir them into the mixture.) Remove the mixture to a bowl, cover, and refrigerate until chilled.

Just before serving, top with a ribbon of red caviar around the outside edge and garnish with parsley.

PER ¼ CUP: Saturated Fat: 0.5 gm   Total Fat: 3 gm
Cholesterol: 58 mg   Sodium: 287 mg   Calories: 69

Tofu-Yogurt Vegetable Dip

Makes 1 1/2 cups

Silky tofu takes on the tang of lemon and the heat of Tabasco in this chunky vegetable dip. I use silken tofu for the texture and because it contains the least fat (although there is nonfat tofu if you can find it).

8 ounces silken tofu

3 tablespoons fresh lemon juice

1/2 teaspoon sugar

1/2 tablespoon cider vinegar

1/2 teaspoon Tabasco, hot sauce, or finely chopped seeded jalapeño

1 tablespoon low-sodium soy sauce

1/4 cup nonfat yogurt cheese or yogurt

1 small onion, chopped

1/4 cup chopped carrots

1/4 cup chopped celery

1/4 cup chopped green bell pepper

1/4 cup plus 2 tablespoons chopped parsley

2 tablespoons chopped red bell pepper, for garnish

In a food processor or blender, blend the tofu, lemon juice, sugar, cider vinegar, Tabasco, soy sauce, and yogurt 3 to 4 minutes until very smooth. Remove the mixture to a small bowl. Add onion, carrots, celery, green bell pepper, and 1/4 cup parsley and stir until combined. Cover and refrigerate for several hours. Before serving, sprinkle with the remaining parsley and red bell pepper. Serve chilled.

PER 1/4 CUP: Saturated Fat: Trace   Total Fat: 1 gm
Cholesterol: Trace   Sodium: 151 mg   Calories: 50

Tonnato Dip

Makes 2¹/₄ cups

This makes a delicious spread for toasted baguettes or any flat bread. It is also an excellent filling for hard-cooked egg whites. To serve as a dip with vegetables, stir in ¹/₄ cup nonfat sour cream.

1 clove garlic, chopped
2 tablespoons fresh lemon juice
1 teaspoon anchovy paste
2 tablespoons egg substitute
3 tablespoons capers plus 2
   teaspoons caper liquid
¹/₂ teaspoon Worcestershire
1 6-ounce can tuna packed in
   water, undrained, or 6 ounces
   fresh

Freshly ground black pepper
1 large slice fresh white bread,
   torn into pieces
2 tablespoons olive oil
¹/₄ cup fresh chopped parsley

In a food processor or blender, puree garlic, lemon juice, anchovy paste, egg substitute, 1 tablespoon capers and caper liquid, Worcestershire, tuna and its liquid, pepper, and bread. With the motor running, drizzle in the olive oil. Remove to a serving bowl, cover, and refrigerate until chilled. Garnish with remaining capers and parsley, surrounded with fresh vegetables and crackers.

PER ¹/₄ CUP: Saturated Fat: 0.5 gm   Total Fat: 1 gm
Cholesterol: 7 mg   Sodium: 198 mg   Calories: 65

Bull's-eye Cucumbers

These bite-size cucumber circles filled with guacamole disappear quickly at my parties. These should chill overnight. Use fringed toothpicks so they can be easily seen and removed.

2 burpless cucumbers, each about
    12 inches long
1 envelope unflavored gelatine
1/4 cup low-sodium defatted
    chicken stock or vegetable stock
2 teaspoons fresh lemon juice
1 clove garlic
1 small onion
1 teaspoon chopped pickled
    jalapeño

1 scallion
1 avocado, diced
1/2 teaspoon salt (optional)
1/4 cup salsa or several drops
    Tabasco
1/2 cup red bell pepper, diced
Several lettuce leaves

Score the outside of the cucumbers lengthwise with the tongs of a fork to make a design. Cut off the ends, and with a long, narrow knife or a vegetable peeler, hollow out the center containing the seeds, making a tunnel all the way through and leaving about 1/4-inch cucumber wall. Stuff the inside of the cucumbers with paper towel to absorb excess moisture, cover, and let stand for 15 minutes to 1/2 hour.

In a medium bowl, dissolve the gelatine in the chicken stock and lemon juice for 5 minutes, then microwave on high for 30 seconds to dissolve completely. In a blender or miniprocessor, finely chop the garlic, onion, and jalapeño. Add the scallion, avocado, and salt, if using, and blend until smooth. Add the gelatine mixture. With a wooden spoon, stir in the salsa or Tabasco, and 1/2 cup red pepper.

Remove the paper towel from the cucumbers and fill each cucumber with the avocado mixture. Place the cucumbers on a platter, cover, and refrigerate 2 hours or overnight.

When ready to serve, cut the cucumbers into 1/2-inch circles. Spear each piece with a fringed toothpick making sure it is put through the filling. The toothpick is now the "handle" for each hors d'oeuvre and will prevent the filling from slipping out. Place the cucumber rounds on lettuce leaves, and sprinkle with remaining ¼ cup diced red bell pepper.

■■   PER 3 PIECES: Saturated Fat: 0.5 gm   Total Fat: 4 gm   ■■
Cholesterol: 0 mg   Sodium: 59 mg   Calories: 69

Vegetable-Onion Dip

■■   *Make 3 cups*   ■■

If you don't want to chop the vegetables by hand, use a food processor. To avoid pureeing vegetables in the food processor, cut the vegetables into large chunks, remove them to the food processor, and pulse——on and off quickly——3 or 4 times until the size desired. Adjust the vinegar and Tabasco to your taste.

2 cups nonfat sour cream
½ cup chopped onions
¼ cup chopped scallions
¼ cup chopped carrots
¼ cup chopped red bell peppers
1 teaspoon finely chopped seeded jalapeño

Dash cider vinegar
1 teaspoon Tabasco (optional)
Salt (optional)
Sprigs parsley, for garnish

In a small bowl, combine the sour cream, onion, scallions, carrots, red peppers, and jalapeño and mix thoroughly; add vinegar, Tabasco, and salt, if using, to taste. Remove to a serving bowl, cover, and refrigerate until chilled. Garnish with parsley before serving.

■■   PER ¼ CUP: Saturated Fat: 0 gm   Total Fat: 0 gm   ■■
Cholesterol: 0 mg   Sodium: 31 mg   Calories: 29

Hummus Spirals

Hummus is spread on snow-white flour tortillas, covered with green spinach and red bell peppers, and rolled and sliced into bite-size spirals. This is better chilled overnight.

*4 8-inch flour tortillas or soft, thin
    lavash cut into 8-inch sheets
2 cups Hummus (page 20)
4 cups shredded fresh spinach*

*1 cup (4 ounces) bottled roasted
    red bell peppers or pimientos,
    drained and blotted dry*

Place the tortillas in a plastic bag and microwave at high for 10 to 15 seconds, until softened. Remove and cover with a damp towel (or leave on the plastic wrap) to keep warm and moist while working.

Spread each tortilla with ½ cup hummus. Spread 1 cup shredded spinach (on top of the hummus), pressing down firmly. Place ¼ cup of the roasted red bell peppers along one edge of the tortilla and roll up the tortilla firmly. Wrap each roll tightly in plastic wrap, ends covered, and refrigerate at least 1 hour or preferably overnight. Just before serving, slice each spiral into 3 or 4 bite-size rounds. Spear each roll-up with a toothpick and serve cold.

PER 3 PIECES: Saturated Fat: 2 gm   Total Fat: 11 gm
        Cholesterol: 0 mg   Sodium: 758 mg   Calories: 294

New Deviled Eggs
à la Virginia Von Fremd

This is one of my signature dishes, borrowed from a friend who very successfully fools her low-fat-eschewing party guests with this healthful and tasty version of traditional deviled eggs. Garnish as desired with tiny shrimp, a small sprig of parsley, capers, or paprika.

12 hard-cooked eggs
Vegetable oil spray
10 egg substitute (or 2½ cups)
½ cup nonfat mayonnaise or
   sour cream
4 tablespoons cider vinegar
1½ teaspoons dry mustard

¼ teaspoon turmeric
¼ teaspoon cayenne
½ teaspoon salt (optional)
4 tablespoons sweet pickle relish,
   drained for 20 minutes, or
   1½ tablespoons sugar
Paprika, for garnish

Slice the hard-cooked eggs lengthwise and discard the yolks. Lightly spray a large nonstick skillet with vegetable oil and place over medium heat. Cook the egg substitute, stirring occasionally to loosen from the sides. Cover and continue cooking over very low heat until very firm, about 10 minutes.

In a food processor or blender, blend the eggs, mayonnaise, vinegar, mustard, turmeric, cayenne, and salt, if using, until smooth, occasionally scraping the sides of the container with a spatula. Add either the pickle relish or its drained juice sugar, and blend to combine. Remove to a bowl, cover, and refrigerate 2 hours.

Fill the egg halves generously with the chilled mixture, sprinkle with paprika or decorate with an attractive garnish.

PER 2 HALVES: Saturated Fat: 0 gm   Total Fat: 0.5 gm
Cholesterol: 0 mg   Sodium: 276 mg   Calories: 56

Sweet Potato Bundles with Yogurt Cheese and Pineapple Salsa

These self-contained and slightly sweet bundles may be served hot, warm, or at room temperature. Traditionally, potato pancakes are fried, but this baked version gives you the flavor without all the fat. Yogurt cheese is made by draining the whey from nonfat plain yogurt. This can be done ahead of time by placing the yogurt in a cheesecloth or coffee filter and allowing it to drain for several hours.

Vegetable oil spray

2 large sweet potatoes, peeled or unpeeled

1 teaspoon ground ginger or 2 teaspoons fresh minced

2 tablespoons all-purpose flour

1 teaspoon salt (optional)

2 large egg whites, beaten to stiff peaks

Pineapple salsa

4 scallions, minced (including the green part)

1 cup (4 ounces) candied pineapple, finely chopped

⅔ cup minced red bell pepper

½ teaspoon ground ginger

4 tablespoons fresh lime juice

1 cup nonfat yogurt cheese

Preheat the oven to 375°F.

Lightly spray a baking sheet with vegetable oil. Cook the sweet potatoes in a microwave oven at high for 2 to 3 minutes, turning once. In a food processor with the shredder blade attached (or with a hand shredder), shred the sweet potatoes.

In a large bowl, combine the sweet potatoes, ginger, flour, salt, if using, and beaten egg whites and mix well. Drop mixture by heaping table-spoonfuls, 2 inches apart, onto the prepared baking sheet. Bake 20 to 25 minutes or until lightly browned on the bottom. Remove to a wire rack to cool. With a spoon, press a well in each warm potato bundle.

Meanwhile, prepare the salsa (which can also be made several days in advance). In a small bowl, combine the scallions, pineapple, red bell pepper, ginger, and lime juice and mix well.

Place a dollop of yogurt cheese in the well, and top with ½ teaspoon salsa.

■■   PER 3 PIECES: Saturated Fat: 0 gm   Total Fat: 0.5 gm   ■■
Cholesterol: 1 mg   Sodium: 66 mg   Calories: 133

Pepper Wedges
with Romesco Filling

■■   *Makes 47*   ■■

These bright pepper wedges are filled with our version (reduced fat, of course) of the Spanish classic Romesco sauce. Usually it's loaded with calories from nuts and olive oil. We've streamlined it but added extra taste pizzazz!

*½ cup (2 ounces) bottled roasted
    red bell peppers, drained
4 tablespoons sliced almonds,
    toasted
2 cloves garlic
1 tablespoon fresh lemon juice
1¼ cup fresh bread crumbs
2 tablespoons olive oil
1 cup diced fresh tomatoes*

*2 or more drops Tabasco
½ cup thinly sliced scallions
Salt (optional)
Freshly ground black pepper
3 or 4 large bell peppers, yellow,
    red, or orange, seeded (seeds
    reserved) and cut into 1½ to
    2-inch wide wedges*

In a food processor or blender, puree the peppers, 2 tablespoons almonds, garlic, lemon juice, bread crumbs, and olive oil. Remove to a bowl and set aside.

Sprinkle the tomatoes with Tabasco. Stir the tomatoes and ¼ cup scallions into the red pepper mixture. Add salt, if using, and pepper to taste and mix well. Mound the filling into the pepper wedges. Cut each pepper wedge in thirds (or bite-size pieces); sprinkle with remaining scallions, reserved pepper seeds, and remaining almonds.

■■   PER 1 WEDGE OR 3 PIECES: Saturated Fat: 0.5 gm   ■■
Total Fat: 3 gm   Cholesterol: 0 mg   Sodium: 80 mg   Calories: 48

Tuna Won Tons

Ginger, peanuts, and freshly crushed black peppercorns give these open-face won tons an Indonesian flavor. You can substitute shrimp, scallops, or thin slices of lean chicken, beef, or pork for the tuna. To crush peppercorns, place them in a plastic bag and crush them with an iron skillet or by rolling a heavy jar over them. Won ton skins are square and available prepackaged in supermarkets and Asian markets.

1 4-ounce tuna fillet, skin removed	Vegetable oil spray
2 cloves garlic, minced	16 won ton skins
¼ cup low-sodium soy sauce	1 tablespoon crushed green peppercorns
2 teaspoons freshly grated ginger	2 teaspoons hot mustard or wasabi
1 tablespoon low-fat peanut butter, melted in a microwave oven at high for about 30 seconds	¼ cup pickled ginger
	1 ounce enoki mushrooms
2 teaspoons vinegar	3 tablespoons chopped peanuts
1 tablespoon honey	Snipped chives or thinly sliced scallions, for garnish

In a medium plastic bag or a shallow dish that can be covered with plastic wrap, marinate the tuna in garlic, soy sauce, ginger, peanut butter, vinegar, and honey and refrigerate for at least 2 hours.

Preheat the oven to 300°F.

Lightly spray a baking sheet with vegetable oil and place the won ton skins ½ inch apart on the sheet. Bake 10 to 15 minutes until evenly browned, and very dry and crisp.

Remove the tuna from the marinade and blot dry with a paper towel. Press the crushed peppercorns into the surface of the tuna. Lightly spray a medium nonstick skillet with vegetable oil and place over high heat. When hot, dry-sear the tuna until brown on both sides and slightly rare in the center, about 1 to 2 minutes per side. Remove to a plate and let cool for 10 minutes, then slice as thinly as possible into 16 slices.

To assemble, spread each won ton skin with a small amount of mustard. Top with a slice of tuna, a piece of pickled ginger, and 2 or 3 enoki mushrooms. Sprinkle sparingly with chopped peanuts. Garnish with chives or scallions. Serve at room temperature.

■■   PER 3 PIECES: Saturated Fat: 1 gm   Total Fat: 5 gm   ■■
              Cholesterol: 13 mg   Sodium: 370 mg   Calories: 167

Cucumber-Ribboned Scallops
■■   *Makes 20*   ■■

If you like sushi, you'll enjoy the delicate flavors of these elegant rolled bundles of cooked scallops and cucumbers. If you aren't a sushi fan, omit the wasabi (Japanese horseradish) and soy sauce.

1 pound (about 20) sea scallops	*1 teaspoon salt*
¼ cup oyster sauce	*⅓ cup pickled ginger*
3 tablespoons fresh lime juice	*Wasabi (optional)*
2 burpless cucumbers	*Low-sodium soy sauce (optional)*

Marinate the scallops in oyster sauce and lime juice for 2 hours in a covered bowl, or in a sealed plastic bag, in the refrigerator. Cut the cucumbers in half and slice lengthwise into very thin (no more than ¼ inch thick) "ribbons," which are at least 4 inches long (a Feemster slicer or mandoline helps). Salt, and let drain, covered, about 1 hour, and rinse. Cucumber ribbons will be quite pliable.

Preheat a broiler, grill, or nonstick skillet. Sear the scallops on each side, until they are done, about 2 minutes per side, being careful not to overcook.

Separate the cucumber ribbons and lay them flat. Place a slice of pickled ginger on one end, cover with a pearl-size piece of wasabi, if using, and top with a cooked scallop. Sprinkle the scallop lightly with soy sauce, roll up jelly-roll style, and secure with a fringed toothpick. Serve immediately.

■■   PER 3 PIECES: Saturated Fat: 0.5 gm   Total Fat: 3 gm   ■■
              Cholesterol: 26 mg   Sodium: 549 mg   Calories: 109

Corn Coins on Shrimp

This is a flashy circle of corn topped with a succulent shrimp that everyone loves. Cooked corn pancakes freeze well and can be reheated in a 350°F. oven for 10 minutes or in a microwave oven at high for 1 minute. Make extra to have on hand for unexpected guests or to serve with your favorite Mexican meal. If you toast the cornmeal first on an oven sheet in a 360°F. oven for 10 minutes, it deepens the corn flavor.

½ onion	1⅓ cups beer
½ leafy rib stalk	¾ cup canned corn or fresh whole
1 small jalapeño, seeded	kernel (drained if canned)
Several drops Tabasco	Vegetable oil spray
1 cup yellow cornmeal	⅓ cup jalapeño jelly, melted
½ cup all-purpose flour	30 fresh cilantro leaves or chopped
¾ teaspoon salt (optional)	scallions, for garnish
2¼ teaspoons baking powder	30 medium shrimp, steamed and
4 teaspoons sugar	peeled
2 egg whites	

In a food processor, chop onion, celery, jalapeño, and Tabasco. Remove and set aside ⅓ of the mixture for garnish (if garnish is desired).

In the same food processor, add cornmeal, flour, salt, baking powder, sugar, egg whites, beer, and mix well. Stir in the corn.

Heat a large nonstick skillet over medium heat and spray lightly with vegetable oil. Drop the batter by tablespoonfuls into the pan. (The coins should be about 1½ to 2 inches in diameter.) Cook until golden brown, turning coins once. Remove and cool on a wire rack. Repeat until all the coins are cooked.

Preheat the broiler. Brush the top of each corn coin with melted jalapeño jelly and lightly brown under the broiler, about 1 minute, watching carefully.

Top each coin with a cilantro leaf and a small shrimp. Garnish with the reserved jalapeño mixture. Serve immediately or at room temperature.

■■   PER 3 PIECES: Saturated Fat: Trace   Total Fat: 1 gm   ■■
Cholesterol: 27 mg   Sodium: 243 mg   Calories: 158

Pesto Pita Triangles
■■   *Makes 32*   ■■

These crispy baked pita triangles suggest the flavor of fresh pesto without the fatty pine nuts. They taste good all by themselves, or when served with Hummus (page 20) or Hunky Caponata (page 15).

¾ cup finely chopped fresh basil | *1 tablespoon grated nonfat*
1 tablespoon olive oil | *Parmesan cheese*
¾ teaspoon cracked black pepper | *4 8-inch pitas*

Preheat the oven to 400°F.

In a food processor, combine the basil with the olive oil, pepper, and cheese. Lightly spread the mixture on the top of each pita. Cut each pita into 8 triangles.

Place the triangles on a baking sheet, and bake for 5 to 8 minutes. Serve immediately.

■■   PER 3 TRIANGLES: Saturated Fat: Trace   Total Fat: 2 gm   ■■
Cholesterol: 0 mg   Sodium: 194 mg   Calories: 110

Phyllo Pizza

This unique party pizza takes advantage of the versatility and low-fat quality of phyllo pastry. Use kitchen shears rather than a knife to cut phyllo and keep the dough covered with a damp towel while using to prevent drying out. Be sure frozen phyllo dough is completely thawed before using.

Vegetable oil spray

4 sheets phyllo pastry

4 tablespoons corn-bread stuffing, finely crushed

½ cup (or 2 ounces) shredded part-skim mozzarella

1 small eggplant, sliced crosswise into ¼-inch rounds and grilled or baked

1 medium tomato, diced

½ cup (or 2 ounces) marinated artichoke hearts, drained and coarsely chopped

2 tablespoons capers

1 tablespoon finely chopped fresh basil

1 small clove garlic, minced

¼ cup grated nonfat Parmesan cheese

Preheat the oven to 350°F.

Lightly spray a 10-inch round tart or cake pan with vegetable oil. Lightly spray one sheet of phyllo with vegetable oil, and sprinkle with 1 tablespoon corn-bread crumbs.

Fold the pastry in half and place it in the tart pan with the folded edge resting against the side of the pan. Repeat with remaining pastry and crumbs, layering the sheets with folded edges against the side of the pan. Tuck in the corners of the pastry so they do not extend over the edge of the tart pan. Bake for 10 minutes, remove, and sprinkle with the mozzarella cheese.

Cut the cooked eggplant slices into small cubes. In a small bowl, combine the eggplant, tomato, artichoke hearts, capers, basil, and garlic. Spread mixture over the phyllo crust and bake for 15 minutes. Remove and sprinkle evenly with Parmesan cheese. Let the pizza rest, keeping it warm near the oven, for 5 minutes before cutting with shears into wedges. Serve hot.

PER SLICE: Saturated Fat: 1 gm   Total Fat: 3 gm
Cholesterol: 6 mg   Sodium: 256 mg   Calories: 93

Phyllo Tartlets with Sun-Dried Tomatoes and Olive Filling

These bite-size tarts take less than 30 minutes to prepare. If you don't have minitins, make them with foil. Cut several 4-inch by 2-inch rectangles out of tin foil. Fold the foil (for more stability) in half to form a 2-inch by 2-inch square. Mold each 2-inch piece of foil around a large bottle-top cap about 1 inch in diameter, cup side down, flaring the edges of the foil and placing them, cup side up, on a baking sheet. Minimuffin tins work well.

Vegetable oil spray
¼ cup egg substitute
2 cloves garlic, minced
1 cup nonfat ricotta cheese
½ cup (about 10) chopped sun-dried tomatoes (not oil-packed)
1 teaspoon oregano

½ teaspoon balsamic vinegar
3 tablespoons (12 to 15 olives) chopped Kalamata olives
2 sheets phyllo pastry
2 tablespoons cornbread stuffing, finely crushed

Preheat the oven to 350°F.

Lightly spray 24 2½-inch by 1¼-inch muffin-pan cups with vegetable oil.

In a medium bowl, combine the egg substitute, garlic, ricotta, sun-dried tomatoes, oregano, vinegar, and 2 tablespoons olives and mix well.

Lightly spray 1 sheet of phyllo with vegetable oil. Sprinkle the phyllo with the corn-bread crumbs, top with the second sheet of phyllo, and lightly spray again. Carefully cut phyllo into 24 equal squares. Press each phyllo square into a muffin cup and fill with a heaping teaspoon of sun-dried tomato mixture. Bake 10 to 15 minutes or until the edges are golden and the filling is slightly firm. Remove to a wire rack to cool for 5 minutes. Remove from cups and garnish with remaining olives and serve warm.

PER 3 TARTLETS: Saturated Fat: Trace   Total Fat: 1 gm
Cholesterol: 2 mg   Sodium: 257 mg   Calories: 57

Polenta Pissaladière

Pissaladière is a flat pizzalike tart from the South of France. Here, polenta (cornmeal) is used for the crust, and a savory creamy filling is spread on top and garnished with slivers of red pepper. Serve it hot, cut into 1½-inch wedges.

3 cups nonfat milk
1 cup cornmeal
1 teaspoon salt (optional)
Vegetable oil spray
2 tablespoons grated nonfat
  Parmesan cheese
3 cups fresh spinach, finely
  chopped

1 clove garlic, minced
2 tablespoons minced fresh basil
¾ cup nonfat ricotta
¾ cup sliced roasted red bell
  peppers

In a large microwave-safe container, cook milk, cornmeal, and salt, if using, at high for 5 minutes. Stir to mix. Continue cooking and stirring in 5-minute increments for a total cooking time of 15 to 20 minutes or until the polenta is very thick and a spoon will stand up straight.

Line a baking sheet or broiler tray with heavy foil and lightly spray with vegetable oil. Pour the hot polenta onto the baking sheet and spread into a 12-inch circle, ½ inch thick. Sprinkle with Parmesan cheese.

Preheat the broiler. In a small bowl, combine the spinach, garlic, basil, and ricotta, and mix well. Set aside. Broil the polenta crust until brown and crispy, about 20 to 25 minutes. Remove the crust and reduce the oven temperature to 400°F. Spread the spinach mixture over the polenta crust, leaving a ½-inch edge around the rim. Place the pepper strips sideways around the outer edge of the polenta. Bake for 15 to 20 minutes, or until lightly browned. Remove to a wire rack to cool for 10 minutes before cutting into 8 wedges. Serve hot.

PER SERVING: Saturated Fat: 0.5 gm   Total Fat: 1 gm
Cholesterol: 5 mg   Sodium: 135 mg   Calories: 127

Potato Bouchées with Caponata

These hot, slightly spicy potatoes are the healthful answer to cheese-stuffed potato skins. Be sure to cut the potatoes into small pieces. Use baking potatoes if you can't find the baby bliss. They take less than 30 minutes to prepare and make an excellent addition to a hearty winter buffet.

Olive oil spray
12 baby bliss (small red) potatoes, (about 1½ inches in diameter) or 3 regular baking potatoes
¼ teaspoon salt (optional)
¼ teaspoon freshly ground black pepper

⅙ recipe Hunky Caponata (page 15) or 1 cup canned
¼ cup fresh snipped chives or fresh chopped parsley, for garnish

Preheat the oven to 475°F.

Spray a baking sheet with olive oil. If using tiny potatoes, cut them in half. (If using baking potatoes, make ¾-inch slices and cut each slice in half.) With a melon ball cutter, scoop out a dime-size shallow "well" from each potato half and discard the scooped pieces. Place the potatoes on the baking sheet well side up and lightly spray with olive oil until coated on all sides. Sprinkle with salt, if using, and pepper, and turn cut side down on the baking sheet. Bake for 10 minutes.

When cool enough to handle, fill each well with caponata and bake 10 to 15 minutes more. Garnish with chives or parsley and serve hot.

PER 3 PIECES: Saturated Fat: 0 gm Total Fat: Trace
Cholesterol: 0 mg Sodium: 22 mg Calories: 58

Potato Galette

A savory potato tart (which is something like scalloped potatoes) is best when made in a springform pan and cut into wedges. This is also an excellent side dish for dinner.

Vegetable oil spray

3 cups wafer-thin, unpeeled sliced baking or Yukon gold potatoes divided into 4 parts

1¼ cups (1 large onion) wafer-thin sliced onions divided into 3 parts

1 cup finely diced pimento

¼ cup all-purpose flour

Salt (optional)

Freshly ground black pepper

¼ cup grated nonfat Parmesan

Olive oil spray

1 5-ounce can evaporated skimmed milk or ⅔ cup nonfat dairy creamer

1 tablespoon Dijon mustard

2 cloves garlic, minced

¼ cup egg substitute

Paprika, for garnish

¼ cup chopped scallions, for garnish

Chopped parsley, for garnish

Preheat the oven to 375°F.

Line a 9-inch springform pan with foil and lightly spray with vegetable oil. You will be making 4 layers of potatoes and 3 layers of onions. Starting with ¼ of the potatoes, line the bottom of the pan. Add ⅓ of the onions and ⅓ of the pimentos. After each layer, sprinkle evenly with 1 tablespoon flour, salt, if using, pepper, and 1 teaspoon of Parmesan and spray lightly with olive oil. Repeat the layering process ending with the potatoes.

In a small bowl, combine the milk, mustard, garlic, and egg substitute and pour the mixture over the potatoes. Sprinkle with remaining Parmesan. Cover with foil and bake 1 hour and 15 minutes.

Preheat the broiler. Remove the foil from the galette and place under the broiler until lightly browned, about 5 minutes, watching carefully. Remove to a wire rack and cool at least 15 minutes. Cut into wedges and garnish with paprika, scallions, and parsley.

PER WEDGE: Saturated Fat: Trace   Total Fat: 0.5 gm
Cholesterol: 3 mg   Sodium: 148 mg   Calories: 118

Sesame Shrimp Spheres

These delicately seasoned shrimp balls are a favorite and take about 20 minutes to make. Serve on a platter with a selection of colorful garnishes.

Vegetable oil spray

1 large clove garlic

2 teaspoons fresh grated ginger or
  ½-inch piece

1 egg white

2 teaspoons fresh lemon juice

1 teaspoon sesame oil

1 tablespoon hoisin sauce

10 ounces fresh shrimp, shelled
  and deveined

2 cups fresh bread cubes

¾ cup sesame seeds

DIPPING SAUCE:

¼ cup hoisin sauce

1 tablespoon low-sodium soy sauce

2 teaspoons fresh lemon juice

Parsley or watercress, radishes, or
  olives, for garnish

Preheat the oven to 375°F.

Lightly spray a baking sheet with vegetable oil. In a food processor or a blender, mince the garlic and ginger. Add the egg white and process until frothy, about 3 minutes. Add the lemon juice, sesame oil, hoisin sauce, shrimp, and bread cubes, and pulse only until just combined. (The shrimp should be *very* chunky).

Using a teaspoon, shape the shrimp mixture into 1-inch balls. Place the sesame seeds in a bowl or on a plate, and roll the shrimp balls in the seeds to coat. Place on the baking sheet and bake 10 minutes.

In a small bowl, combine the hoisin sauce, soy sauce, and lemon juice. Serve the shrimp balls with fringed toothpicks accompanied by the hoisin dipping sauce. Garnish as desired.

PER 3 SHRIMP BALLS: Saturated Fat: 1 gm
Total Fat: 8 gm   Cholesterol: 54 mg   Sodium: 333 mg
Calories: 154

Salmon Mousse

This pretty mousse can be served hot, cold, or warm as part of a buffet table or individually plated as a first course with toast points for a formal dinner.

¾ cup nonfat cottage cheese, drained for 15 minutes	3 ounces smoked salmon, minced
½ pound salmon fillet, skinned and cut into pieces	2 teaspoons grated lemon zest
½ pound flounder or sole fillet, cut into pieces	3 tablespoons fresh lemon juice
1 tablespoon bread crumbs	2 tablespoons chopped onion
1 envelope unflavored gelatine	⅛ teaspoon salt (optional)
¼ cup (about 2 sprigs) fresh dill	⅛ teaspoon white pepper
2 large egg whites, lightly beaten	Vegetable oil spray
	Dill sprigs and cherry tomatoes, for garnish

Preheat the oven to 325°F.

In a food processor, process cottage cheese, salmon, flounder, bread crumbs, gelatine, dill, and egg whites for 3 to 4 minutes, until smooth. Spoon mixture into a large bowl and add the smoked salmon, lemon zest, lemon juice, onion, salt, if using, and pepper and mix thoroughly.

Lightly spray a 4-cup mold or loaf pan with vegetable oil. Spoon the salmon mixture into the mold, and tap the mold on a hard surface to expel any trapped air bubbles. Cover with foil and place in a baking pan filled with 1 inch of boiling water. Bake for 25 to 30 minutes or until a knife inserted in the center comes out clean.

If serving cold, chill first in mold, covered, overnight. Immerse the sides 2 to 3 seconds in hot water, place a serving platter over the mold, and invert the mousse onto the platter (pouring off any excess liquid). (If serving hot, don't immerse in hot water, just invert on a platter.) Garnish with dill sprigs and whole or halved cherry tomatoes.

PER SERVING: Saturated Fat: Trace   Total Fat: 2 gm
Cholesterol: 23 mg   Sodium: 146 mg   Calories: 70

Stuffed Mushrooms

I use large mushrooms and serve three to each guest as a first course, but bite-size mushrooms are preferable for a buffet. Stuffed mushrooms are great party food; they can be prepared ahead of time and baked just before the guests arrive (don't freeze them, however). Garnish with fresh chopped parsley, red bell pepper strips, grated nonfat Parmesan, or sprigs of watercress.

Olive oil spray

12 large mushrooms, cleaned, stems removed, and chopped

1 shallot or small onion, finely chopped

1 tablespoon finely chopped parsley

3 tablespoons herbed bread crumbs

½ teaspoon salt (optional)

Freshly ground black pepper

1 teaspoon Madeira (optional)

Lightly spray a large nonstick skillet with olive oil and place over low heat. Add the chopped mushroom stems, shallot, parsley, bread crumbs, salt, if using, and pepper and stir until well combined. Add the Madeira (or 1 teaspoon water) and cook, about 6 minutes. Move the mixture to one side of the skillet and place the mushrooms top down in the same skillet; spoon the cooked stuffing into each mushroom. Add a few teaspoons water and cook, covered, 15 to 30 minutes (depending on the size of the mushrooms), over very low heat until mushrooms are tender. Garnish and serve hot or keep warm on a heated tray on the buffet.

PER 3 PIECES: Saturated Fat: 0 gm   Total Fat: Trace
Cholesterol: 0 mg   Sodium: 136 mg   Calories: 34

Tabletop Cocktail Party
Hors d'Oeuvre

This giant sit-down cocktail hors d'oeuvre is spectacular. Once the food is arranged on table, there's no additional work for the host. The whole meal takes about 3 hours to prepare, 15 minutes to arrange. The guests sit down to what is actually a fancy cold supper artfully arranged on the table. You can increase or reduce it for more or less people, but I think it works best for no more than six people. It is a seated cocktail party with a large chilled dinner on your table. The mounds of food are always topped with something spectacular such as a grouping of very large shrimp, or crab claws. You could also use lobster or a skinned, roasted Cornish game hen or chicken (page 253) or Roast Quail with Grapes (page 254).

TRAY BASE:
1 large (30 to 35 inches in diameter) tray (omit tray if your table is glass)
4 or 6 long, thin, white candles
30 to 50 shiny, dark green leaves (magnolia, grape, or oak)
1 head Boston or Bibb lettuce
1 head escarole or curly lettuce
1 head radicchio

VEGETABLES, SAUCE, AND MEAT:
24 to 30 cooked thin asparagus spears, wrapped in plastic and chilled
6 to 12 strips pimento, 4 inches by ½ inch (for "tying" the asparagus spear bundles)

6 artichoke hearts
1 6-ounce jar ratatouille or vegetable paté (to fill the artichoke hearts)
9 hard-cooked eggs, cut in half, yolks discarded
1 6-ounce jar nonfat bean dip or Black Bean Dip (page 14) (to fill egg halves)
Paprika
18 baby carrots with leaves, parboiled
36 broccoli florets, parboiled
12 scallions, 6 raw, 6 parboiled
24 wax beans, parboiled
18 cherry tomatoes
18 yellow cherry tomatoes
1 avocado, sliced lengthwise ½ inch wide, coated with lemon juice

18 colossal, pitted black olives
  (optional)
12 whole hot pickled okra or other
  pickle (optional)
12 to 15 sweet pickles or
  watermelon rind (optional)
18 cocktail-size cooked, spiced
  crab claws or shrimp
1 lemon cut in 8 wedges
1 bunch watercress
1 bunch parsley
3 small bunches black grapes
3 small bunches green grapes
3 small bunches red grapes
10 to 20 brightly colored small
  flowers (any kind, each head
  about 2 to 3 inches in
  diameter—pansies, roses,
  marigolds, Queen Anne's
  Lace), stems removed

DIPS:
Cocktail Sauce (page 290)
Classic Vinaigrette (page 116)
Blue Cheese or Roquefort
  Dressing (page 115)
Lillian Smith's Five-Vinegar Dill
  Dressing (page 122)
Salmon and Red Caviar (page
  21)

CONTAINERS:
5 very small (wooden, ceramic, or
  glass) ramekins or scooped-out
  summer squashes, tiny
  pumpkins, anything that can
  hold the 5 sauces and dips

Early in the day, prepare hard-cooked eggs. Parboil vegetables and refrigerate.

An hour before the guests arrive, remove all the ingredients from the refrigerator, including the grapes and flowers. On a large tray (the same shape as the table or if a glass top, arrange directly on the table), arrange the darkest leaves to make the outer edge, hanging off the tray edge (measure beforehand so you can leave at least 6 to 8 inches of table edge for guests to rest their beverages and to set the napkins (no forks—this is all finger food). Place the darker leaves around the edge, overlapping so the edge of the tray doesn't show. Arrange the lighter Boston lettuce on top of the darker leaves but so 3 inches of the darker leaves still show. Arrange radicchio, escarole, and other lighter leaves on the Boston leaves so some of the Boston lettuce leaves show but so the whole tray is covered with greens and no tray part shows.

Arrange the candles evenly and secure them to the tray with modeling clay or low holders, hiding the clay with lettuce leaves.

(continued)

Make 6 bunches (for 6 servings) of 5 asparagus each. Cross the middle of each bundle with 2 strips of pimento and place the bunches all facing the same way around the edge of the tray, about where people will be sitting, near the edge of the tray.

Stuff the artichokes with ratatouille, and place one near each asparagus bunch. Generously fill the hard-cooked eggs with bean dip, and garnish with a shake of paprika. Place the eggs in groups of 3 on the other side of each asparagus bundle.

Place 3 carrots next to the eggs, and half the broccoli tucked in, floret side up, all over, and place 1 raw scallion at each asparagus bundle serving site. Tie each bundle of 4 wax beans with a soft parboiled scallion and place 3 on each side. For the top and center of the arrangement, place the broccoli in the middle, leaving a 3-inch by 3-inch empty circle in the center of the broccoli. Tuck in tomatoes, avocado slices, olives, okra, and pickles randomly throughout the arrangement.

In the very center of the broccoli, where you left the space, sink a tiny cocktail sauce holder, and place the cold crab claws (or shrimp) on the broccoli. Surround the broccoli with lemon wedges.

Nestle the 5 small dipping bowls (or vegetable containers) into the vegetables, taking care to just move the food aside and not mash it. Tuck in watercress or parsley, place a few grape clusters around the very outer edge, and tuck flowers in everywhere. Move the filled tray to the serving table, turn on the music, light the candles, and serve immediately.

■■   PER SERVING (not including dips):   Saturated Fat: 2 gm   ■■
Total Fat: 9 gm   Cholesterol: 37 mg   Sodium: 1231 mg   Calories: 433

Smoked Salmon, Leek, and Dill Strudels

Makes 36 appetizers

Spray phyllo pastry with butter-flavored vegetable oil rather than brushing them with butter to avoid unnecessary fat. Place a slightly damp towel over the phyllo to keep it moist while working and use kitchen shears to cut the dough.

Vegetable oil spray	2 teaspoons fresh lemon juice
1 clove garlic, minced	Freshly ground black pepper
4 ounces smoked salmon, minced	6 sheets phyllo pastry
1 scallion, finely sliced	Butter-flavored vegetable oil spray
½ cup nonfat ricotta	3 tablespoons corn-bread stuffing,
¼ cup nonfat sour cream	finely crushed in a processor
1 teaspoon grated lemon zest	Parsley sprigs or dill for garnish

Preheat oven to 375°F.

Spray a baking sheet with vegetable oil. In a medium bowl, combine the garlic, salmon, scallion, ricotta, sour cream, lemon zest, lemon juice, and pepper and mix well.

Spray 1 sheet of phyllo with vegetable oil and sprinkle with 1 tablespoon of corn-bread crumbs. Top with a second sheet of phyllo. Cut phyllo into 6 equal strips, about 1½ inches wide and 8 inches long. Place 2 teaspoons of the salmon mixture at one end of each strip and fold the corner over the filling, making a triangle. Continue folding (as if folding a flag) to create a many-layered filled triangle. Lightly spray the triangle and place on a baking sheet. Repeat the process to yield 20 to 24 triangles. Do not crowd on the baking sheet. Bake 12 to 17 minutes or until light brown and crispy.

Cut each triangle in half and garnish with parsley or dill.

PER 3 PIECES: Saturated Fat: Trace   Total Fat: 1 gm
Cholesterol: 3 mg   Sodium: 165 mg   Calories: 55

SOUPS
AND STEWS

Almost as soon as humans figured out how to fashion a cooking pot, they also figured out how to combine meats and vegetables to make a good soup. Food historians know soups were enjoyed thousands of years before Christ. There is evidence meat-filled liquids were cooked in hollowed-out wood or rocks and, later, in animal stomachs suspended on poles and slung over fires. For spices, there are signs that our early ancestors discovered coriander seeds and other aromatic leaves such as bay laurel. There is a reason we have always loved soups of all kinds. They are simple to make, take just one pot, and they satisfy.

■ Raison d'Etre ■

Soups (from "soupe") became immensely popular in the Middle Ages in France. In Italy and the British Isles, the contents of what was left in the cooking pot were commonly poured over a six-inch block of coarse bread (or trencher), and the one who ate the sop bread was a trencherman. The French call soup *potage,* the Americans call it soup, and sop bread in both France and England has gone out of style (except for French onion soup where the bread is toasted and placed on the top).

Soup is an easy way to enjoy several good foods at once. Cooking foods together develops and changes their flavors.

Even on the most extreme low-fat eating plan, soups can be made with fatty meat such as salt pork, marrow bones, fat-filled knuckles, smoked ham bones, fatty fish, and you throw everything in the pot—bones, skin, fat, back, neck, wings, even butter. You just need to defat the stock or broth completely (page 48).

Soup liquids can include mixtures of water, wine, juices, vegetable juice or stock, canned consommés, bouillon cubes dissolved in liquid, and other numerous liquids. With so many interesting ingredients, soup never suffers from the lack of fat; in fact, the lack enhances soup.

■ Defatting Stock ■

To defat soups made with animal products, simmer, for 30 minutes to 1 hour, a couple of quarts of water and whatever meat, bacon, fatback, skin, and bones of meat, fish, or poultry, along with herbs, spices, and vegetables such as onions, carrots, celery, etc., you wish. Discard or rinse the vegetables and defat the stock by refrigerating for 3 to 4 hours and picking off the fat (which rises to the surface and congeals). (Be careful not to stir or disturb the stock as it cools because the fat will become incorporated into the liquid.) For more immediate results, spoon off the fat or use a large glass defatting pitcher (available in most kitchen stores or by calling 1-800-8-FLAVOR for my free catalog). The defatting pitcher has a spout on the bottom, so as soon as the fat of a hot liquid rises to the top (about 10 seconds), you can pour off the tasty broth, which is at the bottom. (In a pinch, I've used a watering can because removing the fat is really important.)

Wash the meat pot, add the defatted, flavored broth, then whatever new vegetables, beans, herbs and spices, and any other ingredients you want. You now have a fat-free soup.

Incidentally, regarding bean soup and intestinal problems (or gas), *don't* soak the beans. Just cook them from scratch (which has an additional benefit over the canned or soaked beans of having more texture and less salt.) It takes 3 hours to simmer the longest-cooking bean (dried garbanzo, lima, or pisole [corn]); 10 minutes for the shortest (red lentils, which aren't really lentils but pulses, or seeds).

■ Winning Combinations ■

Once you have defatted the stock, you can either freeze it until you are ready to make soup, use it right away for your favorite soup recipe, or invent a new recipe from scratch. When you are inventing soup, there are a few basic combinations of ingredients that are bound to succeed:

Most dried beans will combine with carrots, onion, garlic, and celery and steep well in a good defatted ham stock with perhaps some Madeira or Cajun spice mixture to give it some kick.

Leeks or onions and potatoes are classic partners. Leeks also go well with rice and beans. Potatoes also go well with other onions, such as scallions, pearl onions, and shallots, and even garlic.

Tomatoes enhance most beans, meats, poultry, fish, shellfish, and vegetables.

Beef, pork, chicken, and vegetable soups are greatly enhanced by adding cooked potatoes, pasta, rice, corn, or dumplings in the last several minutes of cooking.

∎ Seasonings ∎

This is a delicate matter. I suggest that when you experiment with seasonings other than salt and pepper that you pour ¼ cup of the soup into four small bowls. Add a pinch of the herb or spice, a dash of the pepper sauce, a few drops of the wine or liqueur (like Pernod) you think you might like in the soup, and taste. Use the bowls to vary your amounts until you get something you like.

SALT AND PEPPER Nearly everyone wants a little salt in his soup and, frankly, most soups taste better with it. For a salty flavor without using pure salt, you can add a tablespoon or two of vinegar, lemon or lime juice, Worcestershire, low-sodium soy sauce (both contain salt), sherry peppers, several kinds of wine, crushed red pepper, fresh chili peppers, celery (which contains natural salt), olives (also salty), hot pepper sauce, or a combination of half salt and half potassium (has a salty taste without all the sodium) to enhance soups that now use smaller amounts of sodium (check with your physician about potassium). Be sure you realize that pepper's flavor expands with time in any liquid, so best to use it at the table unless the soup is to be eaten immediately.

∎ Wine in Soup ∎

Use any wine that is medium priced as low-priced wine will not taste good. Wines that work best are dry and sweet, red and white, Champagne, sherry, vermouth, Pernod, Madeira, Marsala, and Riesling, as well as many others. Alcohol widens the range of the flavors of a soup. Don't use cooking wine because it often contains salt and is of extremely poor quality.

∎ Garnishes ∎

As with all served foods, the eye eats first. Soups are more appetizing when garnished, even very simply with a sprinkle of paprika, chopped parsley, or shredded carrots. Garnishes not only please the eye but they can also add special unexpected flavor too. I like to add finely chopped parsley, jalapeño, chives, shredded carrots, lime juice, or olives to many of my bean recipes. A shallow traditional soup bowl is best for seeing the garnish. Deeper bowls and cups have a way of engulfing the garnish. For a thin and clear soup in particular, anything heavier than finely chopped chives, scallion, cilantro, or parsley will disappear, sinking to the bottom.

Low-Fat Soup Thickeners

We judge soup by its texture as well as by its flavor. When thickening soup, use a whisk to distribute the thickener evenly and break up lumps.

For clear or translucent soups, use cornstarch or arrowroot. For thick, opaque soups, use flour, potato flour, rice flour, mashed or shredded potatoes, pureed rice, carrots, or lentils.

Most thickeners can be added to the soup anytime during cooking. Cornstarch is the exception: Add it during the last 2 or 3 minutes of cooking.

The following ingredients will thicken 2 to 3 quarts of soup.

Flour: Flour-thickened soups are opaque, can be reheated, and usually remain thick. Whisk 2 to 4 tablespoons all-purpose flour into 1 cup warm or cooled soup stock until smooth. Add to the hot soup and whisk over medium heat for at least 3 minutes (so the flour cooks or the soup will taste doughy).

Cornstarch or arrowroot: Arrowroot behaves like cornstarch and can be found in most health-food stores but it is more expensive. Use these thickeners during the last 3 minutes of cooking. Whisk 2 tablespoons cornstarch or arrowroot with ½ cup (only) cooled soup stock until smooth. Add to the hot soup and whisk over medium heat at least 2 to 3 minutes. If clear, the soup will remain clear rather than opaque and usually needs rethickening when you reheat it.

Tapioca flour: This is made from the cassava plant and can be found in most health-food stores or Asian markets. It is semiclear. Sometimes it's called cassava flour. Follow the directions for thickening with flour. It takes about 30 seconds to thicken the broth.

Flour and cornstarch mixture: Use as you would flour, whisking equal parts of flour and cornstarch in 1 cup of cool liquid until smooth (or shake in a small jar with a lid), and whisk into the soup, over medium heat, for at least 3 minutes. (You can vary the proportions.)

Potato flour: Also called potato starch, it makes an excellent thick, opaque soup. Whisk 2 or more tablespoons into 1 cup cooled soup stock until smooth. Add to the soup and whisk over medium heat about 4 minutes or until thick.

Mashed potatoes: Add 1 cooked and mashed potato for each quart of liquid, and stir over medium heat about 4 minutes or until thick. Mashed potatoes make a soup more dense. For a thicker soup, cook another 15 minutes over low heat.

Raw potatoes: These create a light thickener that is slightly opaque. Add 1 cup grated or shredded potatoes for each quart of liquid to the soup, whisking or stirring occasionally, and cooking over medium-low heat until the potato releases its starch, which take about 20 minutes.

Bread or bread crumbs: Add finely ground bread crumbs, about 4 to 6 tablespoons per quart of liquid, and stir over medium heat for 3 to 5 minutes or until thick.

Cooked rice: Add ½ cup of pureed cooked rice and whisk over medium heat about 4 minutes or until thick.

Raw carrots: Stir ½ cup grated or shredded raw carrots for each ¾ quart of liquid into the soup and cook over medium-low heat, stirring occasionally, for about 15 minutes.

Red/orange lentils: Stir about ½ cup dried red lentils for each quart of liquid into the soup and cook, stirring occasionally, over medium-low heat for at least 15 minutes, when they will disintegrate.

Chicken Stock

Stock is easy to make and easy to defat with a defatting cup (page 7). Use every part of the cleaned chicken except the liver (or you can use leftover bones and skin). Skimming the stock often helps keep it clear but it isn't necessary. I put herbs in my stock. You can tie the herbs and spices in a square of cheesecloth if you like. Extra stock can be frozen for up to 6 months.

1 1- to 3-pound whole chicken	OPTIONAL HERBS:
2 large onions, quartered	1 sprig thyme
3 shallots	1 sprig rosemary
2 carrots	6 basil leaves or 1 teaspoon dried basil
4 cloves garlic	3 oregano leaves or ½ teaspoon oregano
3 ribs celery	1 bay leaf
	Salt (optional)

In a stockpot with a lid, combine all ingredients and add 3½ quarts water. Simmer, covered, over medium-low heat for 1½ hours. Strain the soup through a colander. Reserve the chicken for another use—chicken soup (versus stock), keeping vegetables in the soup. Defat the stock and refrigerate until needed.

PER 1 CUP: Saturated Fat: 0 gm   Total Fat: 0 gm
Cholesterol: 5 mg   Sodium: 23 mg   Calories: 21

Beef Stock

Use marrow or bones, with or without meat. I like herbs in my stock. Herbs and spices tied in a cheesecloth or wrapped in the green part of a leek and tied with clean string will add bouquet and flavor to the stock. Trace amounts of marrow won't affect fat amount.

1 or 2 large beef neck bones with meat	OPTIONAL HERBS:
2 large onions, quartered	1 sprig thyme
3 shallots	1 sprig rosemary
2 carrots	4 basil leaves or 1 teaspoon dried basil
4 cloves garlic	3 oregano leaves or ½ teaspoon dried oregano
3 ribs celery	2 bay leaves
	Salt (optional)

In a stockpot with a lid, combine all ingredients, and add 3½ quarts water. Simmer, covered, over low heat for 1½ hours. Strain through a colander. Reserve the meat for another use. Defat the stock (page 48) and refrigerate until needed.

PER 1 CUP: Saturated Fat: O gm   Total Fat: O gm
Cholesterol: 1 mg   Sodium: 11 mg   Calories: 17

Fish Stock

The best bones for fish stock are from any lean white fish, such as halibut, sole, or flounder. Fatty or salty fish, such as cod, bluefish, pollock, salmon, and swordfish, make inferior fish stock. You can substitute bottled diluted clam juice for some of the liquid in this recipe and if you are fond of sage, add 1 or 2 leaves.

2 to 3 pounds white fish bones and trimmings
1 large leek, thoroughly rinsed and sliced
1 onion, quartered
3 leafy ribs celery, cut in half
2 carrots, cut up
3 bay leaves

2 sprigs fresh thyme or 1 tablespoon dried thyme
4 or 5 parsley sprigs
½ teaspoon whole black peppercorns
1 cup dry white wine
Salt (optional)

In a 4-quart Dutch oven, combine all ingredients except salt and add 6 cups water. Simmer, covered, for 25 minutes, skimming the foam off as necessary. Let stand for ten minutes. Add salt, strain, discard the bones and vegetables. Defat the stock (page 48) and refrigerate till needed.

PER 1 CUP: Saturated Fat: 0 gm Total Fat: 0 gm
Cholesterol: 0 mg Sodium: 49 mg Calories: 28

Ham Stock

Ham stock is a perfect base for bean soup and when cooking Southern greens and green beans. Use it wherever you want a sweet and salty soup base. If you use a Smithfield or country ham, be aware that they're especially salty. The ham can be smoked. Defat the stock (page 48) and refrigerate till needed.

1-pound ham bone or hock, with meat	*1 carrot*
	1 onion

In a large saucepan, combine the ham bone or hock, carrot, and onion and 2 quarts water. Bring to a boil and simmer over medium-low heat, covered, 45 minutes. Discard the vegetables.

PER 1 CUP: Saturated Fat: Trace   Total Fat: 1 gm
Cholesterol: 5 mg   Sodium: 167 mg   Calories: 69

Vegetable Stock

Vegetable stock can be used instead of water for soups, risottos, sauces, and gravies. I often steam vegetables in a little vegetable stock as well. The ingredients don't need peeling or cutting up if they are removed after cooking. Just make sure to scrub them clean with a vegetable brush.

2 onions, cut in fourths	1 sprig thyme
3 shallots (optional), cut in half	3 sprigs parsley
3 carrots, cut in half	2 bay leaves
4 cloves garlic	6 to 10 peppercorns
3 leafy ribs celery	

In a large stockpot, combine all ingredients and add 3½ quarts water. Cover and simmer for 1 hour. Strain the stock in a colander and discard the herbs and vegetables.

PER 1 CUP: Saturated Fat: 0 gm   Total Fat: 0 gm
Cholesterol: 0 mg   Sodium: 18 mg   Calories: 13

Chicken Soup

This is a full-bodied world-class soup. For a velvety rich bisque version, puree the soup with a hand, or immersion, blender or in a food processor and thicken it with flour, cornstarch, or arrowroot (page 50).

1 1½- to 3-pound whole chicken	¼ cup chopped parsley
3 carrots	Salt (optional)
1 large onion, cut into eighths	Freshly ground black pepper
3 leafy ribs celery, cut in half	4 tablespoons flour or
2 leeks, thoroughly rinsed and	4 tablespoons cornstarch
sliced	(optional for thickening)
5 cloves garlic	

In a 5- to 8-quart Dutch oven, combine all ingredients except salt, pepper, and flour and add enough water to cover, about 3 to 4 quarts. Simmer, covered, for 1½ hours over very low heat. Remove chicken and vegetables and set aside. Defat the stock (page 48).

Discard skin, fat, and bones from the chicken; cut meat into large pieces, removing any visible or hidden fat, especially in the thigh. With hot tap water, rinse the oily surface of the meat and vegetables; cut the vegetables and chicken into bite-size pieces; and return them to the stock.

If you wish a thick soup, in a small bowl, blend the flour and cornstarch with 1 cup cooled stock, whisk together, stir into the soup, and cook on medium high for 4 to 5 minutes, until flour is cooked and soup is thickened. Season with salt and pepper, garnish, and serve hot.

PER 1½ CUPS: Saturated Fat: 2 gm   Total Fat: 6 gm
Cholesterol: 68 mg   Sodium: 94 mg   Calories: 188

Chicken Soup with Noodles, Pasta, or White, Brown, or Wild Rice

::

Add ½ cup cooked noodles, pasta shells, orzo, or white, brown, or wild rice to each bowl and pour the hot soup over the grain just before serving. Unless you are going to use all the soup at one time, don't add the noodles or rice directly to the soup or they will get mushy, especially if the soup is to be further cooked, stored, or reheated.

:: PER ¼ CUP with 1½ CUPS SOUP: Saturated Fat: 2 gm **::**
Total Fat: 6 gm   Cholesterol: 68 mg   Sodium: 95 mg   Calories: 229

::

Matzoh Balls

Serves 6

These feather-light matzoh balls, which are a delicately seasoned type of dumpling to be placed in chicken soup, are shaped from dough that must chill for several hours or overnight. They will expand by one third during cooking, so shape them accordingly. If you prefer a heavier matzoh ball, omit the egg whites altogether.

¼ cup canola oil	Salt (optional)
¼ teaspoon nutmeg	½ cup egg substitute
¼ teaspoon ground ginger	2 stiffly beaten egg whites
3 tablespoons grated onion	(optional)
2 tablespoons chopped parsley	Vegetable oil spray
¼ tablespoon paprika	1 recipe Chicken Soup (page 57)
1 cup matzoh meal	

In a medium nonstick saucepan over very low heat, combine the oil, 1 cup boiling water, nutmeg, ginger, onion, parsley, and paprika. Stir in the matzoh meal and salt and cook for 4 to 5 minutes, stirring and scraping the bottom of the pan to blend ingredients well. Add the egg substitute a little at a time in a stream, mashing it in and mixing well. Chill the dough thoroughly for at least 2 hours.

Using your hands (a spoon won't work), fold in the beaten egg whites, by squeezing them into the chilled dough. Spray a large square of foil with vegetable oil. Divide the dough into 12 parts and shape into 1- to 1½-inch balls. (Remember, they expand when cooked.) Place them on the foil. Carefully slip the balls into the chicken soup and cover (don't stir). Simmer on very low for 10 minutes (a fast boil will disintegrate the matzoh balls), and serve hot.

PER 1½ CUPS SOUP and 2-BALL SERVING: Saturated Fat: 2 gm
Total Fat: 15 gm   Cholesterol: 68 mg   Sodium: 124 mg   Calories: 331

Grandma Gracie's Corn Chowder

My grandmother Gracie Gibson Connor was famous for her corn chowder. Her stock of corn on the cob, clean husks and all, simmered with either a whole chicken or chicken skin, wings, and backs. Don't bother peeling the potatoes; they are a good source of fiber.

5 ears fresh corn, silk removed,
   with husks peeled back
1½ to 3 pounds chicken or
   chicken parts (but not the liver)
2 leafy ribs celery, chopped
2 carrots, chopped
3 cloves garlic, minced
1 large onion, chopped
3 potatoes, diced
2 tablespoons minced parsley
½ teaspoon sugar
Salt (optional)

1 teaspoon Worcestershire
   (optional)
1 cup fresh or frozen peas
Pinch nutmeg
1 to 3 tablespoons sherry or
   Madeira (optional)
1 cooked potato, diced or mashed
   (optional)
4 tablespoons all-purpose flour
Salt (optional)
Paprika, for garnish

In a stockpot, combine the corn with husks, chicken, celery, carrots, garlic, onion, potatoes, and parsley. Cover with 2 quarts water and simmer, covered, over low heat for 1½ hours. With a slotted spoon, remove chicken and vegetables to a colander and rinse with hot water. Defat the stock (page 48). Discard the skin, fat, and bones from the chicken. Cut meat into bite-size pieces and return to the stock. Add the sugar, salt, Worcestershire, if using, peas, nutmeg, and sherry. Simmer for 15 minutes. Remove corn, cool under water, cut off the kernals, and return to the soup, discarding the cobs and husks. If using mashed potatoes and flour, stir in the potatoes, or in a bowl, whisk the flour into 1 cup stock until there are no lumps, and return the mixture to the stock. Adjust seasoning. Cook until the soup thickens, about 4 to 5 minutes. Garnish with nutmeg and paprika. Serve hot.

PER 1½ CUPS: Saturated Fat: 0.5 gm   Total Fat: 3 gm
Cholesterol: 28 mg   Sodium: 73 mg   Calories: 183

Magenta Beet Soup

This is a smooth soup with a full beet taste and a beautiful ruby color.

4 to 6 (12 ounces) fresh beets,
  scrubbed, ends removed
6 to 8 (12 ounces) fresh carrots,
  scrubbed and chopped
2½ cups low-sodium vegetable
  stock or defatted chicken stock
½ cup fresh orange juice
½ teaspoon freshly ground nutmeg

Salt (optional)
2 teaspoons raspberry or cider
  vinegar
1 tablespoon dry sherry (optional)
Freshly ground black pepper
¾ cup nonfat sour cream or plain
  yogurt
Dash nutmeg, for garnish

In a large saucepan, combine beets, carrots, stock, orange juice, and nutmeg. Bring to a boil, cover, reduce heat, and simmer on low 30 to 45 minutes, or until the vegetables are tender.

Remove the soup to a food processor (or use an immersion, or hand, blender, and puree the soup in the pot. Add salt, if using, vinegar, and sherry. Thin with additional stock if the soup is too thick. Serve hot with pepper, 3 tablespoons of nonfat sour cream, and a grinding of fresh nutmeg for garnish.

PER 1½ CUPS: Saturated Fat: Trace   Total Fat: 0.5 gm
Cholesterol: 0 mg   Sodium: 137 mg   Calories: 128

Asparagus Soup

When asparagus is in season, making this soup is one of my favorite ways to celebrate early spring. Choose bright green or pale white asparagus with tight, closed tips. The extra twist of lemon when serving rounds out the flavor.

1½ cups low-sodium vegetable
   stock or defatted chicken stock
1 pound asparagus, tough ends
   removed, cut into ½-inch pieces
1 leek (white part only), chopped
½ teaspoon dried tarragon or
   1 teaspoon chopped fresh
2 tablespoons all-purpose flour
⅓ cup nonfat ricotta cheese

2 teaspoons fresh lemon juice
1 teaspoon grated lemon zest
Salt (optional)
Freshly ground white pepper
1 teaspoon sugar
4 strips lemon zest, for garnish
¼ cup nonfat yogurt or sour
   cream, for garnish

In a medium saucepan, combine the stock, asparagus, and leek. Cover and simmer 10 to 12 minutes, or until the asparagus is very tender. Add the tarragon, flour, ricotta, lemon juice, lemon zest, salt, if using, white pepper, and sugar. Using an immersion, or hand, blender or food processor, puree for several minutes and, if serving hot, return to the saucepan, heating just until hot but not boiling. Garnish with lemon strips and a tablespoon of nonfat yogurt. Serve hot or cold.

PER 1½ CUPS: Saturated Fat: Trace   Total Fat: 0.5 gm
Cholesterol: 2 mg   Sodium: 65 mg   Calories: 73

Cream of Broccoli Soup

A delicious all-new rendition of a classic. For a more dense soup, add noodles or rice and this becomes a whole meal in itself. Garnish with wafer-thin slices of lemon or orange.

2 cups low-sodium vegetable stock, defatted chicken stock, or water
1 small onion, finely chopped
2 shallots, minced
1 fist-size bunch broccoli, chopped
1 fist-size bunch broccoli, cut into florets with ½-inch stems
½ cup nonfat milk
½ cup evaporated skimmed milk
½ cup whipped nonfat cottage cheese

3 tablespoons all-purpose flour
Juice of 1 lemon
½ teaspoon grated orange zest (optional)
¼ cup grated nonfat Cheddar cheese (optional)
2 tablespoons pitted chopped black olives (optional)

In a large nonstick saucepan, combine 1 cup stock or water, onion, shallots, and chopped broccoli, and cook for 6 or 7 minutes. Add the second cup of stock and heat. Add the remaining broccoli, stir, and heat for 2 to 3 minutes. Whisk in the nonfat milk, evaporated skimmed milk, and nonfat cottage cheese and heat over medium low until hot, but don't allow to boil.

With a fine mesh sieve held over the saucepan, shake the flour into the soup, continuously whisking for 3 to 4 minutes, until the soup is very thick. Pour into serving bowls, and add ½ teaspoon lemon juice. Garnish with zest, cheese, olives, if desired, and serve hot.

PER 1½ CUPS: Saturated Fat: Trace   Total Fat: 1 gm
Cholesterol: 5 mg   Sodium: 229 mg   Calories: 131

Cream of Pumpkin or Squash Soup

A mug of hot pumpkin soup, a salad, and some crusty bread makes a satisfying autumnal lunch or light supper. This soup can be pureed until smooth or left with some texture. (An immersion, or hand, blender allows you to puree in the pan.) Butternut, acorn, Hubbard, turban, or pureed spaghetti squash can be substituted for the pumpkin. Garnish with chopped apple, toasted pumpkin seed, or orange zest.

½ cup diced celery

½ cup diced onion

½ cup diced carrot

2 cups low-sodium vegetable stock, defatted chicken stock, or water

2 cups canned pumpkin or 1 cup pumpkin and 1 cup diced, cooked, and pureed acorn, butternut, or other winter squash

½ teaspoon salt (optional)

¼ teaspoon white pepper, coarsely ground

1½ teaspoons maple syrup or brown sugar

¼ teaspoon ground ginger

¼ teaspoon ground allspice

⅛ teaspoon ground nutmeg

½ cup evaporated skimmed milk

½ cup nonfat cottage or ricotta cheese, whipped in a processor or blender until smooth

2 tablespoons fresh orange juice

1 teaspoon orange zest

In a large nonstick saucepan over medium heat, cook the celery, onion, and carrot in ¼ inch of water, stirring constantly, adding more water if necessary, for 5 minutes, until the vegetables are cooked. Add the stock, pumpkin, salt, if using, pepper, maple syrup, ginger, allspice, and nutmeg, and simmer, partially uncovered, until slightly thickened, about 15 minutes.

In a food processor or with an immersion, or hand, blender, puree the soup in batches until almost smooth. Return the mixture to the saucepan; add the evaporated milk, whipped cottage cheese, orange juice, and orange zest, and cook over low heat, for 5 minutes, taking care not to boil the soup as it will curdle. The flavor of pumpkins varies, so taste and adjust seasonings if necessary.

Avocado-Zucchini Soup

Serves 4

In this thick, creamy soup, the heat comes from the jalapeño jelly, which also adds a subtle sweetness. This soup is delicious hot or cold.

1 cup low-sodium vegetable stock
  or defatted chicken stock
1 large zucchini, peeled and diced
2 medium shallots, minced
1 large ripe avocado, peeled,
  pitted, and diced
2 tablespoons fresh lime juice
1 cup low-fat buttermilk
½ teaspoon cumin

¼ cup dark rum (optional)
4 teaspoons to 2 tablespoons spicy
  green jalapeño jelly
Salt (optional)
4 red and 4 yellow cherry
  tomatoes, sliced, for garnish
1 tablespoon chopped, seeded
  jalapeños, for garnish

In a large saucepan, bring the stock to a boil. Add the zucchini and shallots, cover, and cook 6 to 8 minutes, or until tender. Place the avocado, lime juice, and buttermilk in a blender or food processor, puree and set aside. Add the hot zucchini mixture to blender or use an immersion, or hand, blender right in the pot; and puree.

Combine the 2 purees in the same saucepan, and heat gently until very warm but not too hot. Add the cumin, rum, jalapeño jelly, and salt, if using, and continue heating for 2 to 3 minutes. Adjust the seasonings. Garnish each serving with the tomato slices and jalapeños if you want more heat.

Curry Crookneck Soup with Croutons

A traditional potage is thickened with cream or egg yolks. I substitute pureed sweet potatoes, which give it a nice texture. You can substitute zucchini or pattypan if no crookneck is available.

Vegetable oil spray

1 medium sweet potato, peeled and chopped

1 large onion, chopped

1½ tablespoons freshly grated ginger

2 pounds crookneck squash, stems removed, and sliced

3 cups low-sodium, defatted chicken or vegetable stock

1 tablespoon curry powder

Salt (optional)

Freshly ground black pepper

Snipped chives or scallions, for garnish

CURRIED CROUTONS:

8 slices (¼-inch thick) French bread

Vegetable oil spray

2 teaspoons curry powder

2 tablespoons freshly grated nonfat Parmesan cheese

Preheat oven to 325°F.

Spray a large heavy saucepan with vegetable oil and place over medium-high heat. Add the sweet potato and onion and sauté for 5 minutes stirring, adding several tablespoons of water to prevent sticking, if necessary. Add the ginger, squash, stock, and curry powder. Bring to a boil, reduce the heat, cover, and simmer for 45 minutes.

Meanwhile, prepare the croutons: Coat the bread slices generously with vegetable oil spray and place on a baking sheet. Sprinkle with curry powder and Parmesan. Bake for 2 to 25 minutes, or until crunchy and lightly browned and cut into croutons.

In a food processor or with an immersion, or hand, blender, puree the soup until smooth. Ladle into individual serving bowls, top with croutons and sprinkle with chives.

PER 1½ CUPS: Saturated Fat: Trace   Total Fat: 2 gm
Cholesterol: 6 mg   Sodium: 300 mg   Calories: 234

Onion Soup with Cheese

Once aboard a sailboat on the Chesapeake, our party got caught in a sudden squall and we couldn't make our expected port. We were all wet, cold, exhausted, and hungry as the temperature dropped. In the galley, I found a bag of onions, some garlic, suspicious-looking bread, a slice or two of beef, cheese, a few spices, and some cognac. Strapped to a gimbaled stove on a berserk boat, I was able to turn out a mighty fine onion soup. I've made it many times since, with bouillon cubes (instead of meat) as the only added ingredient.

Vegetable oil spray
5 large onions, sliced
3 cloves garlic, minced
¼ cup red wine, port, or Madeira (optional)
½ cup cognac or brandy (optional)
2 quarts water, low-sodium vegetable stock, or defatted beef stock
1 beef bouillon cube

¼ teaspoon sugar
Salt (optional)
Freshly ground black pepper
½ teaspoon thyme
8 1-inch thick rounds of French bread
8 slices low-fat Swiss cheese or 8 extremely thin slices whole milk Swiss or Gruyère cheese

Preheat the oven to 350°F.

Spray a large saucepan with vegetable oil and place over high heat. Add the onions, garlic, a few tablespoons of water, and brown, about 3 minutes. Add the wine, cognac, if using, water, bouillon cube, sugar, salt, if using, pepper, and thyme. Reduce the heat and simmer, covered, for 1 hour.

Meanwhile, heat the bread on a baking sheet in the oven, or toast it in the toaster. Pour the soup into individual ovenproof bowls (ladling lots of onions in each bowl), add the toast, cover with cheese, and place in the oven or under a broiler until the cheese melts. Serve hot.

PER 1½ CUPS: Saturated Fat: 1 gm   Total Fat: 2 gm
Cholesterol: 5 mg   Sodium: 368 mg   Calories: 165

Fresh Tomato Soup

For those who think that tomato soup comes only in a can, this will be a revelation! Use the freshest and ripest garden tomatoes you can find.

1 medium onion, quartered
1 large clove garlic, minced
1 leafy rib celery, cut into 1-inch
*   pieces*
8 large fresh basil leaves, torn
4 to 8 leaves fresh oregano
1 teaspoon brown sugar
4 tablespoons all-purpose flour
Salt (optional)

5 large ripe tomatoes
2 cups low-sodium vegetable stock,
*   defatted ham stock, chicken*
*   stock, or water*
Juice of ½ lemon or 3 tablespoons
½ cup nonfat sour cream,
*   for garnish*
1 jalapeño, seeded and finely
*   chopped, for garnish*

In a food processor, combine the onion, garlic, celery, basil, oregano, sugar, flour, and salt, and pulse only until very chunky.

Add the tomatoes and pulse again, keeping mixture chunky. Transfer the tomato mixture to a large saucepan. Add stock, and simmer, covered, over low heat, for 15 minutes. Add ½ tablespoon lemon juice on top, garnish with sour cream and jalapeño, and serve hot.

PER 1½ CUPS: Saturated Fat: 0 gm   Total Fat: 0.5 gm
Cholesterol: 0 mg   Sodium: 37 mg   Calories: 80

Watercress Vichyssoise

This traditional cold French soup is made with leeks, cream, and potatoes, but this rendition gets its creamy texture from whipped nonfat cottage cheese. It is usually served as a first course, but a large bowl can be a refreshing summertime lunch or dinner when accompanied by French bread, an English muffin, or even a toasted bagel.

2 leeks, white part only
½ large onion, diced
1 large or 2 medium potatoes,
*   peeled (optional) and diced*
2 cups low-sodium vegetable stock
*   or defatted chicken stock*
1 cup nonfat milk
⅓ cup nonfat cottage cheese,
*   whipped in a processor or*
*   blender until smooth*

¼ teaspoon mace
Salt and freshly ground white
*   pepper, to taste*
1 cup evaporated skimmed milk
½ cup chopped watercress
½ cup diced cucumbers
Watercress for garnish

In a large saucepan over medium-high heat, combine the leeks, onion, potatoes, stock, and nonfat milk, and bring to a boil. Reduce the heat, cover, and simmer gently for 20 minutes, being careful it doesn't burn. Transfer the mixture to a food processor or use an immersion, or hand, blender. Add the cottage cheese, mace, salt, if using, and pepper and puree. Add the evaporated skimmed milk until desired consistency, remove to a container, and refrigerate 2 hours.

Just before serving, stir in the watercress and cucumbers and garnish with a sprig of watercress.

PER 1½ CUPS: Saturated Fat: Trace   Total Fat: Trace
Cholesterol: 3 mg   Sodium: 162 mg   Calories: 148

Tomatillo Soup

The satisfying zest of this soup makes searching for this Mexican green tomatolike fruit well worth the effort. The tomatillo is smaller than a tomato, covered with a tight-fitting paperlike husk, and tastes best when green. It can be found in specialty food stores, Latin American markets, and some supermarkets. Substitute green tomatoes if you can't find tomatillos. Orzo is a small rice-shaped pasta that cooks in just a few minutes.

Vegetable oil spray
1 cup onion, chopped
3 cloves garlic, chopped
1 pound tomatillos, husks
 removed and quartered
1 jalapeño, seeded and chopped

1 beef, chicken, or vegetable
 bouillon cube
1 pound orzo, cooked according to
 package directions and drained
½ cup nonfat sour cream

Lightly spray a nonstick 4-quart Dutch oven with vegetable oil and place over medium heat. Add the onion, garlic, a few teaspoons water, and cook, stirring constantly about 5 minutes until the vegetables are tender. Add 3 cups water, tomatillos, jalapeño, and bouillon cube and bring to a boil. Reduce the heat and simmer 8 to 10 minutes. Cool slightly.

Transfer the mixture to a food processor, or use an immersion, or hand, blender, and puree until smooth. Return the mixture to the Dutch oven, stir in the orzo, and heat through but don't boil. Either stir in the sour cream in the pot or add a dollop on each serving.

PER 1½ CUPS: Saturated Fat: 0 gm Total Fat: 2 gm
Cholesterol: 0 mg Sodium: 122 mg Calories: 248

Mushroom-Barley Soup

This is a tasty, very thick and filling soup good on autumn days.

1½ pounds button mushrooms
1 large onion, chopped
3 shallots, minced
3 cloves garlic, minced
1 carrot, chopped
1 leafy rib celery, chopped
¼ cup uncooked pearl barley
8 cups low-sodium vegetable stock
  or defatted chicken stock, beef
  stock, or water
¼ teaspoon freshly grated nutmeg

¼ cup Madeira, Marsala, white
  wine, dry vermouth, or sherry
  (optional)
½ teaspoon dried basil
3 tablespoons all-purpose flour
Freshly ground black pepper
1 lemon cut into 4 wedges,
  for garnish
½ cup chopped parsley,
  for garnish
Paprika, for garnish

In a 4-quart Dutch oven, combine the vegetables, barley, and stock, and bring to a boil. Add the nutmeg, half the wine, and basil. Reduce the heat and simmer, covered, for 30 minutes.

Place the flour in a colander or sifter, and shake over the soup, stirring or whisking until incorporated, and cook, stirring, on medium high for at least 3 to 4 minutes or until thick. Add 1 cup more stock or water as desired. Add the rest of the wine and heat but do not boil. Adjust seasoning and serve hot, garnished with lemon wedges, parsley, and paprika.

PER 1½ CUPS: Saturated Fat: Trace   Total Fat: 1 gm
Cholesterol: 7 mg   Sodium: 52 mg   Calories: 136

Creamy-Style Mushroom-Barley Soup

Substitute 1 cup evaporated skimmed milk for 1 cup stock. Add after cooking with ¼ cup whipped nonfat cottage cheese; heat, but do not boil.

PER 1½ CUPS (Creamy Version):   Saturated Fat: Trace
Total Fat: 1 gm   Cholesterol: 8 mg   Sodium: 132 mg   Calories: 172

Italian Bulgur Soup

Bulgur is made of tender wheat kernels that have been steamed, dried, and crushed and is available in most stores. It has a mild nutty flavor and texture of short-grain brown rice and when combined with vegetables, it makes a soup a meal in itself. Nearly any kind of summer or winter squash can be used, and it can be more spicy if you add a few shakes of a Cajun mixture.

Vegetable oil spray

1½ cups coarsely chopped summer
    squash or crookneck pattypan
    squash or diced winter squash
    such as butternut, zucchini

1 10-ounce package frozen lima
    beans or 10 ounces fresh

1 yellow onion, chopped

½ cup bulgur, coarse or medium

3 tablespoons chopped parsley

3 cloves garlic, finely chopped

2 teaspoons chopped fresh basil

1 28-ounce can low-sodium
    tomatoes, undrained and
    broken up

1 beef bouillon cube

2 tablespoons slivered Parmesan
    cheese (optional)

Salt (optional)

Freshly ground black pepper

Lightly spray a nonstick 5-quart soup pot with vegetable oil. Add the squash, lima beans, onion, bulgur, parsley, garlic, and basil and sauté over medium heat for 5 to 8 minutes, adding a tablespoon or two at a time of water to prevent sticking. Add the tomatoes, 3 cups water, bouillon cube, and bring to a boil. Reduce the heat to very low, and simmer, uncovered, for 15 minutes. Add Parmesan cheese and salt, if using, and pepper to taste.

PER 1½ CUPS: Saturated Fat: Trace Total Fat: 1 gm
Cholesterol: 0 mg Sodium: 193 mg Calories: 137

Triple Lentil Soup

For lentil lovers, here is all the nutrition, taste, and texture of yellow and brown lentils. (The red disintegrate and thicken the soup.) You can use any three lentil mixtures, including the tiny French green lentils. This recipe is ready in one hour, start to finish, most of it unattended.

Vegetable oil spray
3 cloves garlic, minced
2 leafy ribs celery, diced
1 large onion, diced
3 carrots, diced
1 cup brown or black lentils,
  rinsed
½ cup yellow or green lentils,
  rinsed
½ cup orange or red lentils, rinsed

5 cups low-sodium vegetable or
  defatted beef stock
2 teaspoons Worcestershire
1 teaspoon dried thyme
Salt (optional)
Freshly ground black pepper
½ cup crumbled reduced-fat feta
  cheese
1 tomato, chopped

Spray a 4-quart Dutch oven with vegetable oil and place over medium-high heat. Combine the garlic, celery, onion, and carrots and cook for about 6 minutes; add a few tablespoons at a time of water as needed to prevent sticking. Add the lentils, stock, Worcestershire and thyme, and bring to a boil. Reduce the heat and simmer for 45 minutes to 1 hour or until the lentils are softened. Add salt, if using, and pepper to taste. Top each serving with a sprinkling of feta cheese and diced tomatoes.

PER 1½ CUPS: Saturated Fat: 3 gm   Total Fat: 5 gm
Cholesterol: 18 mg   Sodium: 312 mg   Calories: 323

Cajun Bean Soup

Here is a hearty soup replete with smoky-rich ham but without the fat. While it is traditional to flavor this soup with an anise liquor, such as Herbsaint or Pernod, it is optional here. Zatarain's Creole seasoning makes this an authentic Louisiana soup but your favorite Creole or Cajun mixture substitution will do fine.

½ pound smoked ham bone or
   ham hock with a few ounces
   of meat
1 pound dried red beans
2 onions, chopped
3 cloves garlic, chopped
2 leafy ribs celery, chopped
½ red bell pepper, seeded and
   chopped (reserve 1 tablespoon
   seeds for garnish)
2 carrots, diced or processed
   coarsely
1 teaspoon dried coriander

½ to 1 teaspoon Zatarain's
   Creole seasoning
1 cup chopped parsley
¼ cup Pernod or 2 tablespoons
   Herbsaint (optional)
1 tablespoon jalapeño slices, for
   garnish
2 tablespoons chopped scallions,
   for garnish
1 small, cooked crayfish, shrimp,
   or piece of lobster, for garnish
   (optional)

In a large saucepan, cover the ham bone with 4 to 4½ quarts water and let simmer uncovered on medium low for 30 minutes. Remove the ham and bone and set aside. Defat the stock (page 48).

Cut the meat from the bone; discard the bone and fat and dice the meat. Rinse the meat. Return the defatted stock to the saucepan and add the beans, onions, garlic, celery, pepper, carrots, coriander, Creole seasoning, and parsley and simmer, covered, on low, for 2 hours or until the beans are tender. Add Pernod and cook for another 2 minutes. Remove half the soup to a food processor or blender and puree, or use an immersion, or hand, blender. Be careful as hot liquid expands when it is processed. Return pureed soup to saucepan, stir to blend, garnish, and serve hot.

PER 1½ CUPS: Saturated Fat: Trace   Total Fat: 1 gm
Cholesterol: 5 mg   Sodium: 136 mg   Calories: 205

New England Clam Chowder

This creamy-thick chowder packed with hunks of potato is especially warming on a chilly day. The traditional texture comes from the pureed cottage cheese (or ricotta). Don't allow the soup to boil after the cheese has been added.

3 cups potatoes, peeled and cut up

1 large onion, cut up

1 leafy rib celery, cut up

3 tablespoons all-purpose flour

2 cups nonfat milk

1 cup chopped fresh clams

Salt (optional)

½ teaspoon sugar

2 tablespoons herbed bread crumbs

½ cup nonfat cottage cheese

1 cup evaporated skimmed milk or nonfat dairy creamer

Freshly ground black pepper

12 to 14 drops Tabasco

Freshly ground nutmeg

¼ cup chopped parsley

In a food processor, coarsely chop potatoes, onion, celery, and flour. Remove to a large saucepan, add milk, cover, and simmer over low heat, stirring occasionally, for 15 minutes. Stir in the clams, salt, if using, sugar, and bread crumbs, and cook 5 minutes.

In a blender or with an immersion, or hand, blender, puree the cottage cheese and evaporated skimmed milk until completely smooth, or for about 3 to 4 minutes. Add the mixture to the soup and heat but don't boil. Stir in the pepper and cook for a minute more. Add the Tabasco, and serve hot, garnished with a grinding of fresh nutmeg and parsley.

PER 1½ CUPS: Saturated Fat: Trace   Total Fat: 1 gm

Cholesterol: 22 mg   Sodium: 228 mg   Calories: 211

Crab and Avocado Gazpacho

Gazpacho is a no-cook soup, perfect for hot summer days when ripe tomatoes are in season. This indulgent version is dressed up with a garnish of crab and avocado. It can be thinned with more tomato juice.

½ large cucumber (peeled if
   waxed)
½ green bell pepper, seeds reserved
⅓ red bell pepper, seeds reserved
½ medium-large yellow or
   Spanish onion
1 large ripe tomato
5½ tablespoons fresh lemon or
   lime juice plus additional, for
   garnish
3 tablespoons cider vinegar

1 clove garlic, minced
1½ cups low-sodium tomato juice
⅛ teaspoon Tabasco plus
   additional, for garnish
2 tablespoons chopped cilantro
Salt (optional)
1 avocado, diced, divided into four
   parts
½ pound lump crabmeat
4 sprigs cilantro, for garnish

In a food processor, puree half of the cucumber, peppers, onion, tomato, and 1½ tablespoons lemon juice, vinegar, all of the garlic, tomato juice, Tabasco, cilantro, and salt, if using, until fine; remove to a large serving bowl and set aside. In the same food processor, pulse the remaining vegetables just until coarsely chopped. Combine the pureed and coarsely chopped vegetables in the bowl, cover, and refrigerate until chilled.

To serve, ladle the soup into shallow dishes or wide mugs. In a small bowl, combine the avocado and 4 tablespoons lemon juice. Add some avocado and crab to each serving of soup. Sprinkle each with Tabasco and additional lemon juice to taste and garnish with cilantro.

PER 1½ CUPS: Saturated Fat: 1 gm   Total Fat: 8 gm
Cholesterol: 35 mg   Sodium: 218 mg   Calories: 138

Asian Lobster Soup
with Emerald Pesto

This lush, low-calorie soup gets a flavor kick from a dab of emerald green cilantro pesto spooned on top.

4 cups low-sodium defatted
    chicken stock or vegetable stock
1 tablespoon freshly grated ginger
1 tablespoon oyster sauce
2 tablespoons fresh lemon juice
1 ounce dried shiitake (or other)
    mushrooms, stems removed and
    cut into small pieces
1 7-ounce frozen lobster tail,
    thawed and uncooked
1 cup fresh peas, stemmed, or
    1 9-ounce package frozen sugar
    snap peas

2 scallions, finely sliced
Sprinkle of crushed red pepper
Salt (optional)

EMERALD PESTO:

1 large clove garlic
½ cup fresh cilantro leaves,
    loosely packed
1 medium scallion
1 tablespoon toasted almonds
1 teaspoon sesame oil
2 tablespoons water, low-sodium
    vegetable stock, or defatted
    chicken stock

In a large saucepan or Dutch oven, over medium-high heat, heat the stock, ginger, oyster sauce, lemon juice, and mushrooms until it just comes to a boil. Reduce the heat and add the lobster tail; poach for 3 to 5 minutes. Remove the lobster tail from the stock to cool, and reduce the heat to low.

Meanwhile, prepare the pesto. In a food processor, puree all ingredients until smooth.

Remove the lobster from its shell, and chop into ½-inch pieces. Just before serving, return the lobster pieces to the soup, add the sugar snap peas, and cook until hot but not boiling. Add the scallions, red pepper, and salt, if using, to taste. Serve immediately, garnished with a dollop of emerald pesto.

PER 1½ CUPS (with Pesto):   Saturated Fat: 1 gm
Total Fat: 4 gm   Cholesterol: 43 mg   Sodium: 507 mg   Calories: 171

She-Crab Soup

She-crab soup, made with the tender, sweet meat and roe from the female crab, is frequently served in restaurants on the mid-Atlantic coast. Since most store-bought backfin blue crab isn't identified by gender, add ¼ to ½ teaspoon of sugar to achieve the sweet taste.

½ cup chopped leeks

½ cup chopped onions

1 cup chopped celery, including leaves

2 cups (10 ounces) sliced mushrooms

1 cup diced, cooked potatoes

2 cups nonfat milk

½ teaspoon salt (optional)

¼ teaspoon mace

¼ cup cream sherry, white wine, or dry vermouth (optional)

Drops Tabasco

3 tablespoons all-purpose flour

1 cup evaporated skimmed milk

1 cup (8 ounces) backfin or lump crabmeat

1 cup (8 ounces) crab claw meat

¼ cup (1½ ounces) crab roe (if available)

½ teaspoon sugar

½ cup chopped watercress

In a large nonstick skillet, simmer the leeks, onions, celery, and mushrooms in ¼ inch of water, adding more water if necessary to prevent sticking, until the vegetables are cooked, about 5 minutes. Add the cooked potatoes, nonfat milk, salt, if using, mace, sherry, and Tabasco, and stir well.

In a small bowl, whisk the flour into the evaporated milk until smooth. Add the mixture to the soup, stirring until soup is thickened. Do not boil as milk mixture will curdle. Turn the heat to very low and add the crab pieces, being careful to break them up, and roe and sugar and stir carefully, heating until just hot. Serve with additional drops of Tabasco to taste and a sprinkle of watercress.

PER 1½ CUPS: Saturated Fat: 1 gm   Total Fat: 7 gm
Cholesterol: 162 mg   Sodium: 544 mg   Calories: 268

Oyster Rockefeller Soup

Inspired by the oysters Rockefeller, which was named for John D. Rockefeller, this is a special occasion stew. In spite of its creamy elegance, it takes only 30 minutes to prepare.

1 teaspoon olive oil

1 cup minced onion

1 large potato, peeled and minced

2½ cups low-sodium, defatted
   chicken stock

1 10-ounce bag fresh spinach,
   rinsed and stemmed

2 tablespoons fresh lemon juice

1 teaspoon tarragon

1 cup evaporated skimmed milk

1 pint fresh shucked oysters,
   drained

Salt (optional)

Freshly ground black pepper

Dash Pernod (optional)

4 strips cooked bacon, blotted, all
   fat discarded, meaty portion
   crumbled

In a medium nonstick saucepan, over medium-high heat, heat the olive oil. Add the onion and potato and sauté for 4 minutes, until brown adding water by the tablespoon if needed. Reduce the heat to low, cover, and cook for 4 minutes. Add the stock and simmer covered for 10 minutes.

To the saucepan, add the spinach, lemon juice, and tarragon, and cook just until the spinach is wilted, about 1 minute. Using an immersion, or hand, blender, puree the soup in the pot. (Or in a food processor, puree the soup in batches and return it to the pot.) Stir in the milk and oysters and cook over medium heat, for 3 minutes, being very careful not to boil. Add salt, if using, pepper to taste, and a splash of Pernod. Just before serving, sprinkle with the crumbled bacon.

PER 1½ CUPS: Saturated Fat: 1 gm   Total Fat: 5 gm
Cholesterol: 75 mg   Sodium: 519 mg   Calories: 239

Mu Shu Pork Soup

This easy cross-cultural soup features Chinese flavors and Mexican tortillas. It is topped with a nest of crinkly, crunchy tortilla strips that must be made first as they take time to bake. Hoisin sauces vary in intensity, so to achieve the fullest flavor ask for a full-bodied strong and thick variety. Canned straw mushrooms make this dish authentic, but they also raise the salt content.

HOISIN TORTILLA
STRIPS:
2 6-inch flour tortillas
2 teaspoons hoisin sauce

8 ounces lean, boneless center-cut
    pork loin, cut into ¼-inch by
    1-inch pieces
4 tablespoons hoisin sauce
½ cup dry sherry (optional)
1 teaspoon sesame oil
Vegetable oil spray
3 cloves garlic, minced
2 large carrots, shredded
3 cups shredded cabbage

1¼ cups fresh mushrooms, sliced
    or 1 15-ounce can straw
    mushrooms, drained
3 tablespoons cornstarch whisked
    into 5 cups low-sodium,
    defatted chicken stock
2 tablespoons low-sodium soy
    sauce
2 tablespoons Worcestershire
2 tablespoons freshly grated ginger
2 tablespoons fresh lemon juice
½ cup diced red bell peppers
4 scallions thinly sliced plus
    2 tablespoons chopped scallions,
    for garnish

Preheat the oven to 300°F.

Spread each tortilla with 1 teaspoon hoisin sauce. Using scissors, cut each one into ⅛-inch wide strips. Arrange the strips on a baking sheet and bake for 30 minutes, until crispy. Set aside until needed.

In a small bowl, toss the pork with 2 teaspoons hoisin sauce, 1 tablespoon sherry, and sesame oil. Marinate for 1 hour in the refrigerator.

Spray a Dutch oven or large nonstick saucepan with vegetable oil and place over medium–high heat. Drain the pork, discard the marinade and add the pork and sauté for about 2 to 3 minutes. Remove the pork to a separate dish. To the saucepan, add the garlic, carrots, and cabbage and sauté for 4 minutes, stirring, adding a few teaspoons water, as needed to prevent sticking. Add the mushrooms, the rest of the sherry, cornstarch-stock mixture, soy sauce, Worcestershire, ginger, lemon juice, and peppers. Bring to a boil, stirring until thickened. Return the pork to the soup and add the scallions. Top each portion with the tortilla strips and scallions.

■■ PER 1½ CUPS: Saturated Fat: 0.5 gm Total Fat: 2 gm ■■
Cholesterol: 18 mg Sodium: 401 mg Calories: 139

French Bean Soup

Serves 6

The pale green flageolet, grown primarily in France, is a small, tender bean that is taken from the pod before fully grown. It is prized for its mildly sweet flavor. Do not presoak these flageolets. Navy beans can be substituted here.

1 smoked ham hock
1 cup flageolets
1 carrot
1 leafy rib celery
10 pearl onions or 1 cup chopped
   yellow onions

2 cloves elephant garlic or 8 cloves
   regular garlic
½ cup chopped parsley
Several shakes Cajun spices or
   pinch cayenne and sugar
Coarsely ground black pepper

In a large soup pot, over medium heat, simmer the ham hock in 2 quarts water, covered, for 1 hour. Remove the ham hock and defat the broth (page 48). Skin the hock, remove the meat, and transfer to a clean soup pot or wipe any fat clinging to the old. Add the defatted stock, flageolets, carrot, celery, onions, garlic, parsley, and spice to the pot and bring to a boil. Reduce the heat and simmer for 2 hours and 35 minutes. Remove the onions with a slotted spoon and peel, and return to the soup. Add pepper to taste.

■■ PER 1½ CUPS: Saturated Fat: 1 gm Total Fat: 3 gm ■■
Cholesterol: 9 mg Sodium: 105 mg Calories: 166

Beef and Barley Soup

My former mother-in-law taught me to make her version of this soup when I was nineteen years old. I began making it again recently, this time defatting the liquid, and it is as good as I remember.

1 beef knuckle or marrow bone
  with a few ounces of meat on
  the bone
1 beef bouillon cube (optional)
3 quarts low-sodium vegetable
  stock or water
1 onion, chopped
3 cloves garlic, finely chopped
2 leafy ribs celery, chopped
1 carrot, chopped

¼ cup chopped parsley
½ cup pearl barley
1 cup dried lima beans
Salt (optional)
Freshly ground black pepper
2 tablespoons chopped parsley, for
  garnish

In a stockpot with a lid, over medium heat, simmer the beef bone and bouillon cube in the stock for 30 minutes, occasionally skimming the top to remove the foam. Remove the meat and bone and set aside. Defat the stock (page 48) and return it to the pot. Dice the beef, discarding all fat.

To the stock, add the onion, garlic, celery, carrot, parsley, barley, lima beans, and beef and cook, covered, over very low heat for 2½ hours, depending upon the dryness and size of the beans. If too much liquid evaporates during the cooking, add more. If the soup is too watery, remove the lid for the last half hour of cooking. This soup should be thick. Add salt, if using, and pepper to taste, and serve garnished with parsley.

PER 1½ CUPS: Saturated Fat: Trace   Total Fat: 1 gm
Cholesterol: 9 mg   Sodium: 160 mg   Calories: 173

Portuguese Pork and Garbanzo Bean Sopa

A café in Portugal served this stew that celebrates the Portuguese taste for pork. Called *sopa*, it may become as favorite a soup in your repertoire as it is in mine (defatting took away none of the flavor).

1 pound pork, trimmed of all fat
    and cut into 1-inch cubes
3 tablespoons all-purpose flour
Vegetable oil spray
Salt (optional)
Freshly ground black pepper
2 medium onions, diced
4 cloves garlic, minced
6 plum tomatoes, diced
3 cups low-sodium, defatted
    chicken stock

⅔ cup Madeira (optional)
2 16-ounce cans garbanzo beans
    (chickpeas), drained
1 teaspoon dried oregano
½ cup pimiento-stuffed green
    olives, coarsely chopped
¾ cup raisins
½ cup finely chopped tomatoes,
    for garnish
¼ cup chopped parsley, for
    garnish

Toss the pork cubes in a plastic bag with the flour until coated. Spray a 5-quart Dutch oven or large soup pot with vegetable oil and place over medium-high heat. Season the pork with salt, if using, and pepper and sear in batches, taking care not to overcrowd, until well browned. As the pieces brown, remove them to a bowl and set aside. Reduce the heat to medium, add the onions and garlic, and several tablespoons of water if needed for moisture, and cook for 8 minutes or until softened. Add the plum tomatoes, chicken stock, Madeira, garbanzo beans, oregano, and olives, and reserved pork. Bring to a boil. Cover, reduce the heat, and simmer for 45 minutes, stirring occasionally.

Skim any fat from the surface of the stock into a defatting pitcher and pour the defatted liquid back into the pot. Add the raisins and simmer, uncovered, for 15 minutes. Serve in bowls and garnish with tomatoes and parsley.

PER 1½ CUPS: Saturated Fat: 2 gm   Total Fat: 6 gm
Cholesterol: 38 mg   Sodium: 577 mg   Calories: 342

Tuscan Beef
and Vegetable Stew

Tuscany is the center for beef and vegetables, and this classic soup is typical of the region. The secret to this highly aromatic and savory stew is the custom of roasting the meat and marrow bones. If you can't find the bones cut up and packaged, ask the meat cutter to do it for you.

Vegetable oil spray

½ pound lean top round, all fat removed, cut into ¾-inch cubes

1 pound beef or veal marrow bones, cut up

½ cup all-purpose flour

Salt (optional)

¼ teaspoon freshly ground black pepper

2 quarts water, low-sodium vegetable stock, or defatted beef stock

2 tomatoes

1 large onion, cut into eighths

10 to 12 pearl onions, peeled

6 to 8 cloves garlic

3 carrots, sliced into 2-inch rounds

½ cup chopped parsley

½ teaspoon dried thyme

½ teaspoon dried oregano

½ teaspoon dried tarragon

½ teaspoon dried rosemary leaves or 1 teaspoon fresh

Preheat the oven to 350°F.

Lightly spray a nonstick baking sheet with vegetable oil (or line a baking sheet with foil and do not spray).

In a plastic bag, combine the meat, bones, flour, salt, if using, and pepper and toss until well coated. Remove from the bag and place on the baking sheet and bake for 1½ hours.

In a large nonstick soup pot, bring 2 quarts water to boiling. Plunge the tomatoes into the water for 1 minute. Remove, peel the skin, and set aside. To the pot add the onions, garlic, carrots, parsley, thyme, oregano, tarragon, rosemary, and the meat and bones. Simmer, on very low heat, covered, for 1½ hours.

Remove the meat and reserve. Remove the marrow from the center of the bones and reserve (there should be about 2 teaspoons); discard the bones. Remove the vegetables and reserve. Defat the broth completely using a defatting pitcher (page 7). Combine the broth, marrow, and vegetables in the pot. With a spoon, mash the whole garlic against the side of the pot. Coarsely chop the tomatoes and add to the pot. Simmer, covered, on low heat for 10 minutes. Adjust the seasonings and serve.

■: PER 1½ CUPS:　Saturated Fat: Trace　Total Fat: 2 gm ■:
Cholesterol: 25 mg　Sodium: 109 mg　Calories: 138

■:

Italian Bean Soup

The Italian word for bean eaters is *mangiafagioli,* and you taste the Italian influence. Thick, savory, and pungent, this soup is a breeze to assemble and is an absolute delight for bean lovers. Cook the pasta during the last 10 minutes that the soup is cooking. The dried scarlet runner is an especially sweet lima-type flat bean. If you can't find it, use large lima or pinto beans.

2 quarts water or low-sodium,
    defatted chicken stock
½ pound dried scarlet runner
2 carrots
1 leafy rib celery
½ onion
2 cloves garlic
¼ cup cream or milk sherry
    (optional)

Cajun seasonings
Salt (optional)
Crushed red pepper
1 ripe tomato, diced
2 cups cooked pasta such as small
    noodles, shells, orzo, or riso
½ cup finely chopped chives

In a 5-quart Dutch oven, combine the water, beans, carrots, celery, onion, and garlic, and bring to a boil. Reduce the heat and simmer, covered for 2 hours. Using an immersion, or hand, blender, partially puree in the bean pot. Alternately, transfer ⅔ of the bean mixture to a food processor, puree, and add back to the pot. Stir in the sherry, spices, and tomato, and cook for 5 minutes. Divide the pasta into six bowls, and ladle the bean soup over the pasta. Sprinkle with chives and serve immediately.

PER 1½ CUPS: Saturated Fat: Trace   Total Fat: 1 gm
Cholesterol: 0 mg   Sodium: 34 mg   Calories: 229

SALADS AND DRESSINGS

***

S alads can be so totally satisfying that our passion for them must be in the bones. Hot or cold, cooked or raw, before the meal or after, salads satisfy.

The first humans (as well as our closest ancestors) have always eaten greens, nuts, berries, roots, and vegetables. No surprise, but five hundred years ago in Europe, we ate salads nearly identical to our basic salads and salad dressings of today.

Lettuce (which comes from ancient China) is the base of most Western-style salads. Summertime in the British Isles in the early fourteenth century, people ate their "salds" mushy and flavored with salt (where "salad" comes from). Sometimes they added a little vinegar.

The landed gentry's *saladas, salets, salatas, salates,* and *salats,* however, were considerably fancier, served in very tiny dishes or occasionally for banquets on large wooden, ceramic, or leather serving platters. By the eighteenth century, salads commonly used lettuce, watercress, lightly cooked and chilled baby asparagus spears, hearts of artichokes, onion slivers, cucumbers, pickled beets, many kinds of marinated mushrooms and truffles, radishes, carrots, baked eggs, caviar, a variety of olives, plus choices of cold crisp-cooked wild duck, baked chicken, venison, even smoked salmon or trout (which were cleverly kept alive in castle moats until needed).

The favorite dressing then? Imported Italian, cold-pressed extra-virgin olive oil combined with an elegant vinegar such as balsamic from Modena, Italy. Also not uncommon was French cheese from the caves of Roquefort, maybe a few slices of apple or chestnuts from a stand well known for good nuts, a sprinkling of some precious herb or spice, and of course they had salt and pepper. The preferred way of eating salads was fingers or on a long two-pronged spear. Forks weren't common until the 1800s, and then it was only among priests, royalty, and the wealthy.

Ancient Asians ate several forms of salad thousands of years B.C. Some were cooked, some cold, and nearly all were made largely of vegetables with a few slices of fish or morsels of fowl. Sprouts and cucumbers were flavored with unusual sauces made from fermented wheat, fish, beans, and rice.

In 2000 B.C., the South American tomato was no bigger than a nut, leaves were used as plates, and avocados were common.

▪▪ Avocados, Nuts, and Seeds ▪▪

Avocados (an original Aztec word) were eaten in places near Mexico City by primitive Aztec tribes. First called *ahuacatl,* then *aguacate,* a mash was made of avocados, chopped onions, tomatillos, and a form of capsicum or hot peppers. The improvement of lemon or lime juice (which keeps the color and heightens the flavor) wasn't made until citrus was brought to the Mexican and Central American Indians from East India sometime in the Middle Ages.

In the 1950s, rich Americans tinkered with a basically healthy combination, adding gratuitous oil, sour cream, mayonnaise, and sometimes even cheese, reversing much of the health benefits of the vitamin- and fiber-filled avocado (whose fat is largely monounsaturated and not important except for calories).

Hass avocados (small and dark with crinkly skin) are from California and have to, by law, contain at least 8 percent fat (less fat than meat and meat fat, unlike avocado fat, is saturated). Florida's Fuerte (light green, smooth-skinned, and sometimes as big as a football) contains less fat. Other kinds of avocados, like the red-skinned and cocktail varieties (which are smooth-skinned, light green, and tiny as a finger but with no pit), as well as those from Israel and South America are all similar in taste. Although higher in calories than most vegetables or fruit, the avocado has little artery-damaging fat.

It has become popular to add nuts, seeds, and grains to salads, which give greater variety and nutrients. To keep the calories and saturated fats down (nuts have a few), keep the amount between one and two tablespoons, chopped, all you need for flavor and crunch. Knowing what our ancestors ate is intriguing. You discover historically how we evolved so well as a species (where nutrition obviously played a major part), and it serves to remind us we have always sought out the best food we could find (or afford).

Five hundred years ago, the Spanish were amazed to find the Aztecs had greenhouses for growing exotic vegetables, fruits, and herbs (long before the Europeans, who prized themselves as the world's greatest epicureans), and thousands of years before that, primitive tribes worldwide cultivated choice roots and seeds. Salads make this urge for good food especially easy to indulge in because there is such a great variety. Almost any food can be used in a salad.

■■ Salad Dressings ■■

When only one dressing goes with a salad, it is included with the salad, but most of the dressings are listed at the end of this chapter. Discovering that salad dressings are the single greatest source of weight gain for American women caught many by surprise. This is according to a 1994 report from the Center for Science in the Public Interest in Washington, D.C. This isn't surprising since most women, and men for that matter, who love salads eat them with ravenous abandon, unmindful of the fats hidden in the dressings. Meanwhile, the oils used (or should we say overused) in prepared and homemade salad dressings are 100 percent fat.

The good news is that almost any dressing can be made with very little oil (about two tablespoons for a salad for four people) and some of the most flavorful oils are actually low in saturated fat. These include walnut, canola, and safflower. Cold-pressed olive oil and corn oil are about 100 percent higher than these in saturated fat.

■■ Oil ■■

There's no reason to give up oil on salads and in dressings. Merely reduce the amount by drizzling a teaspoon of oil on a salad rather than pouring on an unmeasured amount.

Try spraying a few spritzes of oil on a salad instead of pouring it on. Olive oil spray is available in most markets. Or you can fill a plastic or glass bottle with olive oil or your favorite oil blend. Refrigerate it to keep the oil from turning rancid. Just before using, warm the bottle by placing it under hot running water for a minute or so.

For cream-style dressings, substitute low-fat or nondairy products such as yogurt, cottage cheese, and ricotta cheese for cream, milk, or sour cream. Buttermilk, which is naturally low in fat or nonfat despite its name, is delicious in ranch-style dressings. Substitute nonfat mayonnaise for regular mayonnaise. All of these substitutes blend well with vinegar and citrus or vegetable juices.

FLAVORED OIL I don't like most flavored oils, which are now so popular. They lose the best of both properties. I do like the oil from sun-dried tomatoes to cook in or to baste on peeled potatoes to bake.

▪▪ Vinegar ▪▪

One of the best ways to cut down on the use of oil in salad dressings is to increase the use of good-tasting vinegars. Sometimes a dash of a sweet and mellow balsamic or a fruity raspberry vinegar is all a salad needs for flavor and character. Experiment with the many varieties available in the markets today. Substitute the ones you haven't tried before for the one you always use. If you find one vinegar with a taste you like but it is too strong, you can dilute it with water. All commercial vinegars have water as the first ingredient.

Better yet, create flavored vinegars to suit your own tastes (below).

HOMEMADE FLAVORED VINEGARS These are very inexpensive specialties that you can make to suit your own tastes. Their unique flavors can enhance the character of your salads and most definitely reduce the amount of oil you use.

There are a variety of glass bottles suitable for homemade vinegars. Use the 1-quart size for each of the following recipes. It need only be clean and have a tight-fitting cork or cap. Fill the bottle with a scant quart of vinegar, allowing room for the flavorings. Slip in the herbs, spices, vegetables, or fruits.

Here is a caveat: Be cautious about adding dried black peppercorns or crushed red pepper to flavored vinegar. The hot pepper flavor will grow stronger with time and can overpower the vinegar.

The last item in each recipe is the garnish, which is used for visual appeal and is especially important for the vinegar you may wish to display or give away. Cork the bottle and allow the vinegar to sit on a shelf for a week before using. If you feel the flavor needs heightening, add about ⅛ teaspoon sugar.

Basil vinegar Add 2 tablespoons chopped dried basil, a pinch of sugar, ½ teaspoon minced garlic, and several leaves or a sprig of fresh basil to 2 to 4 cups cider vinegar.

Beet vinegar Use ½ cup of juice from canned beets or water that beets have boiled in. Add 1 cup cider vinegar, 1 tablespoon pickling spices,

1 teaspoon sugar, several peppercorns, ½ teaspoon dry mustard, some small beets or beet slices to the bottle.

Blueberry vinegar Add ¼ cup frozen blueberries, pureed and sweetened, if necessary, ¼ teaspoon pickled peppercorns, shake well, and add a pinch of celery seed and 10 whole blueberries to 2 to 4 cups white vinegar.

Caper vinegar Add 2 teaspoons finely chopped onion, 2 tablespoons fresh lemon juice, ½ teaspoon Worcestershire, 2 tablespoons drained capers, and ¼ teaspoon celery seed to 2 to 4 cups cider vinegar. You can use capers with long stems or add some long uncut chives for decoration.

Dill vinegar Add 3 tablespoons chopped fresh dill, ½ teaspoon prepared mustard, a pinch of celery seed, a small amount of minced garlic, and a large dill sprig to 2 to 4 cups white wine vinegar.

Garlic vinegar Add 3 cloves minced garlic, 2 cloves garlic sliced wafer-thin lengthwise, and 5 small whole peeled garlic cloves to 2 to 4 cups cider, red wine, or white wine vinegar.

Hot pepper vinegar Add 2 teaspoons chopped mixture of hot peppers, such as ancho, habanero, jalapeño, Scotch bonnet (the hottest), and a dash of Tabasco (depending on how hot you like it), plus 3 small hot red peppers to 2 to 4 cups of white vinegar. This vinegar isn't for salads but is used drop by drop for spicing up potatoes, fajitas, sandwiches, tacos, meat, wilted spinach.

Italian vinegar Add 2 cloves minced garlic, 1 teaspoon dried or 2 teaspoons chopped fresh sweet basil, 1 teaspoon dried oregano or 1½ teaspoons chopped fresh oregano, ½ teaspoon dry mustard, ½ teaspoon sugar, salt, and 2 tablespoons fresh lemon juice to 2 to 4 cups red wine vinegar. If you want leaves in the bottle, omit either the oregano or the basil and use a small sprig with leaves or add a small sprig of parsley.

Mustard vinegar Add 2 tablespoons prepared French mustard, ½ teaspoon mustard seed, ½ teaspoon Dijon mustard, ½ teaspoon dry mustard, 1 teaspoon sugar, and a large sprig of parsley to 2 to 4 cups cider vinegar.

Onion and chive vinegar Add ½ cup chopped onions, 1 teaspoon dehydrated onions, 10 chopped chives, ¼ teaspoon celery seed, ½ teaspoon finely minced garlic, and 15 or 20 whole chives to 2 to 4 cups of unseasoned rice vinegar.

Oregano vinegar Add 2 tablespoons dried oregano, a pinch of sugar, some salt (optional), and several leaves or an oregano sprig with leaves to 2 to 4 cups cider vinegar.

Raspberry or cider vinegar Add ½ cup mashed, frozen, sweetened raspberries, ¼ teaspoon pickled peppercorns, a pinch of celery seeds, and 10 to 15 whole fresh raspberries (to sit in the bottom of the bottle) to 2 to 4 cups cider vinegar. If your raspberries aren't frozen (or sweetened), add 1 teaspoon sugar.

Tarragon vinegar Add 2 tablespoons dried tarragon, 1 clove minced garlic, a pinch of sugar, ½ teaspoon fresh lemon juice, and a large sprig of fresh tarragon to 2 to 4 cups white wine vinegar.

▪ In Place of Vinegar ▪

For those who can't tolerate vinegar, try a teaspoon of diluted plain, herbed, or spiced fresh lemon or lime juice with a pinch of freshly chopped dill. Or experiment with any number of other juices—tomato, celery, carrot, tomatillo, cabbage, pureed bell peppers, tangerine—mixed with nonfat yogurt, low-fat buttermilk, or lemon juice.

▪ Eating Out: Salads ▪

When ordering salads in a restaurant, ask for cruets of oil and vinegar or the dressing on the side. Be sure to ask for cruets because asking for just oil and vinegar usually produces a prepared mixture and you can't control the amount of oil or vinegar you use. If you like the house dressing, order it on the side, and dilute it with lemon, vinegar, or water. For certain dressings, you can request that they go light on the dressing. You can also use the "dip and stab" method: Dip your fork in the dressing, then stab the salad. I was surprised at the nice (scant) amount of dressing I got compared to a friend's whose salad was drenched.

Any menu salad can be ordered without the cheese, eggs, bacon, or other fatty foods. The low-fat meats to include in your salad are white-meat poultry, Canadian bacon, very lean beef, or defatted Smithfield or country ham; water-packed tuna and salmon are fine. In a restaurant, all you have to do is ask.

■ Nuts and Seeds in Salads ■

Salad bars often feature large containers of nuts and seeds to sprinkle on salads. While high in nutrients, they are also high in fat, so keep your portion to 1 or 2 teaspoons.

When serving salads at home, use 2 tablespoons chopped nuts or seeds for a salad for four to six people. Toast them for 5 minutes in the oven if you want a more intense flavor while using fewer nuts. Naturally appearing oils, for the most part, are fine.

■ Oil and Fat ■

All oil and pure fat have the same number of calories. Butter has about 20 percent less fat and therefore slightly fewer calories than stick margarine (but not diet margarine, which can have half again the amount of fat as stick margarine), but ounce for ounce, butter has 100 percent more saturated fat (the fat to avoid) than margarine.

The oil with the lowest saturated fat content (that we currently know of) is canola. Originally, it was called rapeseed and has 4 grams of saturated fat for ¼ cup (butter has 29). Avocados have about the same saturated fat as canola. Coconut oil has 47 grams of saturated fat, more than any other animal fat or vegetable oil. As you can see from the chart, corn oil, peanut oil, and olive oil are higher than canola or safflower. Oils contain no carbohydrates and, if vegetable, no cholesterol.

The oils below are listed from **low** (diet margarine) to **high** (coconut), in order of saturated fats only. The calories (except for butter) are the same.

40-percent diet margarine (part water)	Corn	Turkey fat
	Sesame	Duck fat
	Soybean	Lard (pig fat)
Canola	Peanut	Lamb fat
Safflower	Stick margarine	Tallow (beef fat)
Walnut	Wheat germ	Palm
Sunflower	Chicken fat	Butter
Avocado	Rice bran	Palm kernel
Olive	Cottonseed	Coconut

Caesar Salad

Romaine lettuce was first grown on the island of Cos in the Aegean Sea probably around 2000 B.C. and is sometimes called cos lettuce. Look for a firm crisp perfect head with dark outer leaves and a pale center. The midrib should be crunchy and the leaves should have a mild, slightly bitter taste. The secret to a low-fat Caesar is to serve it very cold, use fresh lemon juice, and the top quality both grated nonfat Parmesan cheese and extra-virgin olive oil. If you don't have an olive oil spray, add 1 teaspoon oil to the dressing. It doesn't need any egg, but luckily, with the pasteurized egg substitutes available (one should *never* use a raw egg) you can add it. You can add capers, ripe olives, diced avocado, and diced cooked poultry to vary the flavors and make it a heartier salad, but I eat it plain without croutons most often.

SALAD:
1 head romaine lettuce, chilled
Olive oil spray

DRESSING:
2 large garlic cloves, minced
1 teaspoon Worcestershire
1 teaspoon anchovy paste or 4
   anchovies, drained and
   patted dry
4 to 6 tablespoons fresh lemon
   juice
¼ cup egg substitute (optional)

¼ cup freshly grated nonfat
   Parmesan cheese
Black peppercorns, cracked

GARLIC CROUTONS
(OPTIONAL):
Lightly spray with olive oil both
   sides of 2 pieces white toast,
   rub with a cut piece of garlic,
   lightly salt, and brown under a
   broiler for 2 minutes and cut
   into croutons.

Leave the leaves whole or cut or tear into bite-size pieces. Spray the romaine leaves lightly with the oil and place them in a large chilled salad bowl and set aside.

In a small bowl, whisk the garlic, Worcestershire, anchovy paste, lemon juice, and egg substitute, if using, until well blended. Pour over the

romaine and toss to mix well. Sprinkle with cheese, pepper, and croutons
and serve immediately.

■■ PER SERVING: Saturated Fat: 0 gm   Total Fat: 0.5 gm ■■
Cholesterol: Trace   Sodium: 280 mg   Calories: 66

Spicy Corn and Tomato Salad

■■   *Serves 4*   ■■

Although I usually serve this salad at room temperature, it is also delicious
when served slightly warm. Cover the salad with plastic wrap and heat in
the microwave on low for 1 to 2 minutes.

DRESSING:
*3 tablespoons white wine or cider
    vinegar*
1 teaspoon Dijon mustard
2 tablespoons chopped parsley
2 tablespoons chopped fresh basil
*1½ teaspoons dried summer
    savory (optional)*

2 drops Tabasco

SALAD:
*2 cups whole kernel corn, fresh or
    frozen*
2 tomatoes, diced
Salt (optional)
¼ teaspoon white pepper

Bring a large nonstick skillet filled with ¼ inch of water to a boil. Add
the corn and cook for 1 to 2 (for frozen, 3 to 4) minutes, covered, or until
just tender; drain and cool.

In a small bowl, whisk the vinegar, mustard, parsley, basil, savory, if using,
and Tabasco, and set aside. In a salad bowl, mix the corn and tomatoes.
Pour the dressing over the corn and tomato mixture and toss lightly. Add
salt, if using, and pepper to taste. Serve warm or chilled.

■■   PER SERVING: Saturated Fat: Trace   Total Fat: 1 gm ■■
Cholesterol: 0 mg   Sodium: 53 mg   Calories: 105

Amalfi Coast Salad with Sausage and Fennel

Serves 4

The Amalfi coast is rugged and dramatic. A rich combination of classic Italian delicacies—artichoke hearts, turkey sausage (which tastes just like regular sausage but without the fat), fennel, and capers—this is a satisfying entrée salad.

BASIC VINAIGRETTE:

2 tablespoons red wine vinegar

1 teaspoon fresh lemon juice

¼ cup low-sodium, defatted chicken or vegetable stock

½ teaspoon salt (optional)

Freshly ground black pepper

1½ tablespoons olive oil

SALAD:

4 ounces sweet Italian turkey sausage

1 bunch arugula or one head Boston lettuce

2 6-ounce jars marinated artichoke hearts packed in water and drained

1 teaspoon capers

1 medium red onion, chopped

½ cup matchstick slices of fresh fennel

½ cup Basic Vinaigrette

2 cloves garlic, minced

½ teaspoon anchovy paste

2 teaspoons Dijon mustard

3 tablespoons chopped parsley

½ pound ziti or penne pasta, cooked and drained

2 large fresh plum tomatoes, quartered, for garnish

In a food processor or blender, combine the vinegar, lemon juice, stock, salt, if using, and pepper. With the motor running, slowly drizzle in the olive oil until thick and smooth, about 1 minute. Set aside.

In a small saucepan filled with boiling water, cook the sausage for 10 minutes and cut into ¼-inch slices. Line a serving platter or individual salad plates with lettuce and chill.

In a large bowl, mix the cooked sausage, artichoke hearts, capers, onion, fennel, ¼ cup of the vinaigrette, garlic, anchovy paste, mustard, and parsley. Cover and refrigerate for 30 minutes. To serve, toss the pasta with the remaining vinaigrette and arrange on lettuce leaves. Top the pasta with the sausage mixture and garnish with the tomato wedges.

■■   PER SERVING: Saturated Fat: 1 gm   Total Fat: 9 gm   ■■
Cholesterol: 1 mg   Sodium: 666 mg   Calories: 362

Wild Rice and Wilted Spinach Salad

East meets West with an Asian sweet sesame dressing and water chestnuts tossed with all-American red bell pepper and wild rice. Gently wilted spinach steamed for a few minutes, then drained and chilled, lends texture as well as flavor.

FUSION SALAD
DRESSING:
2 cloves garlic
1 tablespoon fresh lemon juice
1 tablespoon freshly grated ginger
1 tablespoon plus 2 teaspoons low-sodium soy sauce
1 tablespoon dark sesame oil
½ cup fresh diced pineapple
⅓ cup pineapple juice

SALAD:
2 cups cooked wild rice
1 8-ounce can sliced water chestnuts, drained
1 large yellow or red bell pepper, diced, seeds reserved
10 ounces fresh spinach, cleaned and lightly wilted
1 cup diced fresh pineapple
2 cups torn mixed salad greens with a small amount of shredded red cabbage or radicchio for color
½ cup fresh snipped chives, for garnish
Freshly ground black pepper

In a food processor or blender, puree the garlic, lemon juice, ginger, soy sauce, sesame oil, ½ cup pineapple, and pineapple juice until smooth.

In a large bowl, mix the wild rice, water chestnuts, bell pepper, spinach, and 1 cup pineapple. Pour ½ cup of the dressing over the rice and spinach mixture and toss to mix well.

Line a bowl or individual plates with salad greens, mound the salad, sprinkle with snipped chives for garnish, and drizzle the remaining dressing over the top. Serve and sprinkle on the seeds and pepper.

PER SERVING: Saturated Fat: Trace   Total Fat: 3 gm
Cholesterol: 0 mg   Sodium: 210 mg   Calories: 137

Oriental Cucumber Salad

I first ate this salad when I was sixteen years old and working as a model for George Kawamoto, one of Detroit's finest photographers. His wife, Louise, was not only his stylist and manager, but she also prepared lunch as well. This refreshing, no-fat salad uses tender-skinned burpless cucumbers.

1 large burpless cucumber
2 tablespoons sugar
½ cup rice wine vinegar

1 teaspoon sesame seeds, lightly toasted

Using a fork, run the lines down the sides of the cucumber to create stripes. Then slice into ¼-inch rounds and place in a salad bowl.

In a small bowl, whisk the sugar and vinegar together until the sugar dissolves; add to the cucumbers, cover, and refrigerate for 30 minutes. Spoon the cucumbers into small individual bowls and sprinkle with the sesame seeds.

PER SERVING: Saturated Fat: 0 gm   Total Fat: 0.5 gm
Cholesterol: 0 mg   Sodium: 5 mg   Calories: 43

German Potato Salad

This salad offers all the traditional flavors of German potato salad, but without the fat. Although it is usually served hot or warm, I find that this salad tastes better cold.

6 strips fat bacon or salt pork

2 strips lean bacon

6 medium red or white new potatoes (about 2 pounds), peeled or unpeeled and cut into fourths

1 small onion, coarsely chopped

1 leafy rib celery, coarsely chopped

⅓ cup chopped low-sodium (if available) kosher dill pickle

¼ cup wine vinegar

½ teaspoon sugar

Salt (optional)

¼ teaspoon freshly ground black pepper

½ teaspoon dry mustard

2 tablespoons nonfat mayonnaise

2 teaspoons coarse mustard

2 tablespoons snipped chives or chopped scallions

Paprika, for garnish

In a large nonstick saucepan with 6 cups water, simmer the fat bacon for 15 minutes. Remove and discard the bacon; reserve the liquid and defat (page 48). Wipe the saucepan clean, add the defatted broth, and boil the potatoes until soft. Discard the liquid and place the potatoes in the freezer for 10 minutes to chill. Microwave the lean bacon slices wrapped in paper towel at high for about 1 minute 30 seconds, turning once or twice, until crisp. (If frying, cook until crisp.) Blot and pick off all the fat from the bacon and discard. Crumble the meat and set aside.

In a large nonstick saucepan, combine the defatted stock and the potatoes, and boil for 25 to 30 minutes or until soft when pierced with a fork. Drain and slice into ½-inch pieces.

In a medium bowl, mix the crumbled lean bacon, onion, celery, pickle, vinegar, sugar, salt, if using, pepper, and dry mustard. In a large nonstick skillet, over medium-low heat, cook the potatoes, bacon, and onion mixture for 5 minutes stirring occasionally.

Add the potato mixture, mayonnaise, and coarse mustard to the serving bowl, and toss lightly. Cover and refrigerate for several hours or overnight. Stir in the chives and garnish with a dash of paprika.

■■ PER SERVING: Saturated Fat: Trace   Total Fat: 1 gm ■■
Cholesterol: 2 mg   Sodium: 402 mg   Calories: 224

Cucumber, Orange, Fennel Seed, and Red Onion Salad

■■ *Serves 4* ■■

A lovely refreshing salad. Fennel seed, which has a slight licorice flavor, is available in most supermarket spice sections, and toasting it releases its fragrant oil.

SALAD:
3 burpless cucumbers, thinly sliced
1 red onion, thinly sliced and
   soaked in ice water for 30
   minutes and drained
2 large navel or temple oranges,
   peeled, sliced, and each slice
   quartered

DRESSING:
2 teaspoons fennel seed
2 tablespoons raspberry or cider
   vinegar
2 tablespoons fresh orange juice
1 tablespoon olive oil
Salt (optional)
Freshly ground black pepper
Black olives, for garnish (optional)

In a salad bowl, mix the cucumber, onion, and oranges. In a small bowl, whisk the fennel seed, vinegar, orange juice, and olive oil, until combined. Pour over the salad mixture and toss to mix well. Add the garnish, if using, salt, if using and pepper to taste and serve immediately.

■■ PER SERVING: Saturated Fat: 0.5 gm   Total Fat: 4 gm ■■
Cholesterol: 0 mg   Sodium: 3 mg   Calories: 99

Rock and Roll Potato Salad

This is a robust, colorful salad you can't wait to eat that is so low in fat that you can really indulge. It is also the salad I most often demonstrate on television when I appear as a guest because it is so scrumptious looking. Then the crew devours it and confides to producers I was a great guest. For a sweeter-tasting version use sweet pickles instead of dills. Other taste options: Add ⅛ cup chopped black or green olives, sliced radishes, 2 hard-cooked egg whites diced, or even some diced red, yellow, or green bell pepper.

5 medium red potatoes, skin on, scrubbed, and cut into large (1½-inch) pieces
⅓ cup chopped low-sodium (if available) kosher dill pickles plus 1 tablespoon liquid
2 to 3 scallions, finely chopped
2 large leafy ribs celery, diced
⅔ cup whole kernel corn, fresh or canned

½ cup nonfat mayonnaise
¼ cup nonfat sour cream
2 teaspoons Dijon mustard
¼ teaspoon cumin
1 to 2 teaspoons raspberry or cider vinegar
Freshly ground black pepper
12 cherry tomatoes, halved, for garnish
Watercress, for garnish

In a medium saucepan, cook the potatoes in gently boiling water for 20 to 25 minutes, until soft when pierced with a fork; drain, cut into bite-size pieces, and place in a medium bowl. In a small bowl, mix the pickles and pickle liquid, scallions, celery, corn, mayonnaise, sour cream, mustard, cumin, vinegar, and pepper to taste. Pour over the potatoes and toss gently, being careful not to bruise the potatoes. Cover and refrigerate at least 2 hours. On a platter, place the salad, garnish with cherry tomatoes, and tuck in the watercress around the edges.

PER SERVING: Saturated Fat: 0 gm   Total Fat: 0.5 gm
Cholesterol: 0 mg   Sodium: 301 mg   Calories: 135

Coleslaw with Raisin Vinaigrette

A sweet and sour creamy dressing heightens the taste and texture of this slaw. Adding cooked, skinned, and defatted poultry such as chicken or duck makes this a meal in itself.

SALAD:
- 2 cups (½ pound) finely shredded cabbage, savoy, Chinese, or green
- 1 cup (6 medium) grated carrots
- 2 scallions, thinly sliced
- ⅔ cup golden raisins
- 1½ cups cooked diced chicken or other poultry, skinned and all fat removed (optional)

DRESSING:
- ¼ cup cider vinegar
- 3 tablespoons nonfat sour cream
- 2 tablespoons canola oil
- Salt (optional)
- Freshly ground black pepper
- 4 large outer cabbage leaves to line bowls or plates, for garnish
- ¼ cup toasted chopped pecans (optional)

In a large bowl, combine the cabbage, carrots, scallions, ⅓ cup of the raisins, and chicken, if using. In a small microwave-safe container, combine the remaining raisins and vinegar. Cook at high 1 to 2 minutes and let steep 15 minutes until the raisins are plump. In a food processor or blender, puree the vinegar and raisin mixture, sour cream, and oil until smooth. Pour the dressing over the cabbage mixture and toss to mix well. Add salt, if using, and pepper to taste. Line individual plates with cabbage leaves and mound with slaw. Sprinkle with pecans, if using, and serve.

PER SERVING (Without Chicken):   Saturated Fat: Trace
Total Fat: 5 gm   Cholesterol: 0 mg   Sodium: 28 mg   Calories: 137

Fusilli Vegetable Salad
with Creamy Herb Dressing

A simple and hearty country-style salad, perfect for a quick dinner. Blanching the vegetables in the pasta water saves a lot of time.

SALAD:

8 ounces fusilli or rotelle pasta
2 cups diced mixed vegetables
    (such as carrots, broccoli, red
    bell peppers, green beans, corn)
2 large tomatoes, diced
½ cup pitted sliced black olives
Salt (optional)
Freshly ground black pepper

HERB DRESSING:

1 large clove garlic
3 scallions, cut into pieces
3 tablespoons chopped fresh basil
½ teaspoon dried rosemary
4 tablespoons chopped parsley
¼ cup nonfat cottage cheese
1 tablespoon Dijon mustard
2 tablespoons fresh lemon juice
½ cup low-sodium vegetable stock
2 tablespoons olive oil

Cook the pasta according to package directions. About 6 minutes before it is done, add the 2 cups mixed vegetables and cook for 2 minutes. Drain the pasta and vegetables in a colander; rinse under cool running water and place in a large bowl. Add the tomatoes and olives, and set aside.

In a food processor or blender, mince the garlic. Add the scallions, basil, rosemary, and parsley, and pulse until finely chopped. Add the cottage cheese, mustard, lemon juice, and vegetable stock. With the motor running, slowly drizzle in the olive oil and continue to process about 1 minute. Pour the dressing over the salad and toss to mix well. Add salt, if using, and pepper to taste and serve immediately.

PER SERVING: Saturated Fat: 0.5 gm   Total Fat: 4 gm
        Cholesterol: Trace   Sodium: 179 mg   Calories: 230

Italian Country Ziti Salad

This is an especially satisfying salad during summer, when fresh basil and juicy vine-ripe tomatoes are in great abundance. You can, of course, substitute other pastas. A cherry pitter helps pit olives.

DRESSING:

2 tablespoons Dijon mustard

2 teaspoons chopped fresh basil

2 tablespoons balsamic or cider vinegar

2 cloves garlic, minced

1 tablespoon olive oil

¼ cup nonfat low-fat buttermilk

1 tablespoon chopped parsley

1 tomato, diced

SALAD:

4 cups cooked ziti, rinsed and cooled

2 tablespoons capers

1 6½-ounce can tuna packed in water, drained

½ cup Kalamata olives, pitted, halved, and drained

2 tablespoons chopped sun-dried tomatoes

2 tablespoons minced red onions plus paper-thin onion rings, for garnish

Lettuce (romaine or Bibb) leaves to line plates

4 tomatoes, quartered, for garnish

Parsley sprigs, for garnish

In a small bowl, whisk together the mustard, basil, vinegar, garlic, olive oil, buttermilk, and parsley. Stir in the diced tomato. Place the pasta in a large bowl and toss with dressing to coat. Add the capers, tuna, olives, sun-dried tomatoes, and minced red onions and toss to mix well. Cover and refrigerate for 30 minutes.

Line individual plates with lettuce leaves. Mound salad on each leaf and garnish with tomato wedges, red onion rings, and parsley.

PER SERVING: Saturated Fat: 0.5 gm   Total Fat: 7 gm
Cholesterol: 8 mg   Sodium: 504 mg   Calories: 246

Lentil Salad with Orange-Yogurt Dressing

Serves 6

The tiny lentil has been a staple throughout Europe, India, and the Middle East for thousands of years. It cooks in less than 20 minutes. Combine it with oranges for a mellow taste.

ORANGE-YOGURT
SALAD DRESSING:
1 clove garlic
¼ cup fresh orange juice
1 tablespoon Dijon mustard
½ cup nonfat plain yogurt
1 teaspoon Worcestershire
¼ teaspoon cumin
½ teaspoon ground ginger
2 tablespoons olive oil

SALAD:
3 cups cooked lentils
1 large orange, peeled, seeded,
    and cut into segments

2 hard-cooked egg whites (yolks
    discarded), chopped
4 to 6 carrots, sliced in ¼-inch
    rounds
3 leafy ribs celery, diced
3 scallions, thinly sliced on the
    diagonal
½ cup crumbled low-fat feta
    cheese (optional)
Freshly ground black pepper
1 orange, peeled and sliced, for
    garnish

In a food processor or blender, combine the garlic, orange juice, mustard, yogurt, Worcestershire, cumin, and ginger. With the motor running, slowly drizzle in the olive oil and continue to process about 1 minute.

In a large salad bowl, mix the lentils, orange segments, egg whites, carrots, and celery. Pour the dressing over the lentil mixture. Add ¾ of the scallions, reserving the remaining ¼ for garnish. Add the feta cheese, if using, and toss gently. Sprinkle with the remaining scallions and pepper to taste and top with orange slices.

PER SERVING: Saturated Fat: 0.5 gm   Total Fat: 4 gm
Cholesterol: Trace   Sodium: 107 mg   Calories: 177

Sugar Snap Peas
and Black Bean Salad

This dish is truly a snap to make if you have some leftover rice. If you prefer a spicier dressing, increase the garlic by 2 or 3 cloves and add several drops of hot sauce. To serve for a main course, I add 2 cups skinned, defatted, and julienned smoked turkey or diced lean ham from the deli.

SNAPPY CUBA
DRESSING:
½ orange, peeled, seeded, and separated into segments
1 clove garlic
2 teaspoons fresh lime or lemon juice
2 tablespoons fresh balsamic or cider vinegar
1 tablespoon olive oil
½ cup chunky salsa verde

SALAD:
1 cup cooked rice, at room temperature

1 15-ounce can black beans, drained
1 medium red bell pepper, diced
1 cup fresh sugar snap peas, cut in ¼-inch pieces or 1 9-ounce package frozen, thawed and drained
Salad greens to line the plates
8 ounces skinned and defatted smoked turkey, chicken, or lean ham, diced or cut into matchstick-size pieces (optional)
Freshly ground black pepper

In a food processor or blender, puree the orange segments, garlic, lime juice, and balsamic vinegar. With the motor running, slowly drizzle in the olive oil and continue to process for about 1 minute. Remove the blade and stir in the salsa.

In a large bowl, toss the rice with ¼ cup of the dressing, cover, and refrigerate 1 hour. Just before serving, add the beans, pepper, and peas to the rice mixture and toss to mix well. Line 4 individual dinner plates with salad greens and mound each with the rice salad. Place the smoked turkey or chicken on top, if using, add pepper to taste, and serve immediately with the remaining dressing passed separately.

PER SERVING: Saturated Fat: Trace   Total Fat: 2 gm
Cholesterol: 0 mg   Sodium: 277 mg   Calories: 216

Key Largo Chicken Salad

Full of tropical flavors and colors, serve this salad in hollowed pineapple or mango shells. For pineapple, leave the fronds on and cut lengthwise in 4 shell wedges. If you make the salad a day ahead, omit the pineapple until just before serving. Pineapple enzymes break down protein and will make the chicken soggy.

SALAD:

1 8-ounce can sliced water chestnuts, drained and chilled in ice water
2 medium leafy ribs celery, sliced in thin diagonals and chilled in ice water
2 cups cooked chicken, skinned and all fat removed, diced
2 cups fresh pineapple, cut into chunks
1 papaya, seeded, sliced, plus 3 or 4 slices for garnish
2 shallots, minced

DRESSING:

½ cup spicy hot and sweet mustard
1 teaspoon chives
2 tablespoons capers
2 tablespoons fresh lime juice
1 tablespoon sherry (optional)
½ cup nonfat mayonnaise
½ cup nonfat sour cream
1 head Napa or Oriental cabbage, finely shredded
1 cup mung bean sprouts, crisped in ice water and then drained

Drain the water chestnuts and celery and blot dry. In a large bowl, combine the chicken, pineapple, papaya, and shallots.

In a small bowl, whisk together the mustard, chives, capers, lime juice, sherry, mayonnaise, and sour cream. Pour ½ the dressing over the chicken mixture and toss to mix well. In a separate large bowl, toss the cabbage and bean sprouts to mix well and cover a serving platter with the mixture. Top with the chicken salad. Garnish with 3 or 4 papaya slices and serve immediately with the remaining dressing passed separately.

PER SERVING: Saturated Fat: 0.5 gm   Total Fat: 3 gm
Cholesterol: 37 mg   Sodium: 446 mg   Calories: 165

Sesame-Peanut Chicken and Noodles Salad

The mildly Asian taste combination of peanut and ginger seems to hook everyone. The quick cooking tip of blanching the vegetables in the pasta water saves a lot of time.

8 ounces spaghetti or linguine

2 cups broccoli florets

6 carrots, thinly sliced

2 large cloves garlic

1-inch piece of ginger, peeled

⅓ cup reduced-fat low-sodium peanut butter

1 tablespoon honey

2 tablespoons low-sodium soy sauce

3 tablespoons Worcestershire

2 tablespoons fresh lemon juice

¾ cup low-sodium defatted chicken or vegetable stock

1 tablespoon sesame oil

1 8-ounce can sliced water chestnuts, drained

1½ cups cooked chicken, skinned and all fat removed, diced

4 scallions, sliced on a diagonal

4 large leaves Napa cabbage plus 2 cups thinly shredded

½ cup mandarin orange slices, for garnish

Cook the pasta according to package directions. About 8 minutes before it is done, add the broccoli and carrots to the pasta water and cook for 4 minutes; drain the pasta and vegetables in a colander and rinse with cool water. Remove to a large bowl.

In a food processor or blender, puree the garlic, ginger, peanut butter, honey, soy sauce, Worcestershire, lemon juice, stock, and sesame oil until smooth. Pour the dressing over the pasta mixture, add the water chestnuts, chicken, and all but ¼ cup of the scallions and toss to mix well.

Line individual plates with a large cabbage leaf, sprinkle with ½ cup shredded cabbage, and mound the spaghetti salad on top. Garnish with scallions and mandarin oranges and serve immediately.

PER SERVING: Saturated Fat: 3 gm   Total Fat: 14 gm
Cholesterol: 43 mg   Sodium: 696 mg   Calories: 589

Summer Salad Française

The Dijon mustard, potatoes, tarragon, and olives give this salad a decided French twist. Smoked turkey makes it an entrée.

DIJON SALAD
DRESSING:
1 clove garlic
3 tablespoons coarse grain Dijon
    mustard
1/2 teaspoon tarragon
1/2 cup raspberry or cider vinegar
2 tablespoons olive oil

SALAD:
1 cup baby peas, thawed if frozen
6 carrots, diced and lightly
    blanched

4 medium cooked potatoes (peeled
    or unpeeled), diced
8 ounces smoked turkey,
    skinned and all fat removed,
    diced (optional)
2/3 cup pitted sliced black olives
Salt (optional)
Freshly ground black pepper
4 cups fresh spinach, cleaned and
    stemmed

In a food processor or blender, mince the garlic. Add the mustard, tarragon, and vinegar and puree. With the motor running, slowly drizzle in the olive oil and continue to process for 1 minute.

In a large bowl, mix the peas, carrots, potatoes, turkey, olives, and salt, if using, and pepper. Pour the dressing over the potato mixture and toss to mix well. Line a serving bowl or individual plates with spinach, top with potato mélange, and serve immediately.

PER SIDE SALAD SERVING: Saturated Fat: 1 gm

Total Fat: 11 gm   Cholesterol: 0 mg   Sodium: 607 mg   Calories: 305

Lugano Fresh Seafood Salad

Lugano is an area influenced by both Switzerland and Italy and specializes in seafood. The dill makes it more Swiss and the dressing is like the place, rich and lush. This is a layered salad of potatoes, mushrooms, shrimp, and onions, which can be prepared a day in advance. A food processor saves time as does buying cooked shrimp.

MARINADE:

1 tablespoon fresh lemon juice

4 teaspoons raspberry or cider vinegar

1 clove garlic, minced

Salt (optional)

Freshly ground black pepper

2 tablespoons olive or canola oil

4 ounces mushrooms, sliced

2 large potatoes, sliced into thin rounds

SHRIMP MIXTURE:

1 cucumber, peeled and sliced into thin rounds

6 ounces cooked shrimp

½ red onion, thinly sliced

SOUR CREAM DRESSING:

2 tablespoons Dijon mustard

3 tablespoons raspberry or cider vinegar

1 tablespoon sugar

½ cup nonfat sour cream

Salt (optional)

Freshly ground black pepper

1 teaspoon freshly chopped dill

Salad greens to line dishes

2 hard-cooked egg whites, diced, for garnish

In a small, nonreactive bowl, whisk together the lemon juice, vinegar, garlic, salt, if using, and pepper to taste. Slowly drizzle in the oil while continuing to whisk vigorously. Stir in the mushrooms.

In a medium nonstick saucepan, in boiling water, blanch potato slices for 3 minutes or just until tender. Drain and stir into mushrooms and marinade.

(continued)

In a medium bowl, combine the cucumber, shrimp, and red onion. In a small bowl, whisk together the mustard, vinegar, sugar, sour cream, salt, and pepper, to taste, if using, and dill. Pour the dressing over the shrimp mixture and toss to mix well.

To assemble, line individual plates with salad greens. Arrange potatoes and mushrooms over the greens, top with shrimp mixture, and garnish with grated hard-boiled egg whites. Serve immediately.

PER MAIN COURSE SERVING: Saturated Fat: 1 gm
Total Fat: 8 gm Cholesterol: 83 mg Sodium: 342 mg Calories: 253

Salmon and Jicama Salad with Snow Peas and Watercress

Serves 4

Jicama has a crisp, white, sweet and nutty flavor and can be used raw or cooked. The dressing and salmon can be prepared a few hours in advance or the day before.

SALAD:

3 cups watercress, stems removed
1 cup thinly sliced red cabbage
1 cup jicama, peeled and julienned

DRESSING:

1/2 cup fresh orange juice
2 tablespoons raspberry or cider vinegar
1 tablespoon canola oil
2 tablespoons minced scallions
Salt (optional)

SPICY SWEET ALMONDS:

1/2 cup slivered almonds
Vegetable oil spray
1/4 teaspoon cayenne
1/4 teaspoon seasoned salt (optional)
2 tablespoons sugar

8 ounces skinned salmon fillet, grilled or broiled, or 1 7 1/2-ounce can salmon, drained
1 1/4 cups snow peas, stem end cut, blanched and chilled

Preheat the oven to 300°F.

In a large bowl, combine the watercress, red cabbage, and jicama, and refrigerate until ready to assemble. In a food processor or blender, puree the orange juice, vinegar, oil, scallions, and salt, if using.

Line a baking sheet with foil. Place the almonds on the sheet and spray lightly with vegetable oil. In a small bowl, mix the cayenne, seasoned salt, if using, and sugar. Toss the almonds in the sugar and spice mixture to coat, and return to the baking sheet. Bake for 20 to 25 minutes, or until golden.

To assemble the salad, pour the dressing over the chilled watercress mixture and toss to mix well. Slice or flake the salmon into thin strips and place on top of the salad. Arrange the snow peas around the edge of the salad and sprinkle with almonds. Serve immediately.

PER SERVING: Saturated Fat: 2 gm   Total Fat: 14 gm
Cholesterol: 33 mg   Sodium: 44 mg   Calories: 269

Reggae Salad with Pork, Mango, and Orzo

This salad is a bright and lively island specialty, just like a reggae band. Fresh mango can be found in most supermarkets, but the commercially bottled mango (in the refrigerated section) has lots of taste and is perfectly acceptable. Use it if you want to save the bother of peeling and pitting the fruit.

SALAD:

Vegetable oil spray
8 ounces pork loin, trimmed of fat

DRESSING:

½ teaspoon chopped pickled jalapeño
2 cups fresh mango diced plus ½ cup diced mango reserved for dressing
2 cloves garlic

2 cups cooked orzo or pastita
1 small red bell pepper, minced, plus 2 tablespoons minced red bell pepper, for garnish

½ cup minced red onion plus thinly sliced red onion rings, for garnish
3 tablespoons fresh lime juice
⅓ cup fresh orange juice
½ teaspoon cumin
2 tablespoons olive oil
Drop of Tabasco

¼ cup chopped cilantro plus 2 tablespoons chopped cilantro, for garnish
Thinly sliced romaine lettuce

Spray a nonstick skillet and heat over medium high until hot. Sear the pork about 2 minutes per side until quite brown. Reduce the heat and cook until firm to the touch, about 3 minutes per side. Cool and slice into ½-inch by 1-inch strips.

In a food processor or blender, puree the jalapeño, ½ cup mango, garlic, lime juice, orange juice, cumin, olive oil and Tabasco.

In a large bowl, combine the pork, orzo, red pepper, red onion, the remaining mango, and cilantro. Pour the dressing over the pork mixture and toss to mix well. Line a platter or individual plates with romaine. Mound the salad on top and garnish with reserved red pepper, red onion rings, and cilantro. Serve immediately.

■■ PER SIDE SALAD SERVING: Saturated Fat: 0.5 gm ■■
Total Fat: 3 gm Cholesterol: 15 mg Sodium: 15 mg Calories: 184

Blue Cheese or Roquefort Dressing
■■ *Makes 1 1/2 cups* ■■

If you like blue cheese dressing on your salad, which is the American version of Roquefort (from the Roquefort caves in France), you will love this one. It will keep for a week.

1 cup white wine vinegar
3 tablespoons fresh lemon juice
2 tablespoons olive oil
1 clove garlic, minced
1/2 teaspoon sugar
1/2 teaspoon dry mustard

1/4 teaspoon dried rosemary
1/2 teaspoon paprika
1 teaspoon finely chopped parsley
4 ounces blue or Roquefort cheese,
crumbled

In a small bowl, whisk together the vinegar, lemon juice, olive oil, garlic, sugar, mustard, rosemary, paprika, and parsley. Gently stir in the cheese. Use immediately if you want the parsley to remain a fresh green color as it wilts and darkens quickly in vinegar.

■■ PER TABLESPOON: Saturated Fat: 1 gm Total Fat: 3 gm ■■
Cholesterol: 4 mg Sodium: 67 mg Calories: 29

Herb or Italian Dressing

Redolent with fresh garlic and herbs, serve this on a green salad.

½ cup red wine vinegar	1 teaspoon dried oregano
½ cup cider vinegar	½ teaspoon chopped fresh basil or
2 cloves garlic	¼ teaspoon dried
½ teaspoon dry mustard	Freshly ground black pepper
1 tablespoon fresh lemon juice	2 tablespoons olive oil

In a food processor, pulse the vinegars, garlic, mustard, lemon juice, oregano, basil, and a couple grinds of pepper. With the motor running, slowly drizzle in the oil and continue to process for 1 minute. Serve chilled or at room temperature.

PER TABLESPOON: Saturated Fat: Trace   Total Fat: 2 gm
Cholesterol: 0 mg   Sodium: Trace   Calories: 19

Classic Vinaigrette

This is one of the best dressings for any salad—truly classic! It can easily take small additions of prepared mustard, dry mustard, lemon juice, or fresh herbs, such as oregano, basil, and tarragon. It can also take ½ teaspoon of sugar for those who like sweet salad dressing. Use immediately or the scallions and parsley will wilt.

1 cup white or cider vinegar	½ teaspoon chopped parsley
2 tablespoons water	Salt (optional)
½ teaspoon sugar	2 tablespoons olive oil
½ teaspoon chopped scallions	

In a food processor or blender, pulse the vinegar, water, sugar, scallions, parsley, and salt, if using. With the motor running, slowly drizzle in the oil and continue to process for 1 minute. Serve chilled or at room temperature. Store in the refrigerator for up to 1 week. Shake or stir before using.

PER TABLESPOON:　Saturated Fat: Trace　Total Fat: 1 gm
Cholesterol: 0 mg　Sodium: 0 mg　Calories: 13

Russian Dressing

Makes about 2 cups

This is the traditional American dressing for cold wedges of iceberg lettuce, avocado, and often used as a sandwich spread, that was so popular in the forties and fifties and is making a comeback. It's called Russian because it is bumpy and reminded some of caviar.

1 cup nonfat mayonnaise	2 tablespoons grated onion
1/4 teaspoon Worcestershire	1/4 teaspoon dry mustard
1/2 cup low-sodium chili sauce or salsa	3 to 4 drops Tabasco
	1 teaspoon prepared horseradish
3 tablespoons finely chopped parsley	1 tablespoon nonfat milk

In a small bowl, whisk together the mayonnaise, Worcestershire, chili sauce, parsley, onion, mustard, Tabasco, horseradish, and nonfat milk. Serve chilled. Store in the refrigerator for up to 4 days.

PER TABLESPOON:　Saturated Fat: 0 gm　Total Fat: 0 gm
Cholesterol: 0 mg　Sodium: 142 mg　Calories: 11

Cold Duck Sauce Dressing

This is a very simple dressing that adds creamy enhancement to cold chicken, turkey, or duck salads. It will keep for five days.

½ cup nonfat sour cream
⅔ cup fresh orange juice
1½ teaspoons low-sodium soy
    sauce

1 teaspoon apple or currant jelly
Several drops Tabasco

In a small bowl, whisk together the sour cream, orange juice, soy sauce, jelly, and hot sauce. Serve chilled, just before dressing the poultry salad.

PER TABLESPOON: Saturated Fat: 0 gm   Total Fat: 0 gm
Cholesterol: 0 mg   Sodium: 16 mg   Calories: 7

Thousand Island Dressing

This is the old-time thick and velvety favorite that men in particular love on a wedge of iceberg lettuce, tomatoes, hamburgers, avocado, and even chicken salad. It can be used as a sandwich spread, too. Keep for only four days.

1 cup nonfat mayonnaise

½ cup nonfat milk

3 hard-cooked egg whites, finely
chopped

4 tablespoons chili sauce

2 tablespoons chopped parsley

3 tablespoons sweet pickle relish

2 tablespoons pitted chopped green
olives

3 tablespoons chopped onion

½ teaspoon paprika

In a small bowl, whisk together the mayonnaise, milk, egg whites, chili sauce, parsley, relish, olives, onion and paprika. Store in the refrigerator for up to 4 days.

■■ PER TABLESPOON: Saturated Fat: 0 gm   Total Fat: 0 gm ■■
Cholesterol: 0 mg   Sodium: 146 mg   Calories: 14

Poppy-Seed Dressing
■■ *Makes about 1 cup* ■■

One of my favorite salad dressings, keep it on hand and use on green salads or fresh fruit. I like it on a salad of lettuce, mandarin oranges, celery, onions, raisins, and slivered almonds.

⅓ cup low-sodium, defatted
chicken stock

2 teaspoons cornstarch

¼ scant cup cider or rice vinegar

1 tablespoon sugar

1 tablespoon poppy seeds

1 tablespoon grated onion

½ teaspoon Dijon mustard

1 teaspoon finely chopped parsley

In a small nonstick saucepan, combine the chicken stock, cornstarch, vinegar, sugar, poppy seeds, onion, and mustard. Place over medium heat and whisk until thickened, about 4 or 5 minutes. Cool to room temperature and stir in the parsley. Store in the refrigerator for up to 1 week.

■■ PER TABLESPOON: Saturated Fat: 0 gm   Total Fat: Trace ■■
Cholesterol: 0 mg   Sodium: 5 mg   Calories: 9

Sour Cream Dressing

Use this sparingly on coleslaw, potato salad, and seafood. Substitute fresh lemon juice for the vinegar if you wish. For a sweeter coleslaw dressing, add ¹⁄₄ cup crushed pineapple to your cabbage and top with the sour cream dressing.

¹⁄₂ cup nonfat sour cream	1 teaspoon sugar
¹⁄₄ cup evaporated skimmed milk	Salt (optional)
1 teaspoon cider or white vinegar	

In a small bowl, whisk together the sour cream, milk, vinegar, sugar, and salt, if using. Cover and refrigerate until chilled. Store in the refrigerator for up to 4 days.

PER TABLESPOON: Saturated Fat: 0 gm   Total Fat: 0 gm
Cholesterol: 0 mg   Sodium: 26 mg   Calories: 9

Seafood Dressing

This dressing is excellent on any shrimp salad, crab Louis, or served on the side with cold cooked fish and vegetables. For tangier dressing, substitute nonfat yogurt for the mayonnaise. It will keep for five days.

¹⁄₂ cup nonfat mayonnaise	1 teaspoon chopped dill pickles
2 tablespoons nonfat milk	3 teaspoons chopped chives
3 tablespoons fresh lemon juice	Paprika, to taste
Tabasco, to taste	
¹⁄₂ teaspoon dry mustard	

In a small bowl, whisk together the mayonnaise, milk, lemon juice, Tabasco, dry mustard, dill pickles, chives and paprika. Cover and refrigerate until chilled. Store in the refrigerator for up to 5 days.

PER TABLESPOON: Saturated Fat: 0 gm   Total Fat: 0 gm
Cholesterol: 0 mg   Sodium: 117 mg   Calories: 10

Green Goddess Dressing

Makes ¾ cup

Popular since the Roaring Twenties, green goddess is perfect for fish, shellfish, vegetable salads, and as a spread. Use immediately.

½ cup nonfat mayonnaise
1 tablespoon cider vinegar
1 teaspoon fresh lemon juice
1 teaspoon anchovy paste
2 tablespoons chopped parsley
1 tablespoon chopped fresh chives
  or 1½ teaspoons dried

1 clove garlic, minced
2 tablespoons chopped scallions
1 teaspoon chopped fresh tarragon
  or ½ teaspoon dried

In a small bowl, whisk together the mayonnaise, vinegar, lemon juice, and anchovy paste until smooth. Stir in the parsley, chives, garlic, scallions, and tarragon. If the dressing is too thick, add a few drops of water. Cover and refrigerate until chilled.

PER TABLESPOON: Saturated Fat: 0 gm   Total Fat: 0 gm
Cholesterol: 0 mg   Sodium: 186 mg   Calories: 9

Lillian Smith's
Five-Vinegar Dill Dressing

My good friend Lillian Smith of New Orleans, whose salads and conversation I have enjoyed for years, insists that this dressing needs all of the five vinegars. I have no idea why, but she's right. I've tried to get away with using just one or two and it's never the same.

¾ cup equal parts mixed vinegars (including balsamic, cider, wine, and white vinegar) plus a flavored vinegar, such as raspberry, blueberry, or herbal vinegar

4 sprigs fresh dill
2 sprigs fresh parsley
1 tablespoon Dijon mustard
2 teaspoons honey
2 tablespoons olive oil

In a small bowl, combine equal amounts of the five vinegars. In a food processor, finely mince the dill and parsley; add the mustard and vinegars and honey. With the motor running, slowly drizzle in the olive oil and continue to process for 1 minute. Serve chilled or at room temperature, stirring or shaking before using. Store in the refrigerator for up to 2 days.

PER TABLESPOON: Saturated Fat: 0 gm   Total Fat: 2 gm
Cholesterol: 0 mg   Sodium: 24 mg   Calories: 21

Sesame Soy Dressing

This is a lively Asian-style topping for salads of lettuce, scallions, bean sprouts, alfalfa sprouts, slivered almonds, mandarin oranges, cold poultry, pea pods, chopped jicama, and celery with this soy dressing. Rice vinegar has a pleasant mellow flavor whereas other vinegars, such as cider and white vinegar, are harsher.

⅓ cup unseasoned rice vinegar or cider vinegar	2 teaspoons freshly minced ginger
3 tablespoons dark sesame oil	2 teaspoons sesame seeds, toasted or untoasted
2 tablespoons low-sodium soy sauce	3 teaspoons sugar
	Dash white pepper

In a small bowl, whisk together the vinegar, sesame oil, soy sauce, ginger, sesame seeds, sugar, and pepper, until the sugar dissolves. Store in the refrigerator up to 1 week. Stir or shake before using.

PER TABLESPOON: Saturated Fat: 0.5 gm   Total Fat: 4 gm
Cholesterol: O mg   Sodium: 101 mg   Calories: 40

Tangy Honey-Mustard Dressing

Makes about ¹/₂ cup

Honey and mustard combine to give a nice piquancy to mixed green salads with lean diced ham.

2 tablespoons nonfat mayonnaise

2 tablespoons unseasoned rice or cider vinegar

1 tablespoon fresh lemon juice

1 teaspoon Dijon mustard

1 teaspoon honey

1 clove garlic, minced

Dash white pepper

3 drops Tabasco

1 scallion, finely chopped

1 tablespoon finely minced parsley

In a small food processor, combine the mayonnaise, vinegar, lemon juice, mustard, honey, garlic, pepper, and Tabasco. Add the scallion and parsley and pulse several times to combine. Store in the refrigerator for up to 2 weeks. Stir or shake dressing before using.

PER TABLESPOON: Saturated Fat: 0 gm   Total Fat: 0 gm

Cholesterol: 0 mg   Sodium: 59 mg   Calories: 8

VEGETABLES

The word "vegetable" comes from the Latin "vegere," which means to give life. And we, along with every animal relative, have been eating our vegetables for that very life energy benefit since prehistory. A bountiful source for our early ancestors of simple and complex carbohydrates, fiber, vitamins, and minerals, there are only a few vegetables today that were not around at the dawn of time (broccoli, spinach, cauliflower, and brussels sprouts, for example).

It wasn't until the Middle Ages in Europe, however, that anyone paid attention to the life-giving advantage of eating vegetables. Kings and feudal lords slowly began to notice that soldiers and sailing men performed better in the fall and early winter. The men not only survived long marches and voyages but they also arrived robust and healthy, fought well in battle, and recovered quickly from injury. (They had eaten meat throughout the year.) This, of course, had not been the case during late winter and spring, when the men often fell sick and died by the wayside or at sea.

Since most Europeans then enjoyed a year-round abundance of meat in their diets, it became apparent that vegetables, which were available fresh only during summer and fall, had something to do with the well-being of the king's men.

Until 1900 America and the dawn of the industrialized Western world, everybody enjoyed fresh vegetables in season because if one didn't work on a farm, one most likely lived near one. Leftover fall harvests were then put up in jars and stored for winter vegetable eating. Potatoes and carrots were stored in root cellars common in the east and Midwest.

Then came mechanization, factories, and the move from the farm into large cities. Along with inventions like mass-produced tin cans and frozen foods, fresh vegetables became a rarity—so much so that by 1960, three generations of Americans had grown up eating bland-tasting canned, jarred, or frozen vegetables. Convenient, yes, but Americans had lost touch with the good taste of fresh produce.

By the midseventies, Americans began to demand better-tasting food, and fresh produce started a slow comeback in the produce sections of supermarkets. Now thanks to major agribusiness and the rebirth of small specialty farms, we are inundated with fresh homegrown produce and herbs, which are available every day in the local farmers markets as well as supermarkets. Thanks, too, to global farming there are new vegetable varieties arriving daily from Israel, Chile, and Australia, to name just a few countries. Many of us are already familiar with some of the recent arrivals from south of the border—jicama, tomatillos, and cherimoyas—but there are dozens of new winter (hard) squash varieties showing up in the markets and, in some areas, miniature coconuts, kiwis with no fur, finger-size avocados with no pit, and avocado-size grapefruit.

This chapter is devoted to good vegetable eating with more recipes than any other chapter. From the traditional to the new, they are here: from Mashed Potatoes (page 148) to Stuffed Portobello Mushrooms (page 139) to spicy Shanghai Snow Peas (page 150). Vegetables and grains form the two base areas of the USDA food pyramid, along with legumes, or dried beans (which are also vegetables). Vegetarians have less heart disease and many athletes are vegetarians, so eat your vegetables. This chapter gives you some tasty ways to enjoy them.

▪▪ Vegetable Basics ▪▪

While vegetables vary in color, texture, taste, size, and appearance, and while they differ too in the amount of nutrients they offer, they have several things in common: Nearly all are low in calories and fat; are cholesterol free; and when combined with grains and fruits are an efficient base for a healthful menu plan.

Vegetables are often rich in calcium and important vitamins, such as A, C, and beta-carotene, as well as antioxidants, fiber, and carbohydrates. Broccoli, for example, is a great source of vitamins A, C, and beta-carotene (in fact, the leaves are richer in these nutrients than are the florets). The calcium-rich sources are the cruciferous vegetables, such as cabbage, kale, bok choy, broccoli florets and leaves, brussels sprouts, and the dark green leafy vegetables, such as collard greens, romaine lettuce, turnip and mustard greens, spinach, watercress, parsley, and arugula. Okra, corn, asparagus, kohlrabi, and lima beans are also good sources for calcium.

BUYING Be flexible when you go shopping for vegetables. Buy what is fresh. Rather than going to the market with specific recipe ingredients in mind, pick out the vegetables that are fresh and in season and choose a recipe based on them, or substitute them in your favorite recipe. You may come up with a winner.

If the vegetables you want are prewrapped, the law in most states allows you to unwrap them and take only the amount you need. Produce managers appreciate your telling them so they can reweigh and rewrap the remainders.

STORING Today's refrigerators are still designed with puny produce bins, a remnant of the days when people ate more canned foods than fresh. For those vegetables that must be refrigerated, store them in the bins or in plastic bags to slow the drying process.

•Refrigerate, not in plastic bags: garlic, onions, cabbage.

•Refrigerate unwashed in plastic bags: hot peppers, scallions, leeks, chives, bell peppers, herbs, carrots, lettuce, zucchini, squash, beans, celery, fennel, parsley, cilantro, and watercress.

•Refrigerate in aerated bags, baskets, or loose: shallots, pearl onions, eggplant, mushrooms, and potatoes.

•*Don't* refrigerate: unripe tomatoes, avocados, and pineapples. Put them in brown bags in a dark place or, if nearly ripe, in a basket on the counter. Pineapples do not ripen further once picked. Tomatoes will and avocados will.

The hanging braids of garlic and hot peppers are pretty to look at, but unusable after a few weeks. They get dusty, dry, and filled with bugs. Freeze or spray them with a bug killer first to kill the eggs.

If you want to use them, break off the garlic and refrigerate, crush or flake the peppers in a processor, and store in jars, pick off the bay laurel, sage, or other herbs and store in paper bags. Some herb or pepper wreaths and pepper ropes aren't edible, so I would just use them as decoration (often they have a fixture, varnish, or bug spray on them).

Asparagus with Roasted Shallot and Walnut Sauce

Pureed oven-roasted shallots and garlic are the low-fat base to this creamy sauce. I keep a variety of roasted vegetables in the refrigerator to use as quick bases for many different sauces.

3 to 4 medium shallots, skin on

4 cloves garlic, skin on

Olive oil spray

1 teaspoon fresh lemon juice

2 tablespoons walnuts, toasted and chopped

1 tablespoon canola oil

⅓ cup water or low-sodium vegetable stock

Salt (optional)

Freshly ground black pepper

1 pound fresh asparagus, tough ends discarded

1 teaspoon lemon juice or balsamic vinegar or cider vinegar

Preheat the oven to 350°F.

Line a baking sheet with foil. Place the shallots and garlic on the sheet and lightly spray with oil. Cover with additional foil, crimp the edges, and poke a hole in the top and roast 45 to 50 minutes or until very soft. Set aside until cool enough to handle, then peel. The onions and shallots may be prepared ahead and refrigerated, covered for up to 4 days.

In a food processor or blender, puree the shallots, garlic, lemon juice, 2 tablespoons of the walnuts, and the oil until smooth. Add the water or stock gradually until it is the desired thickness. Salt, if using, and pepper to taste.

In a small saucepan lightly sprayed with oil, over low heat, cook the shallot mixture, stirring occasionally, until warmed through. Meanwhile, in a large nonstick skillet, heat ½ inch water to boiling. Add the asparagus and reduce heat; cover and simmer for 4 to 6 minutes. Drain and place the asparagus on a serving platter or individual serving plates. Top with the warmed shallot sauce, sprinkle with lemon juice or vinegar, and garnish with the remaining 2 tablespoons of chopped walnuts. Serve immediately.

■■ PER SERVING: Saturated Fat: Trace   Total Fat: 6 gm   ■■
Cholesterol: 0 mg   Sodium: 4 mg   Calories: 79

Steamed Artichokes
with Curry Dip

■■ *Serves 4* ■■

Buy deep green artichokes with tight leaf formations that feel heavy for their size. They are available year round but are at their peak in the spring. Serve this dish hot or cold with a dollop of chutney, sprigs of parsley or watercress, and a few sprinkles of paprika. The dip has more flavor if made a day ahead.

4 artichokes, stems and any dark lower leaves removed	*Juice of 1 large lemon*
1 cup nonfat sour cream	*1 to 3 teaspoons curry powder*
	Pinch sugar

Press hard on the stem end of the artichoke (pointed tip on the counter) with the palm of your hand to open the leaves. Rinse the opened leaves under cool running water. Place the artichokes stem side down so that they fit snugly in a large saucepan. Fill with water to cover the artichokes and place over high heat and bring to a boil. Reduce the heat to medium, cover, and simmer 40 minutes, and drain.

Meanwhile, in a small bowl, whisk together the sour cream, lemon, curry powder, and sugar. If serving chilled, cover and refrigerate, or serve the artichoke hot with the dip, which can be made up to 3 days in advance.

■■ PER SERVING: Saturated Fat: 0 gm   Total Fat: Trace   ■■
Cholesterol: 0 mg   Sodium: 193 mg   Calories: 116

Asparagus and Prosciutto

Prosciutto, if lean, is low in both total and saturated fat. Use large, extra-thick asparagus spears to make this wonderful entrée. Serve it with fragrant basmati rice and Baked Stuffed Plum Tomatoes (page 151). The Parmesan can be slivered on the large shredder size of a grater.

1½ pounds asparagus, tough ends
   discarded
1 cup evaporated skimmed milk
2 tablespoons all-purpose flour
Salt (optional)
Pinch cayenne

3 ounces lean prosciutto, trimmed
   of all fat and julienned
Olive oil spray
2 tablespoons slivered Parmesan
   cheese
2 tablespoons chopped parsley

In an asparagus steamer over high heat, heat 2 inches water to boiling. Add asparagus and steam for 4 minutes; drain. Alternatively, in a large nonstick skillet over medium-high heat, heat ¼ inch water. Add asparagus and steam for 5 or 7 minutes; drain.

In a large nonstick skillet over medium-high heat, whisk together the milk, flour, salt, if using, and cayenne and cook, stirring, until thickened. Sprinkle the prosciutto on top.

Arrange the asparagus on a warm serving platter, spray lightly with oil to moisten so they are glossy, and top with the sauce. Garnish with Parmesan cheese and parsley and serve immediately.

PER SERVING: Saturated Fat: 1 gm   Total Fat: 3 gm
Cholesterol: 20 mg   Sodium: 708 mg   Calories: 141

Steamed Bok Choy and Oysters

Bok choy is a versatile loose leaf cabbage that is often used cooked or raw in Chinese cuisine. It resembles celery in looks, flavor, and texture. Both bok choy and the bottled oyster sauce that I use here are available in Asian markets and some supermarkets. If you can't find bok choy, use romaine lettuce or Napa cabbage. Shrimp is also a fine substitute for oysters.

1 pound bok choy, chopped into
  1- to 2-inch pieces
2 tablespoons chopped fresh ginger
  or 1 teaspoon dried
1 clove garlic, minced

3 ounces small shucked oysters
2 tablespoons oyster sauce
2 tablespoons Worcestershire

In a large nonstick skillet over high heat, heat ¼ inch water to boiling. Add the bok choy, ginger, and garlic, and reduce the heat to low; cover and simmer 5 to 7 minutes, adding more water if necessary to prevent sticking. When the bok choy is tender, drain the liquid from the skillet, add the oysters, and turn the heat to medium high. Toss the mixture for 2 to 3 minutes, add the oyster sauce, Worcestershire, and toss to coat. Remove from heat and cover for 1 minute and serve hot.

PER SERVING: Saturated Fat: Trace   Total Fat: 1 gm
Cholesterol: 11 mg   Sodium: 523 mg   Calories: 50

Vegetable-Stuffed Cabbage

This is comfort food but with a little different presentation, that of serving the whole cabbage. Stuffed cabbage is colorful and takes about 1 hour to prepare and cook. If you have leftover filling, bake it in ramekins with a sprinkle of grated Parmesan cheese. Have two to three clean, two-foot-long pieces of heavy string for this dish.

1 large head cabbage	2 tablespoons herbed bread crumbs
Vegetable oil spray	1 tablespoon red wine or cider
1 medium onion, thinly sliced	vinegar
1 small spaghetti squash, cooked	1 tablespoon steak sauce
and cooled (about 1½ cups)	2 teaspoons chopped fresh
6 medium plum tomatoes, diced	rosemary
½ teaspoon salt (optional)	2 to 3 lengths of clean white
Freshly ground black pepper	kitchen string, each 2 feet long

Remove 4 to 5 outer leaves of the cabbage and reserve. Cut the cabbage in half. With a paring knife, cut around the inside half, leaving a ½-inch-thick shell, and remove the inside leaves, forming 2 ½-inch shells of cabbage and set aside. Remove the core and discard; thinly chop the removed inside leaves.

In a 5-quart nonstick sauce pot lightly sprayed with oil, over medium-high heat, heat ½ cup water. Add the chopped cabbage and onion and cook for 10 to 12 minutes or until soft, adding more water by the spoonful to keep moist, if necessary. Drain and rinse out the pot.

In a large bowl, mix together the cabbage mixture, spaghetti squash, tomatoes, salt, if using, pepper, bread crumbs, vinegar, steak sauce, and rosemary. Fill each cabbage shell with half the mixture and push the two halves together to reform the cabbage. Wrap the reserved outer leaves around the cabbage to cover the cracks and tie with the string.

In the same sauce pot, heat 1 inch water to boiling. Reduce heat to low and add the stuffed cabbage; cover and cook for 40 minutes, turning carefully once or twice and adding more water if needed. Let the cabbage cool for 5 minutes before removing from the pot. Slice in half, then in 6 wedges, 3 per half; remove the string, and serve immediately.

PER SERVING: Saturated Fat: Trace   Total Fat: 1 gm
Cholesterol: 0 mg   Sodium: 138 mg   Calories: 80

Gingered Beets with Orange

Serves 4

If you like beets, this colorful and gingery dish abounds with fresh beets, which are simple to prepare. The taste of the fresh ginger is very different from the dried but both are good. It's on the table in 25 minutes.

4 medium beets, peeled and thinly
   sliced
¼ cup raspberry or cider vinegar
1 teaspoon freshly grated ginger or
   ½ teaspoon dried, ground
   ginger

Salt (optional)
⅓ cup orange marmalade
1 teaspoon walnut or canola oil

In a large nonstick skillet in ¼ inch water, over high heat, combine the beets, vinegar, ginger, and salt, if using, and heat to boiling. Reduce the heat, cover, and simmer for 14 to 16 minutes or until tender, adding more water if necessary to prevent sticking. Remove beets to a serving dish, stir in the marmalade and walnut oil, and toss to mix well. Serve immediately or cover and refrigerate to serve cold.

PER SERVING: Saturated Fat: Trace   Total Fat: 1 gm
Cholesterol: 0 mg   Sodium: 78 mg   Calories: 112

Sweet and Sour Red Cabbage

Red cabbage is delicious raw in salads or cooked as in this traditional German rendition. I prefer the rich taste of this dish after it has been refrigerated overnight and reheated for serving the next day. If you prefer a sweeter milder dish, use less vinegar; for a more tart taste, use less sugar.

1 small head red cabbage,
   shredded
1 small onion, finely chopped
1 Granny Smith apple, diced

½ cup cider or red wine vinegar
¼ cup brown sugar
2 tablespoons cornstarch

In a large nonstick saucepan in ¼ inch water, over high heat, combine the cabbage, onion, apple, vinegar, and brown sugar; cover and steam for 15 to 25 minutes, adding more water if necessary, until tender. To eat immediately, in a small bowl, whisk together cornstarch and ¼ cup cool water until blended. Add the mixture to the finished cabbage and cook, stirring, for 30 seconds, until thickened, before adding cornstarch, cover and refrigerate overnight. Then add cornstarch mixture, stirring until thickened, reheat, and serve immediately.

PER SERVING: Saturated Fat: 0 gm   Total Fat: Trace
        Cholesterol: 0 mg   Sodium: 22 mg   Calories: 125

Mediterranean-Stuffed Eggplant

Serves 8

This can be a whole meal with several chopped vegetables stuffed in eggplant halves. In the house where I had a garden, I left the stem end of eggplant attached for presentation. This combination of vegetables nicely fills a hollowed zucchini, summer squash, winter squashes, or small pumpkins with baked seeds sprinkled on top.

2 1-pound Italian eggplants	Dash cayenne
3 cloves garlic, minced	1 tablespoon tahini
1 large onion, finely chopped	¼ teaspoon ground cinnamon
1 stalk celery, finely chopped	½ cup pitted chopped black olives,
2 green bell peppers, chopped,	for garnish
seeds reserved	½ cup chopped parsley, for
1 tomato, roughly chopped	garnish
Salt (optional)	2 teaspoons capers, for garnish

Preheat the oven to 425°F.

Cut the eggplants in half lengthwise. Run a knife (a curved grapefruit knife works for some, or a regular knife) around ½ inch from the shell, to loosen the pulp but not all the way. Place the shells with pulp cut side down on a nonstick baking sheet and bake for 15 to 20 minutes, or until softened. When cool enough to handle, scoop out the flesh.

In a large nonstick skillet in ¼ inch water, over medium heat, steam the garlic, onion, celery, bell peppers, tomato, salt, if using, cayenne, tahini, and cinnamon, adding more water if necessary to prevent sticking. Stir occasionally, for 8 minutes, or until vegetables are tender.

Reduce the oven temperature to 350°F.

Mound the vegetable mixture into the eggplant shells, place on the nonstick baking sheet, return the shells to the oven, and bake for 15 minutes. Garnish with olives, parsley, seeds, and capers, and serve hot.

PER ¼ EGGPLANT: Saturated Fat: Trace   Total Fat: 2 gm
Cholesterol: 0 mg   Sodium: 90 mg   Calories: 63

Chinese Eggplant with Garlic Sauce

Chinese vegetable dishes are traditionally cooked in peanut oil, which is high in saturated fat. I have found that steaming the vegetables in water and adding Chinese hot oil makes up for any taste lost from not frying in oil. The hot oil is available in Asian food markets.

1½ large yellow onions, thinly sliced	4 teaspoons low-sodium soy sauce
4 cloves garlic, minced	6 to 10 drops Chinese hot oil
4 Chinese eggplants, peeled and seeded, thinly sliced into strips about ½ inch wide and 2 to 3 inches long	2 tablespoons brown sugar
	2 tablespoons cornstarch
	5 scallions, chopped

In a large nonstick skillet in 2 or 3 tablespoons water, over medium–high heat, cook the onions and garlic for 1 minute. Add the eggplant, soy sauce, hot oil, and sugar, and cook for 2 to 3 minutes, adding more water if needed, stirring often. Adjust seasoning. It should be very spicy, hot, sweet, and flavorful.

In a small bowl, whisk together ½ cup water and the cornstarch until blended. Tip the skillet to allow the liquid to pool and keep it directly over high heat. Whisk in the cornstarch mixture and cook for 30 seconds, until thick. Set the pan on the stove and toss the vegetables to coat. Sprinkle the scallions over the vegetables and serve immediately.

PER SERVING: Saturated Fat: 0 gm   Total Fat: 0.5 gm
Cholesterol: 0 mg   Sodium: 143 mg   Calories: 101

Southern-Style Green Beans

These beans have all the southern flavor of traditional smoked ham and beans. The stock takes only 30 minutes, and once it is defatted you can use it to make southern-style spinach, collard greens, and okra, too.

1 smoked ham hock
1 pound green beans, washed and
  trimmed

Freshly ground black pepper

In a nonstick saucepan, over high heat, heat 1 quart water to boiling. Add the ham hock and reduce the heat; cover and simmer for 30 minutes. Remove the ham hock and set aside. Defat the stock (page 48). Cut the meat from the ham hock and discard the fat and bone. Dice the meat. You should have about ½ cup.

In a medium saucepan, over medium heat, combine 1 cup defatted stock, the meat, and beans. Cover and cook for about 5 minutes. Reserve any leftover stock for other uses. Add pepper to taste and serve immediately.

PER SERVING: Saturated Fat: 1 gm   Total Fat: 3 gm
Cholesterol: 14 mg   Sodium: 47 mg   Calories: 79

Green Bean Bundles

As elegant as this dish appears on the plate or serving platter, it is the model of simplicity to prepare. If time is of the essence, substitute jarred red peppers for the fresh roasted. Serve hot or cold with a low-fat dressing.

2 cloves garlic, minced
½ pound green beans
½ pound yellow wax beans

Olive oil spray
1 red bell pepper, roasted, peeled,
    seeded, and cut into 8 strips

In a large saucepan in ½ inch water, over high heat, combine the garlic and beans; cover and cook for about 5 minutes, or until the beans are bright and tender. Drain. Lightly spray the beans with oil and return to the heat, tossing lightly, for 30 seconds. Divide the beans by color into 4 bundles each, 4 green, 4 yellow, and place 2 bundles on each serving plate or lay 4 bundles on a serving platter. Place 2 pepper strips crisscross on top of each bundle and tucked under each bundle and serve.

PER SERVING: Saturated Fat: 0 gm   Total Fat: Trace
Cholesterol: 0 mg   Sodium: 7 mg   Calories: 42

Stuffed Portobello Mushrooms

Serves 4

The large portobello mushroom, often 4 inches or more in diameter, has a mild flavor that lends itself to taking on flavorful stuffings. You may also use a large button mushroom at least 4 inches wide. This rather flashy and elegant dish also benefits from a dash of Marsala or Madeira wine.

4 portobello mushrooms, cleaned,
stems removed and reserved
6 shallots, finely chopped
½ cup chopped parsley plus
1 tablespoon, for garnish
6 teaspoons herbed bread crumbs
2 teaspoons chopped fresh basil or
4 teaspoons dried

Olive oil spray
½ cup Marsala or Madeira
(optional)
2 tablespoons grated nonfat
Parmesan cheese

In a food processor, coarsely chop the mushroom stems. Add the shallots, parsley, bread crumbs, and basil and pulse until just combined.

In a nonstick skillet in ⅛ inch water sprayed lightly with olive oil, over medium heat, cook the mushroom mixture until the water evaporates and the mixture is slightly dry. Remove to a plate and keep warm.

Spray the skillet with oil and add the mushrooms, top down, spraying again lightly with oil. Add 2 teaspoons water, and cook, covered, over medium-low heat for 10 minutes. Spoon the stuffing mixture into the mushroom caps, and sprinkle each with about 2 teaspoons wine, and ½ tablespoon Parmesan. Cook, partially covered, for an additional 2 to 6 minutes until warmed through. Sprinkle with parsley and serve immediately.

PER SERVING: Saturated Fat: Trace   Total Fat: 1 gm
Cholesterol: 3 mg   Sodium: 154 mg   Calories: 89

Grilled Portobello Mushrooms

Here, the meaty and mild portobello is the star of the meal. Many supermarkets and almost all specialty food stores carry portobello mushrooms.

4 portobello mushrooms	*Olive oil spray*
1 Lemon-Rosemary Mignonette	
(page 213)	

In a large sealable plastic bag, toss the mushrooms with half of the mignonette until well coated. Marinate at room temperature for 30 minutes to 1 hour.

Preheat the grill. Lightly spray the mushrooms and the grill with olive oil. Place the mushrooms on the grill 2 to 3 inches from the flame, and grill for about 3 minutes per side. Serve whole on individual plates, passing remaining mignonette sauce.

NOTE: The mushrooms can also be broiled by placing them in a broiling pan 2 inches from the heat and broiling 2 to 3 minutes per side, but don't let them dry out.

PER SERVING   Saturated Fat: 0 gm   Total Fat: 0.5 gm
Cholesterol: 0 mg   Sodium: 16 mg   Calories: 60

Caramelized Onions

In the South coffee is commonly partnered with onions. As the two cook, the coffee flavor dissipates yet caramelizes the onions, giving them a beautiful sheen. These onions are wonderful with grilled meats, poultry, fish, or alongside rice, beans, or any vegetable dish. If you like your onions slightly sweet, add a teaspoon of maple syrup or brown sugar with the coffee.

1 pound large yellow onions, peeled and sliced
½ cup brewed black coffee or ½ teaspoon instant coffee or decaffeinated coffee in ½ cup boiling water

Salt (optional)
Freshly ground black pepper

In a large nonstick skillet in ¼ inch water, over high heat, steam the onions, stirring occasionally, for about 8 minutes, until soft. Add the coffee, salt, if using, and pepper and cook down until the coffee evaporates completely. Serve immediately.

PER SERVING: Saturated Fat: 0 gm   Total Fat: Trace
Cholesterol: 0 mg   Sodium: 4 mg   Calories: 44

Heavenly Peas and Onions
in Cream Sauce

I have slimmed down this old-time favorite without stripping away any of its traditional taste. If you substitute bottled onions (which contain lots of salt) for the frozen or fresh ones, use ³/₄ cup onion liquid instead of ³/₄ cup water.

10 ounces frozen or fresh pearl onions
10 ounces frozen or fresh peas
³/₄ cup evaporated skimmed milk
2½ tablespoons cornstarch
1 tablespoon flour
¼ teaspoon freshly grated nutmeg

½ cup nonfat cottage cheese
2 tablespoons nonfat ricotta cheese
Salt (optional)
Pinch sugar (optional)
¼ teaspoon white pepper

Tap the boxes of frozen vegetables on a counter edge to loosen the contents. Open and set aside. In a food processor or blender, puree ¾ cup water or onion liquid, milk, cornstarch, flour, nutmeg, and the cheeses for 3 minutes.

In a medium nonstick saucepan over medium heat, cook the cheese mixture, whisking continually, for about 3 minutes, until thickened. Be careful not to bring it to a boil. Reduce the heat and add the onions, peas, and salt, if using, sugar, if using, and pepper, cooking until heated through. Serve immediately.

PER SERVING:　Saturated Fat: Trace　Total Fat: 0.5 gm
Cholesterol: 4 mg　Sodium: 262 mg　Calories: 169

Creamy Baked Potatoes

One of my favorite meals is a simple baked potato. And the sweetest, fluffiest potato for baking is the russet from Idaho. Buy those that are dark, rough, and thick skinned without eyes or bumps and like a smooth rock or stone.

3 large russet or baking potatoes	¼ cup nonfat sour cream
½ cup nonfat milk	2 to 4 tablespoons chopped
1 cup nonfat cottage cheese	scallions
Salt (optional)	Cayenne pepper or paprika, for
Freshly ground black pepper	garnish

Preheat the oven to 375°F.

Scrub the potatoes and leave wet. Pierce them all over with a fork and bake about 45 minutes until soft when pierced with a fork. Alternatively, microwave them for 3 to 4 minutes and bake for 20 minutes at 350°F.

Using a potholder to hold the hot potato, cut the potato in half lengthwise, squeezing the ends hard to separate the flesh from the skin. Scoop out a few tablespoons of flesh from each potato and place in a medium-size bowl. With a fork, fluff up the remaining potato flesh in each potato.

Remove all the flesh from one potato, reserving the skin, and add the flesh to the potato in the bowl. Stir in the nonfat milk, cottage cheese, salt, if using, and pepper and stir until mixed well and fairly smooth. Spoon the mixture back into each of the 4 remaining potato halves. Add a dollop of sour cream to each, sprinkle with chopped scallions, and garnish with a dash of cayenne or paprika.

PER SERVING: Saturated Fat: 0 gm   Total Fat: Trace
Cholesterol: 3 mg   Sodium: 243 mg   Calories: 184

Twice-Baked
Ratatouille-Stuffed Potatoes

Serves 4

A hearty ratatouille stuffed into baked potatoes makes this a quick meal. You can use your own homemade, or to simplify, use canned or jarred ratatouille.

Vegetable oil spray
1 medium onion, chopped
1 clove garlic, minced
1 small eggplant, cubed, salted, and drained for 20 minutes
1 small red or yellow bell pepper, cut into strips
1 medium zucchini, diced

3 plum tomatoes, diced
1 tablespoon balsamic or cider vinegar
4 medium baking potatoes, baked or microwaved until soft
½ cup nonfat ricotta cheese
½ cup nonfat Parmesan cheese

Preheat the oven to 375°F.

In a large nonstick skillet lightly sprayed with oil, in a few tablespoons water, over medium-high heat, combine the onion, garlic, and eggplant; cover and steam for 4 minutes, adding more water if necessary to prevent sticking. Add the pepper, zucchini, tomatoes, and vinegar. Reduce the heat, cover, and simmer 12 to 15 minutes, stirring occasionally, until all the vegetables are tender.

Meanwhile, slice off the top third of the potatoes lengthwise, and with a spoon, scoop out the flesh, leaving a ½-inch shell. (Reserve the flesh for another use.) Spoon 2 tablespoons ricotta into each potato. Fill the potatoes with the ratatouille. Sprinkle with 2 tablespoons Parmesan and bake 35 minutes. Alternatively, place the potatoes in a microwave-safe dish, cover with wax paper, and cook at high for 4 minutes, rotating once.

PER SERVING: Saturated Fat: Trace   Total Fat: 1 gm
Cholesterol: 12 mg   Sodium: 302 mg   Calories: 184

Cheddar Scalloped Potatoes

Scalloped potatoes are a favorite of midwesterners, southerners, northerners, and everyone else I know. This casserole comes to the table with all the old-fashioned taste. The new nonfat creamers instead of milk, if you like, achieve a richer taste.

2 pounds new potatoes, peeled
and sliced in thin rounds
1 cup nonfat milk or creamer
½ cup evaporated skimmed milk
3 tablespoons all-purpose flour
Salt (optional)
2 tablespoons chopped lean ham

¼ cup coarsely chopped onions
¼ cup nonfat Cheddar cheese
2 tablespoons sharp Cheddar
cheese
Freshly ground black pepper
Paprika

Spread the potatoes in a shallow 2-quart baking dish and set aside. Preheat the oven to 350°F.

In a medium bowl, whisk together the milks and flour. Add the salt, if using, ham, onions, cheeses, and pepper. Pour the mixture over the potatoes, sprinkle with paprika, and bake, uncovered, for 40 to 45 minutes, or until the potatoes are soft and golden with a crust.

PER SERVING: Saturated Fat: 1 gm   Total Fat: 2 gm
Cholesterol: 9 mg   Sodium: 222 mg   Calories: 262

Cowboy Fries

These savory spuds are colorful, something like a hash brown, and baked instead of fried.

Vegetable oil spray

1 medium onion, coarsely chopped

4 medium potatoes cut into
  ½-inch chunks or wedges

3 cloves garlic, minced

1 to 2 teaspoons Cajun spice
  blend or Old Bay seasoning

½ green bell pepper, diced

½ red bell pepper, diced

1 teaspoon paprika

Freshly ground black pepper

Preheat the oven to 450°F.

Line a baking sheet with heavy foil extending over the edges and lightly spray it with oil. Place the onion, potatoes, and garlic on the sheet and lightly spray again. Sprinkle with the Cajun spice blend and toss to mix well. Bring the foil edges together and fold to seal. Bake for 30 minutes.

Remove the packet from the oven and open away from you (be careful of the steam). Add the peppers and toss until well combined. Lightly spray again, and bake, uncovered, for an additional 15 minutes to brown and crisp. Top with paprika and pepper to taste and serve immediately.

PER SERVING:　Saturated Fat: 0 gm　Total Fat: Trace
Cholesterol: 0 mg　Sodium: 40 mg　Calories: 103

Baked Potatoes with Sun-Dried Tomatoes

Serves 4

These rather formal potatoes grace a meal. Peeled and only partially sliced, the whole potato is seasoned with the sweet flavor of sun-dried tomatoes. Serve with beef or lamb plus vegetables.

4 white potatoes
2 tablespoons chopped sun-dried tomatoes, packed in oil and blotted dry, with 2 tablespoons oil reserved

Paprika
Salt (optional)
2 tablespoons chopped chives or parsley

Preheat the oven to 350°F.

Peel the potatoes and carefully make as many ¼-inch-wide cuts widthwise on the potato as you can, cutting to within a ¼ inch of the bottom, so the potato remains whole.

Into a shallow dish, pour the 1 tablespoon tomato oil; add the potatoes, and toss to coat well. Drizzle or gently brush remaining oil into the slits being careful not to break them and sprinkle with paprika and salt, if using. Place the potatoes on a nonstick cookie sheet and bake for 45 minutes, or until soft when pierced with a fork. Sprinkle with chopped chives and sun-dried tomatoes just before serving.

PER SERVING: Saturated Fat: 0.5 gm   Total Fat: 7 gm
Cholesterol: 0 mg   Sodium: 42 mg   Calories: 178

Mashed Potatoes

The secret to successful mashed potatoes is hand mashing or ricing. If you use a food processor or electric beater, usually the potatoes become gluey rather than fluffy. (You can use an immersion, or hand, blender if you only use it with up-and-down movements, never swirling or stirring with the blender.) These are rich and creamy thanks to the nonfat cottage cheese.

3 large boiling potatoes, peeled and cut in eighths	*1 tablespoon margarine (optional)*
¼ cup evaporated skimmed milk	*Salt (optional)*
½ cup pureed nonfat cottage cheese	*Freshly ground black pepper*
	2 tablespoons chopped parsley

In a large nonstick saucepan, over high heat, heat potatoes and enough water to cover them to boiling. Reduce heat to low; partially cover, and simmer for 20 to 30 minutes, or until potatoes are soft when pierced with a fork. Drain. In a large bowl, mash the potatoes with the milk, cottage cheese, and margarine. Add salt, if using, and pepper to taste, and sprinkle with parsley. Or serve with nonfat gravy (page 298).

PER SERVING: Saturated Fat: 0 gm   Total Fat: Trace
Cholesterol: 1 mg   Sodium: 88 mg   Calories: 90

Chunky Potatoes with Turnips and Carrots

This is a real neat vegetable dish with potatoes. Substitute rutabagas for the turnips if you want a buttery color that is even more authentically down-home.

1 quart nonfat milk

1 clove garlic, minced

2 small turnips, peeled and cut into chunks

3 medium potatoes, peeled and cut into chunks

2 medium carrots, peeled and cut into chunks

½ cup nonfat ricotta cheese

1 tablespoon chopped parsley

Salt (optional)

Freshly ground black pepper

Measure ¼ cup milk and set aside. In a large nonstick saucepan, over medium heat, heat the remaining milk to boiling. Reduce the heat to very low, add the garlic and turnips, cover, and simmer, for 10 minutes. Add the potatoes and cook for an additional 10 minutes. Add the carrots and cook another 10 to 12 minutes, making sure all the vegetables are covered with milk, adding more if needed. The turnips and potatoes should be soft and the carrots should be slightly firmer. Drain.

In a food processor, or bowl using an immersion, or hand, blender, in an up and down motion, puree the ricotta, ¼ cup milk, and parsley until smooth. Stir the ricotta mixture into the vegetables, and mash just until chunky. Add salt, if using, and pepper to taste. Serve immediately.

PER SERVING: Saturated Fat: Trace Total Fat: Trace
Cholesterol: 3 mg Sodium: 116 mg Calories: 111

Shanghai Snow Peas

Serves 4

Very simple and fast, this versatile side dish is a perfect accompaniment for rice or pasta dishes. Pickled ginger is available in most Asian markets and many specialty food stores.

2½ cups snow peas
¼ teaspoon sesame oil
1 teaspoon low-sodium soy sauce
1 clove garlic, minced

1 15-ounce can straw mushrooms
1 8-ounce can sliced water
   chestnuts, drained and rinsed
¼ cup chopped pickled ginger

In a medium nonstick skillet, over medium-high heat, heat ¼ inch water to boiling. Add the snow peas, cover, and steam for 1 to 2 minutes; drain and return to the skillet. Add the sesame oil, soy sauce, garlic, mushrooms, water chestnuts, and pickled ginger, and cook, stirring, until heated through. Serve immediately.

PER SERVING: Saturated Fat: Trace   Total Fat: 0.5 gm
Cholesterol: 0 mg   Sodium: 364 mg   Calories: 78

Spinach with Garlic and Olive Oil

Serves 4

Spinach lovers savor this Sicilian-style dish with fresh garlic and tender spinach. Cut the spinach leaves in half if they are more than 5 inches wide.

1 clove garlic, minced
Olive oil spray

1 pound spinach, washed and
   trimmed
Salt (optional)

In a large nonstick skillet, over medium-low heat, cook the garlic with a few teaspoons of water, about 2 minutes, being careful not to scorch the garlic. Lightly spray the garlic with oil and swirl in the pan for 30 seconds. Add the spinach (it will spatter), spray lightly with oil again, and swirl to coat the spinach with garlic and oil. Reduce the heat to low, cover, and cook for about 1 minute, just until the spinach wilts. Sprinkle with salt to taste, if using, and serve hot.

■■   PER SERVING: Saturated Fat: Trace   Total Fat: 1 gm   ■■
Cholesterol: 0 mg   Sodium: 90 mg   Calories: 31

Baked Stuffed Plum Tomatoes

■■ ——————————————— *Serves 4* ——————————————— ■■

Stuffed tomatoes compliment seafood, poultry, or even other starches such as pasta or potatoes. They take about an hour to prepare and bake, much of it unattended.

4 large plum tomatoes (or 8 small), cut in half lengthwise	¾ cup nonfat ricotta cheese
1 clove garlic, minced	Salt (optional)
2 scallions, finely chopped	Freshly ground black pepper
½ cup chopped fresh basil	Vegetable oil spray
½ cup chopped fresh spinach	3 tablespoons pine nuts

Preheat the oven to 375°F.

Scoop out the center of the tomato halves and reserve pulp for another use. In a medium bowl, mix together the garlic, scallions, basil, spinach, ricotta, and salt, if using, and pepper. Stuff the mixture into the tomato shells.

Lightly spray a baking sheet with oil. Place the stuffed tomatoes on the sheet and sprinkle with pine nuts. Bake on a lower rack 20 to 25 minutes, watching to see that the pine nuts do not become too brown. Serve immediately.

■■   PER SERVING: Saturated Fat: 1 gm   Total Fat: 5 gm   ■■
Cholesterol: 3 mg   Sodium: 105 mg   Calories: 101

Baked Mediterranean Tomatoes

These gently spiced tomatoes, named for one of the vegetable centers in Italy, are succulent and easy to prepare. The Italian custom is to enhance these with only a light herbed stuffing, as I do here. You can improvise by filling these with mashed potatoes, orzo, turnips, or spoonfuls of pureed creamed spinach.

4 medium ripe tomatoes
1 teaspoon olive oil
1 teaspoon grated onion
3 tablespoons bread crumbs
1 tablespoon chopped fresh basil
1 teaspoon dried oregano

1 tablespoon chopped parsley
Salt (optional)
Freshly ground black pepper
2 teaspoons grated nonfat
  Parmesan cheese

Preheat the oven to 350°F.

Cut ½ inch off the top (where attached to the vine) of the tomatoes, and, using a knife, make several deep cuts in the top of the tomato, loosening the flesh with a fork. Add several drops of olive oil to each tomato, and spear the loosened pulp again with a fork to force the oil into the tomato.

In a small bowl, whisk together the onion, bread crumbs, basil, oregano, parsley, salt, if using, pepper, and 1 teaspoon water. Fill the tomatoes with the crumb mixture and sprinkle each with ½ teaspoon Parmesan cheese. Place the filled tomatoes on a nonstick baking sheet and bake for 25 minutes, watching to make sure the tomatoes do not collapse. To brown the top, place under the broiler for a few minutes before serving. Serve hot.

PER SERVING: Saturated Fat: 0.5 gm Total Fat: 2 gm
Cholesterol: 1 mg Sodium: 42 mg Calories: 48

Baked Vegetable Medley with Crunchy Polonaise

This is a hearty vegetable-filled baked dish with lots of taste and crunch. Serve it for a cold-weather dinner or on the buffet for parties. The topping can be prepared and the vegetables steamed up to a day ahead. Reheat it all just before serving.

¾ cup corn-bread stuffing, crushed
2 cloves garlic, minced
2 scallions, finely chopped
¼ cup chopped parsley
1 tablespoon fresh lemon juice
2 tablespoons grated nonfat
    Parmesan cheese

Salt (optional)
½ pound baby carrots
½ pound (about 1½ cups) fresh
    cauliflower florets
½ pound (about 1½ cups) fresh
    broccoli florets

Preheat the oven to 375°F.

In a medium bowl, mix together the corn-bread crumbs, garlic, scallions, parsley, lemon juice, Parmesan cheese, and salt, if using, and set aside.

In a medium nonstick skillet, heat ½ inch water to boiling. Add the carrots, cover, and steam for about 5 minutes, adding more water if necessary. Add the cauliflower and broccoli, cover, and cook for an additional 2 minutes. Remove the vegetables to a gratin or casserole dish and top with the crumb mixture. Bake 15 to 20 minutes, or until the crumbs are brown and crispy. Serve immediately and serve hot.

PER SERVING: Saturated Fat: Trace   Total Fat: 1 gm
Cholesterol: 2 mg   Sodium: 430 mg   Calories: 122

Glazed Asian Vegetables

This colorful blend of vegetables is tossed with a spicy sauce. Use a mild pepper jelly instead of the hot peppers and reduce the amount of garlic if you want less heat.

½ pound baby carrots, thinly sliced

1 teaspoon sesame oil

3 scallions, cut diagonally into 2-inch pieces

1 cup broccoli florets

1 cup whole kernel corn, fresh or frozen

1 cup fresh snow peas or green beans

½ medium red bell pepper, thinly sliced, seeds reserved

2 small dried, hot, red peppers (optional) or ½ cup jalapeño jelly

2 tablespoons low-sodium soy sauce

2 teaspoons freshly grated ginger

2 cloves garlic, minced

1 teaspoon cornstarch

In a large nonstick skillet, heat ¼ inch water to boiling. Add the carrots, reduce the heat to medium low, cover, and cook for 4 minutes, stirring once or twice. Raise the heat to high, add the sesame oil, scallions, broccoli, corn, snow peas, pepper and seeds, and hot peppers, and toss continually for 3 to 4 minutes.

Into a small metal bowl, pour 2 tablespoons of the cooking liquid from the skillet and place in the refrigerator for 4 to 5 minutes. If using the red peppers or jalapeño jelly, add to the skillet. Add the soy sauce, ginger, and garlic and cook, tossing continually, about 2 minutes, or until the jelly has melted.

Remove the bowl from the refrigerator and add the cornstarch and whisk until blended. Tip the skillet so the liquid puddles on one side, add the cornstarch mixture, and stir the liquid and cornstarch together until it thickens slightly. Reduce the heat, toss the vegetables in the thickened liquid to coat well, and serve immediately.

PER SERVING: Saturated Fat: Trace   Total Fat: 1 gm
Cholesterol: 0 mg   Sodium: 250 mg   Calories: 69

Ratatouille Provençale

This colorful mixture of traditional tomatoes, eggplant, and onions comes from the South of France where the vegetables that give it character are abundant. Ratatouille is versatile and makes a great side dish, main dish, or a stuffing for vegetables. It can be hot or cold and improves over time, so don't be afraid to make it a day ahead. I don't peel the eggplant because I find so many of them taste sweet. However, peel and seed it if you wish but double the eggplants to 2 large or 4 small as you lose half in the peeling and seeding.

1 large onion, coarsely chopped

2 cloves garlic, minced

1 large or 2 small eggplants, cut into chunks

1 large or 2 medium yellow squash or zucchini, cut into chunks

3 medium tomatoes, chopped

1 green bell pepper, seeded and cubed

½ cup low-sodium, defatted chicken or vegetable stock

Salt (optional)

¼ teaspoon freshly ground black pepper

1 teaspoon chopped fresh basil or 3 teaspoons dried

2 teaspoons chopped fresh oregano or ½ teaspoon dried

2 tablespoons chopped parsley

In a large nonstick skillet, over high heat, heat ¼ inch water to boiling. Reduce heat to medium, add the onion, garlic, eggplants, and squash, and steam, stirring, for about 4 minutes, adding 1 or 2 tablespoons water if necessary to prevent sticking. Drain. Stir in the tomatoes, pepper, stock, salt, if using, pepper, basil, oregano, and parsley, and bring to a boil. Reduce the heat to low, cover, and simmer for about 35 minutes, stirring occasionally, until the vegetables are tender but hold their color and texture. Serve warm, at room temperature, or chilled.

PER SERVING: Saturated Fat: Trace   Total Fat: 1 gm
Cholesterol: 0 mg   Sodium: 20 mg   Calories: 107

Scalloped Root Vegetables

This is a layered winter or fall casserole that makes the most of buttery rutabagas, leeks, and potatoes.

Vegetable oil spray

1 large rutabaga, thinly sliced

3 medium potatoes, thinly sliced

3 medium leeks, thoroughly
  rinsed, white part only, thinly
  sliced

10 to 12 shallots, chopped

3 tablespoons all-purpose flour

½ to 1 teaspoon salt (optional)

Freshly ground black pepper

3 tablespoons grated nonfat
  Parmesan cheese

¼ cup Madeira

1 12-ounce can evaporated
  skimmed milk

1 tablespoon Dijon mustard

3 cloves garlic, minced

¼ cup egg substitute

2 teaspoons freshly chopped thyme
  or parsley

2 tablespoons shredded nonfat
  mozzarella

Preheat the oven to 375°F.

Line an 8-inch springform pan with foil and lightly spray it with oil. Layer the vegetables, beginning with one third of the rutabaga on the bottom of the pan. Add one third of the potatoes, one third of the leeks, and one third of the shallots. Lightly spray again with oil and sprinkle with 1 tablespoon flour, ⅓ salt, if using, and pepper, and 1 tablespoon of the Parmesan cheese. Repeat the layers two more times.

In a medium bowl, mix together the Madeira, milk, mustard, garlic, egg, and 1 teaspoon of the thyme. Pour over the vegetables and sprinkle with mozzarella. Cover with foil and bake 1 hour. Remove the foil and place the pan under the broiler for about 4 minutes, until lightly browned. Sprinkle with the remaining thyme. Set aside to cool for 15 minutes; unmold and slice into 6 or 8 wedges. Serve immediately.

PER SERVING: Saturated Fat: 0 gm   Total Fat: 0.5 gm
Cholesterol: 4 mg   Sodium: 190 mg   Calories: 159

PASTA

There is controversy about the origin of pasta. Five hundred years ago, pasta was a nugget of coarse flour mixed with usually rancid beef or pork fat, fried, then boiled or refried. Today pasta is *very* different—tender, sleek, with all shapes and sizes.

Americans have always enjoyed Italian spaghetti and German noodle specialities, but it's only in the last ten years that we have become wild for pasta in all its shapes and forms. In 1984, average consumption was eight pounds per person per year. Today, according to the National Pasta Association, each of us devours more than nineteen pounds of pasta every year. Thank goodness it is high on the list of healthy indulgences.

Primarily a starch, pasta contains high amounts of complex carbohydrates—the preferred fuel of the body. These carbohydrates break down slowly in the digestive system, converting to glucose over time and providing long-lasting energy. This is why pasta is so popular with marathon runners. Simple, unsauced pasta is also very low in saturated fats, and so low in calories that you would have to eat five bowls of it in order to take in 1,000 calories.

Pasta, however, is rarely enjoyed plain. On the contrary, fine pasta dishes have been traditionally sauced with flavor-rich oils, herbs, and creams, and enhanced with colorful vegetables and a variety of meats and cheeses. High-fat sauces can sabotage a basically healthful dish. All of my recipes adapt the classic creamy, meat, cheese, and herbed oil sauces so that anyone on a healthful menu plan can enjoy all the traditional pasta favorites, including popular offerings like Penne with Sausage (page 166), Spaghetti and Meatballs (page 168), Fettuccine Alfredo (page 160), even the great American favorite, Macaroni and Cheese (page 162).

■ Pasta Basics ■

For a good-tasting finished dish, put some care into selecting and cooking your pasta. Neither fresh nor dried pasta is necessarily better than the other; each cooks differently and produces a unique texture and taste.

DRIED PASTA Dried pasta comes in dozens of shapes and sizes, and keeps for months in the cupboard. Depending on the size and thickness, pasta cooks in 8 to 12 minutes.

Much of the best dried pastas come from Italy. The quality of the imported brands is often superior to some American brands perhaps because of Italy's rigorous standards. Pasta makers there are required by law to use 100 percent semolina flour. Ground from durham wheat, semolina has a high gluten content, which produces a resilient pasta that is less likely to absorb water as it cooks. So, semolina pasta cooks up perfectly to a clean firm texture and is never soft or mushy.

Many American brands are made from softer wheat flour, which unfortunately often cooks to a softer finish. But a few American companies use semolina. Check the labels. I love both American and Italian pasta.

There is a variety of other interesting dried pastas that are made from rice, buckwheat flours, other grain flours, and pureed vegetables such as artichokes and flour. These are usually found in specialty food stores. Experiment with them. There are also several varieties of precooked fast-cooking dried pasta, besides ramen, in some supermarkets. These cook up in about 4 minutes, but the texture of most is a little unusual.

FRESH PASTA Commercial fresh pasta, the kind found in the refrigerator case in the supermarket, and homemade fresh pasta both cook in 2 to 4 minutes to a delicate finish. Its soft and silky texture is very different from the denser texture that dried pasta produces. Commercial fresh and homemade pasta will keep in an airtight container in the refrigerator for four or five days, but it is best to cook it soon after purchase. It can be frozen up to six weeks.

Commercial fresh pasta is generally made with soft wheat flour. If overcooked, it can become gummy. It is also made with egg yolks instead of water, making it higher in fat and cholesterol than dried or fresh pasta made at home with water only.

Fresh pasta is necessary for making stuffed dishes such as ravioli, tortellini, cannelloni, and agnolotti. I also prefer the tender texture of fresh lasagna, pappardelle (an inch-wide very long flat noodle), and fettuccine (a narrow flat noodle). Fresh pasta doesn't stand up well in soups or many dishes that are baked or simmered for long periods because it is too soft and fragile.

COOKING PASTA, KEEPING LEFTOVERS Cooking times vary for dried or fresh, and the package directions are usually reliable.

Most recipe amounts of pasta, 12 ounces to 16 ounces, cook in 3 to 4 quarts of water. Bring the water to a rolling boil. Contrary to popular opinion, it is not necessary to add oil to the water, which adds nothing but calories.

Add the pasta to the boiling water and stir immediately, lifting or scraping any off the bottom, and twirling the longer varieties to separate. Stir or separate again once or twice during cooking. Add very little salt (about ¼ teaspoon) during cooking or, better yet, add none at all. If you want more salt flavor, add it at the table, allowing everyone to sprinkle it on to taste.

For storing leftover cooked pasta, make sure it is unsauced as it will absorb moisture and become mushy. Store in an airtight container or plastic bag; reheat in a steamer, a microwave (right in the storing bag), or a pan with a little liquid.

To store leftover soups and stews that contain noodles or pasta (or rice, barley, etc.), if possible, separate the pasta from the sauce or the soup and refrigerate separately. Combine them when reheating. To store baked lasagna, sprinkle on a few drops of water (or extra sauce), and wrap tightly with plastic wrap.

Fettuccine Alfredo

Fettuccine Alfredo is one of the most satisfying of all the pasta dishes for its high fat content. My low-fat version achieves its creamy texture by using fresh nonfat milk cheeses and just two tablespoons of heavy cream instead of the one cup usually called for. Have all the ingredients measured and ready; the secret to a successful Alfredo is a quick assembly without interruption. For Fettuccine Carbonara, add half a cup diced, very lean cooked ham and one cup fresh or frozen peas to the sauce and cook until warmed through.

¼ cup nonfat cottage cheese	Dash of freshly ground nutmeg
½ cup nonfat ricotta cheese	2 tablespoons Madeira wine
1½ cups nonfat milk	(optional)
2 tablespoons heavy cream	2 tablespoons plus 2 teaspoons
1 clove garlic, minced	freshly grated nonfat Parmesan
¼ cup evaporated skimmed milk	cheese
or nonfat dairy creamer	2 tablespoons chopped parsley
2 tablespoons all-purpose flour	½ teaspoon freshly ground black
¼ teaspoon sugar	pepper
2 tablespoons chopped parsley	12 ounces fettuccine

In a food processor or blender, puree the cottage cheese, ricotta, ½ cup milk, and heavy cream 3 to 4 minutes until smooth; set aside.

In a nonstick saucepan over high heat, cook the garlic in a few tablespoons water, stirring constantly, for 3 minutes, or until the water has nearly evaporated. Reduce the heat to medium low and add 1 cup nonfat milk and evaporated skimmed milk. Whisk in the flour and cook, whisking constantly, for about 3 minutes, or until the mixture is thickened and very hot. Take care not to boil the sauce as it will curdle. (If the mixture becomes too thick, add a little more milk to regain the desired consistency.) Whisk in the pureed cheese mixture, sugar, parsley, nutmeg, wine, if using, and 2 tablespoons Parmesan cheese, and cook until the sauce is thick and hot but not bubbling. Keep warm.

In a large pot of boiling water, cook the fettuccine. Drain in a colander and remove to a warm serving bowl.

Spoon the sauce over the fettuccine and toss well. Add the parsley and toss again. Sprinkle with the pepper and the 2 teaspoons Parmesan cheese. Serve immediately.

PER SERVING: Saturated Fat: 2 gm   Total Fat: 8 gm
Cholesterol: 101 mg   Sodium: 279 mg   Calories: 469

Making Fresh Pasta

Most American and some European recipes for homemade fresh pasta dough call for whole eggs, flour, and water, which can have some cholesterol that you don't want. Italian dried pasta seldom contains eggs.

For a no-egg-yolk pasta, combine 1½ cups all-purpose flour, ½ teaspoon salt, 4 egg whites (or ½ cup egg substitute) in a large bowl and stir until a thick dough forms. Knead the dough, shape into a ball, cover with plastic wrap, and let it sit for 20 minutes before putting it through a hand crank or rolling and cutting the pasta by hand. Follow the directions for these very useful electric pasta makers.

To make pasta dough without egg, combine 1½ cups all-purpose flour with ½ cup cool water in a large bowl and stir until a thick dough forms. Knead the dough, shape into a ball, cover with plastic wrap, and let it sit for 20 minutes before making the pasta.

When making pasta by hand or in a hand-cranked machine, use a good sprinkling of flour on the counter, your knife, and/or your hand cranker. You'll need a rack to dry your pasta. (A couple of clean broom handles resting between chair backs work fine.)

Macaroni and Cheese

An all-American favorite that adapts wonderfully to a healthful menu plan. The turmeric gives the finished dish its traditional yellow/orange color.

2 tablespoons heavy cream

½ cup nonfat cottage cheese

½ cup nonfat ricotta cheese

½ cup shredded nonfat Cheddar cheese

½ cup shredded nonfat mozzarella cheese

¼ teaspoon turmeric

2 cups nonfat milk

3 tablespoons all-purpose flour

1 pound elbow macaroni

Pinch or 2 freshly ground nutmeg

2 tablespoons shredded sharp Cheddar cheese

Several dashes cayenne or paprika

2 tablespoons nonfat Parmesan cheese

Preheat the oven to 350°F.

In a food processor or blender, blend the cream, cottage cheese, ricotta, nonfat Cheddar, mozzarella, and turmeric about 2 minutes until smooth.

In a large nonstick saucepan over medium-high heat, heat the milk. Whisk in the flour and cook, whisking constantly, about 2 minutes, or until mixture is thickened. Reduce the heat and whisk in the cheese mixture; cook, stirring, taking care not to boil the sauce, until hot.

In a large pot of boiling water, cook the macaroni with the nutmeg for about 12 minutes until almost done; drain.

To serve immediately, place the macaroni in a warm serving bowl; spoon the sauce over the pasta and toss well. Sprinkle with Cheddar and cayenne and serve.

For a deep-dish crispy-crust version, place the macaroni in a 2-quart ovenproof casserole. Spoon the sauce over the macaroni, and sprinkle with sharp Cheddar, Parmesan, and cayenne. Bake for 30 minutes. Serve hot.

PER SERVING: Saturated Fat: 2 gm   Total Fat: 4 gm
Cholesterol: 16 mg   Sodium: 396 mg   Calories: 419

Orzo with Chicken and Broccoli

Orzo is the Italian word for "barley" but the tiny pasta most resembles short-grain rice in size. Because orzo cooks so quickly, this hearty entrée takes just 15 minutes to prepare. If you substitute a larger pasta, such as bow tie, anticipate longer preparation time. Four ounces of shrimp or lean pork may be substituted for the chicken.

4 ounces boneless chicken breast or
   thigh cut into 1-inch cubes,
   skinned and all fat removed
1 teaspoon Old Bay seasoning
1 pound orzo
1 pound broccoli, florets and stems
   chopped into ½-inch pieces
3 cloves garlic, minced

2 cups low-sodium, defatted
   chicken or vegetable stock
¼ cup fresh lemon juice
2 tablespoons cornstarch
1 teaspoon dried oregano
¼ teaspoon crushed red pepper
Freshly ground black pepper

Place the chicken in a microwave-safe bag; sprinkle with the seasoning and shake. Place the bag with the chicken in a microwave, pierce the bag, and cook on high for 3 to 4 minutes; drain any juice or fat and set aside.

In a large pot of boiling water, cook the orzo 5 to 7 minutes, or until done, stirring occasionally. After 3 minutes, place a colander containing the broccoli over the pot, and continue cooking the orzo for 3 more minutes while the broccoli steams. Remove the colander and set aside. Drain the pasta and stir in the garlic; cover and keep warm.

In a medium nonstick saucepan over high heat, cook the stock, lemon juice, cornstarch, dried oregano, and crushed red pepper, whisking constantly, about 3 minutes, or until the sauce thickens. Stir in the chicken.

Spoon the orzo onto individual plates, top with a serving of broccoli, and spoon on the sauce. Sprinkle with pepper and serve immediately.

PER SERVING: Saturated Fat: Trace   Total Fat: 3 gm
Cholesterol: 20 mg   Sodium: 173 mg   Calories: 520

Pappardelle with Roasted Red Peppers, Artichoke Hearts, and Cannellini Beans

Pappardelle is my pasta of choice for this and many other savory dishes. It is a long, inch-wide flat pasta. Smaller shapes like fusilli or penne are excellent too. A sure bet for a quick dinner, this recipe takes 20 minutes from start to finish.

3 cloves garlic, minced

1 leek, thoroughly rinsed (white part only), or yellow onion, chopped

1½ cups low-sodium vegetable stock or defatted chicken stock

½ cup white wine

4 tomatoes, diced

1 6-ounce jar marinated artichoke hearts, rinsed and drained

1 7-ounce jar roasted red bell peppers, drained

4 tablespoons cornstarch

1 15-ounce can cannellini (white kidney beans), drained

¼ to ½ teaspoon Tabasco

½ teaspoon dried oregano

½ cup chopped parsley

Freshly ground black pepper

1 pound pappardelle

2 tablespoons grated nonfat Parmesan cheese

In a large microwave-safe bowl, combine the garlic, leek, stock, and wine and cook at high for 5 minutes. In a food processor, coarsely chop the tomatoes, artichoke hearts, peppers, and cornstarch. Add the tomato mixture to the stock mixture, and microwave for 5 minutes, stirring every 2 minutes, until thickened. (You may also heat the mixture in a saucepan over medium heat for 15 minutes.) Add the cannellini, Tabasco, oregano, parsley, and pepper and cook at high for 2 minutes, or until the beans are hot.

In a large pot of boiling water, cook the pasta. Drain and remove to a warm serving bowl.

Spoon the sauce over the pappardelle, sprinkle with Parmesan, and serve immediately.

PER SERVING: Saturated Fat: 0.5 gm   Total Fat: 3 gm   Cholesterol: 3 mg   Sodium: 276 mg   Calories: 444

Linguine with Clam Sauce

Serves 6

It's well worth the effort to search out fresh littleneck clams for this rich dish. If using canned clams, supplement them with bottled clam juice so the liquid measures 1½ cups.

12 to 14 ounces linguine

2 tablespoons heavy cream

¼ cup nonfat ricotta cheese

½ cup nonfat cottage cheese

20 ounces fresh littleneck clams, chopped, or 6 6½-ounce cans chopped baby clams, drained, 1½ cups stock reserved

1½ cups bottled clam juice (if needed)

½ cup dry white wine

2 teaspoons fresh lemon juice

3 large cloves garlic, minced

2 tablespoons cornstarch

½ cup thinly sliced scallions, white and green parts

½ cup fresh or canned sliced mushrooms

¼ teaspoon sugar

Salt (optional)

Freshly ground white pepper

1 cup blanched whole kernel corn or lima beans, for garnish (optional)

In a large pot with boiling water, cook the pasta until firm; drain and keep warm.

Meanwhile, in a food processor or blender, combine the cream, ricotta, and cottage cheese and puree about 3 minutes until smooth; set aside.

In a large nonstick saucepan over medium-high heat, combine the reserved clam stock from the canned clams or the clam juice if you are using fresh clams, the white wine, lemon juice, and garlic. Whisk in the cornstarch, and cook, whisking constantly for 2 minutes, until slightly thickened. Stir in the clams, scallions, mushrooms, sugar, salt, if using, and pepper to taste, and cook, stirring, until very hot. Reduce the heat to medium low and stir in the cheese mixture; cook, stirring, being careful not to boil the sauce as it will curdle, until just heated through.

Place the linguine on individual plates and spoon on equal portions of clam sauce. Sprinkle with corn for garnish. Serve immediately.

■■ PER SERVING: Saturated Fat: 2 gm   Total Fat: 5 gm   ■■
Cholesterol: 69 mg   Sodium: 369 mg   Calories: 412

Penne with Sausage and Roasted Red Bell Pepper Sauce

■■ *Serves 4* ■■

Steve Sappe, a talented and busy chef, says this recipe is so quick and so good that he makes it for himself at home. This adapted version replaces heavy cream and cheese with evaporated skimmed milk and low-fat cottage cheese, making this a true healthy indulgence.

1 7-ounce jar roasted red bell
   peppers
1 15-ounce container nonfat or
   low-fat ricotta cheese
3/4 cup evaporated skimmed milk
1 1/2 tablespoons cornstarch
1 1/4 teaspoons dried basil
1/4 teaspoon crushed red pepper

4 ounces low-fat sausage (or
   reduced-fat Italian-style turkey
   sausage)
Vegetable oil spray
1 cup thinly sliced scallions
1/2 cup diced tomatoes
1 pound penne

In a food processor or blender, blend the peppers, ricotta, milk, cornstarch, basil, and crushed red pepper for 3 minutes, or until thick and creamy; set aside.

Slice the sausage into ¼-inch rounds. In a large nonstick saucepan lightly sprayed with vegetable oil, over medium-high heat, cook the sausages until firm and well browned on both sides.

NOTE: If the sausage still renders fat after it is browned, add 3 cups hot water to the skillet and boil the sausage 2 minutes; drain. If the fat is excessive, repeat the process. Using paper towel, blot the sausage, wipe the pan clean (to remove any excess fat), and rebrown the sausage.

Stir the scallions into the sausage and cook over medium-high heat for 3 minutes. Reduce the heat to medium low and stir in the red pepper mixture and tomatoes. Cook, stirring, for about 1 minute, or until the sauce is fairly thick. Take care not to boil the sauce as it will curdle. Keep warm.

In a large pot of boiling water, cook the penne; drain, and remove to a warm serving bowl.

Spoon the sauce over the penne and serve immediately.

■■ PER SERVING: Saturated Fat: 2 gm   Total Fat: 8 gm ■■
Cholesterol: 32 mg   Sodium: 452 mg   Calories: 630

Spaghetti and Meatballs with Marinara Sauce

This beloved classic is made with meatballs just like it used to be. Buy lean top round steak and ask the meat cutter to remove all the skirt fat before grinding it. With a meat grinder attachment or food processor, you can do it at home. I use an immersion, or hand, blender right in the pan to achieve the sauce consistency I like.

MARINARA SAUCE:

1 onion, coarsely chopped

3 cloves garlic, chopped

1 pound mushrooms, sliced

2 teaspoons dried oregano

5 ripe tomatoes, coarsely chopped

1 16-ounce can low-sodium tomato sauce or crushed tomatoes

4 sprigs fresh basil (about 15 leaves with stems), torn

1 carrot, cut in 1-inch rounds

1 leafy rib celery, cut in 1-inch pieces

Salt (optional)

Freshly ground black pepper

MEATBALLS:

½ pound lean top round, all fat removed, ground

2 egg whites

¼ cup bread crumbs

2 tablespoons finely chopped onions

2 tablespoons finely chopped celery

½ teaspoon Worcestershire

2 tablespoons chopped parsley

¼ teaspoon dried oregano

1 small clove garlic, minced

Freshly ground black pepper

Vegetable oil spray

1 pound spaghetti

2 tablespoons chopped parsley, for garnish

In a large nonstick saucepan, combine all sauce ingredients and cook, covered, for 15 minutes.

While the sauce is cooking, in a large bowl, combine the meatball ingredients and mix thoroughly using your hands. Shape the mixture into 12 meatballs.

In a nonstick skillet lightly sprayed with vegetable oil, heat ½ cup marinara sauce. Add the meatballs and cook over medium-high heat for 10 minutes, turning often. (Or, roll the meatballs in the sauce in a microwave dish and microwave for 6 to 8 minutes, turning once.)

In a large pot filled with boiling water, cook the spaghetti. Drain. Remove the spaghetti to a large serving platter. Spoon the sauce on top of the spaghetti, add the meatballs, and sprinkle with remaining parsley.

■■   PER SERVING (with 2 meatballs):   Saturated Fat: 0.5 gm   ■■
Total Fat: 4 gm   Cholesterol: 25 mg   Sodium: 97 mg   Calories: 442

■■

Bangkok-Style Glass Noodles

This recipe calls for bean threads, which are delicate, translucent noodles made from mung beans. Sometimes called cellophane noodles, they're available in many supermarkets and in Asian markets. To serve, cut the portions of noodles with a scissors. To turn this into an entrée, add skinned, defatted chicken strips, julienned lean beef or pork, or shrimp. Add them when you add the sugar snaps and pepper, and increase the cooking time from 3 minutes to 4.

1½ tablespoons freshly chopped
 ginger
1 to 2 teaspoons minced Thai
 chili or ½ small jalapeño,
 seeded and minced
2 cloves garlic, minced
3 medium shallots, minced
¼ cup low-sodium soy sauce
2 tablespoons fresh lemon juice
2 tablespoons brown or white
 sugar

1½ ounces bean threads
 (cellophane noodles)
10 ounces fresh or frozen sugar
 snap peas, trimmed and cut in
 half
1 red bell pepper, thinly sliced,
 seeds reserved
¼ cup chopped cilantro (optional)
3 scallions (including the green
 part), thinly sliced
Crushed red pepper

In a medium bowl, mix together the ginger, chili, garlic, shallots, soy, lemon juice, and sugar.

In a large pot of boiling water, cook the bean threads 3 to 4 minutes until they are soft. Drain almost all the water, leaving a few tablespoons with the noodles. Return the pan to the stove and reduce the heat to low; stir in the ginger mixture, cover, and cook, for 3 or 4 minutes, occasionally loosening the noodles from the bottom with a spatula. Stir in the peas, pepper, and reserved seeds and continue cooking for 3 minutes, occasionally loosening the noodles from the bottom; toss (it doesn't toss easily). Using a scissors, cut the noodles, dividing them evenly onto 4 individual plates. Sprinkle with cilantro, if using, scallions, and a pinch of crushed red pepper.

PER SERVING: Saturated Fat: 0 gm   Total Fat: Trace
Cholesterol: 0 mg   Sodium: 410 mg   Calories: 194

Sauces for Pasta

STORE-BOUGHT SAUCE When buying commercially prepared sauces found in the cold section, they are as good as any prepared by a chef in a restaurant. However, be sure to read the labels. Oil is often one of the primary ingredients. Although many manufacturers have reduced the oil in their sauces, one label I read revealed that the sauce contained clarified butter (enormously high in saturated fat), chicken livers (which have more cholesterol than nearly anything), shredded coconut (couldn't believe it), and Brie (no comment). Again, read the label.

Those convenient pesto sauces that contain ground walnuts, pine nuts, and olive oil are fatty, but aren't all that high in saturated fat. So, enjoy them judiciously—one tablespoon per person per serving, not four. You can stretch the sauce by adding several tablespoons finely chopped spinach, basil, or parsley, plus a splash of wine to the sauce. Heat a few minutes and add a sprinkle of nonfat Parmesan.

Combine canned or jarred pasta sauces with freshly steamed or blanched vegetables such as chopped onions, garlic, mushrooms, or tomatoes and herbs including basil and oregano.

HOMEMADE SAUCE Any good sauce can be made without the traditional first step of sautéeing vegetables in oil. Just steam them in small amounts of water. Tomato, or marinara, or primavera sauce can begin with sautéeing the vegetables in a nonstick skillet with a few tablespoons of water or low-sodium defatted chicken broth or vegetable stock. You needn't give up the olive oil flavor or aroma. Use an olive oil spray (page 3) to lightly spray the pan before sautéeing the ingredients in water.

For a creamy sauce, puree (for several minutes) combinations of nonfat cottage cheese, nonfat or lite ricotta cheese, nonfat yogurt cheese, hoop cheese, farmer cheese, nonfat cream cheese, nonfat creamers, evaporated skimmed milk, or nonfat milk and heat in a saucepan until warmed through, taking care not to boil the sauce as it will curdle.

For a cheese sauce, heat 2 cups nonfat milk with 3 tablespoons flour. Add 2 tablespoons shredded nonfat meltable cheese (which you won't know until you try as nonfat cheese makers are always changing their formulas), 1 cup pureed nonfat cottage or nonfat ricotta cheese, and 1 tablespoon each of two very strong-flavored cheeses, such as extra-sharp Cheddar or Monterey jack. Cook over very low heat, taking care not to boil the sauce. (If it does curdle, you can save it by pureeing it in the food processor for several minutes.)

Dan Dan Noodles

This vegetarian Asian dish is redolent of ginger and sesame and is delicious hot or cold. For absolute authenticity, don't substitute the sesame paste, which is lighter in color, with tahini. The flavor of the paste is much more pronounced. If you can't find the long thin hollow perciatelli pasta, linguine will do fine. Peanut butter is hardly authentic, but many people like it. The black vinegar is necessary.

16 ounces perciatelli	3 tablespoons low-sodium soy
½ teaspoon sesame oil	sauce
1 tablespoon dark sesame oil	1 teaspoon Chinese black vinegar
6 to 16 drops Chinese hot oil	Pinch sugar
2 teaspoons finely chopped ginger	2 cloves garlic, minced
3 tablespoons sesame paste,	½ cup chopped scallions
tahini, or low-fat peanut butter	½ cup shredded cucumber
4 tablespoons low-sodium,	2 tablespoons chopped cilantro, for
defatted chicken stock or water	garnish

In a large pot of boiling water, cook the noodles. Drain and toss with the sesame oil.

Meanwhile, in a small saucepan over medium heat, cook the dark sesame oil, hot oil, ginger, sesame paste, stock, soy sauce, vinegar, sugar, and garlic for 5 minutes. Pour the sauce over the noodles, add the scallions and cucumber, and toss to mix well. Garnish with cilantro and serve hot or cold.

PER SERVING: Saturated Fat: 2 gm Total Fat: 12 gm
Cholesterol: 0 mg Sodium: 463 mg Calories: 549

Angel Hair Pasta with Spinach and Almonds

This is an elegant company dish. Delicate angel hair pasta cooks in about 4 minutes, so be careful not to overcook. If you want a more country-style dish, use penne or rigatoni and toss all the ingredients before serving.

1 pound angel hair pasta
Olive oil spray
8 ounces mushrooms, sliced
3 cloves garlic, minced
8 ounces fresh spinach, rinsed and coarsely chopped
1 cup low-sodium, defatted chicken or vegetable stock

1 4½-ounce can pitted Kalamata olives, sliced
⅓ cup reduced-fat feta cheese, crumbled
¼ cup toasted sliced almonds

In a large pot of boiling water, cook the pasta for about 3 minutes, until barely done. Drain and return to the pot. Spray the pasta lightly with olive oil and toss. Cover the pasta and set aside.

Meanwhile, in a large nonstick skillet lightly sprayed with olive oil, over medium-high heat, arrange the mushrooms in a single layer. Add the garlic and lightly spray the mixture with olive oil. Cook, stirring, for 7 to 8 minutes until brown. Remove from the heat.

To the pasta, add the spinach, stock, olives, and mushrooms, toss well, and place over medium heat. Cover and cook for 2 minutes until the spinach is wilted and all the ingredients are warmed through. Serve topped with feta cheese and almonds.

PER SERVING: Saturated Fat: 3 gm   Total Fat: 13 gm
Cholesterol: 19 mg   Sodium: 549 mg   Calories: 578

Fresh Tomato Lasagna

This recipe lends itself to meat variations. Add as much as 6 ounces of cooked, drained, and rinsed ground lean beef or lean pork or turkey sausage to the sauce if you like.

12 ounces fresh or dried lasagna	2 tablespoons chopped parsley
1 large onion, chopped	⅛ teaspoon crushed red pepper
2 cloves garlic, minced	Salt (optional)
½ cup chopped sun-dried tomatoes	Freshly ground black pepper
6 tomatoes, diced	Olive oil spray
1 16-ounce can low-sodium	⅓ pound nonfat ricotta cheese
crushed tomatoes	½ (8 ounces) cup shredded nonfat
1 teaspoon dried oregano	mozzarella
3 tablespoons chopped basil or 2	2 tablespoons grated nonfat
tablespoons dried	Parmesan cheese
½ teaspoon fennel seed	

Preheat oven to 350°F.

Cover a work surface with waxed paper or lightly sprayed foil. Into a large pot of boiling water, place the noodles one at a time, stirring carefully after each addition, and cook, stirring several times during the cooking to separate them. Drain and immediately rinse under cold water. Do not let the noodles stick together or tear. Place the noodles in a single layer on the waxed paper.

Meanwhile, in a large nonstick skillet over medium-high heat, cook the onion, garlic, sun-dried tomatoes, and fresh tomatoes in 4 tablespoons water for about 5 minutes until just tender. Add the canned tomatoes, oregano, basil, fennel seed, parsley, crushed red pepper, salt, if using, and pepper. Spray lightly with olive oil, cover, and cook for 5 to 7 minutes stirring occasionally. (Remove the cover if necessary to further reduce the moisture.)

In a 9-inch by 11½-inch baking dish, arrange a layer of 4 noodles, slightly overlapping, and spray lightly with oil. Using the back of a spoon, spread ⅓ the ricotta on the noodles and sprinkle with ⅓ the mozzarella. Spoon ⅓ the sauce over the cheese. Arrange a second layer of noodles over the sauce and spread half of each of the remaining cheeses and slightly less than half of the sauce. Arrange the final layer of noodles and add the remainder of the ricotta and mozzarella, and the remaining sauce. Sprinkle the top with grated Parmesan and bake uncovered for 40 minutes. Let stand for 5 minutes before serving.

■ PER SERVING: Saturated Fat: 0.5 gm   Total Fat: 2 gm ■
Cholesterol: 3 mg   Sodium: 220 mg   Calories: 242

Mushroom Lasagna

■ *Serves 8* ■

This dish is remarkably rich and robust. It has made several appearances on my buffet because it is so satisfying and simple to prepare. If you can find fresh lasagna, by all means use it here. If you can't find three varieties of mushrooms, two or even one variety will do. Be sure to garnish it nicely as the dish is pale in color.

9 ounces lasagna noodles
Olive oil spray

FILLING:
½ ounce dried porcini
3 shallots, chopped
1 pound cultivated mushrooms,
   thinly sliced
½ pound shiitake mushrooms,
   sliced
1 7-ounce jar roasted red peppers,
   drained and chopped

SAUCE:
1¾ cups nonfat milk
5 tablespoons all-purpose flour
Salt (optional)
¼ cup sherry or Madeira
   (optional)
¼ teaspoon cayenne pepper
1 15-ounce package nonfat ricotta
   cheese
4 ounces nonfat mozzarella,
   shredded
2 tablespoons grated nonfat
   Parmesan cheese
2 tablespoons chopped parsley

Preheat oven to 375°F.

Cover a work surface with waxed paper or lightly sprayed foil. Into a large pot of boiling water, place the noodles one at a time, stirring carefully after each addition, and cook, stirring several times during the cooking to separate them. Drain and immediately rinse under cold water. Do not let the noodles stick together or tear. Place the noodles in a single layer on the waxed paper.

In a small bowl soak the porcini in hot water to cover and let stand for 15 minutes or until the mushrooms are rehydrated.

In a large nonstick skillet lightly sprayed with olive oil, over medium heat, heat the shallots; cover and cook, adding a tablespoon or two of water as needed to steam and prevent sticking, for 5 minutes or until tender. Add the sliced mushrooms and continue cooking an additional 10 minutes.

Meanwhile, drain the porcini through a coffee filter or cheesecloth, squeezing to extract excess liquid; reserve all the liquid in a small bowl. Rinse the mushrooms under running water, drain, and chop. Stir the porcini and roasted red peppers into the skillet. Remove to a bowl, and set aside.

In the same skillet over medium heat, heat the milk. Whisk the flour into the reserved porcini liquid and whisk the mixture into the milk. Cook, stirring, for about 3 minutes until thickened. Add salt, if using, sherry, and pepper.

Into a 13-inch by 9-inch baking dish, spoon ½ cup sauce and spread evenly. Arrange a layer of 3 lasagna noodles on top of the sauce and cover with 2 cups mushroom filling. Spoon half the ricotta and half the mozzarella evenly over the filling. Add ½ cup sauce, a layer of 3 noodles, and 2 cups filling. Spoon on the remaining ricotta cheese and top with ¼ cup sauce. Arrange a third layer of noodles on top of the sauce, spoon the remaining filling evenly over the noodles, and top with the remaining sauce. Sprinkle the remaining mozzarella and Parmesan on top. Cover and bake for 40 minutes. Remove the cover and bake for 10 more minutes. Sprinkle on the parsley and serve hot.

■■ PER SERVING: Saturated Fat: 0.5 gm   Total Fat: 2 gm   ■■
Cholesterol: 8 mg   Sodium: 261 mg   Calories: 242

Gnocchi

Gnocchi is a small, light, plump potato and flour dumpling. When making the gnocchi, mix the dough while the potatoes are hot. Too much flour will make them tough, as will using a food processor.

3 large russet potatoes, cooked and peeled	Salt (optional)
2 cups all-purpose flour	¾ cup Marinara Sauce (page 168)

In a large bowl, rice or mash the potatoes until smooth. Add half the flour and knead in the bowl, then place the dough on a lightly floured surface and knead for 2 to 3 minutes. Place the dough back in the bowl and knead in the remaining flour. Turn out onto a lightly floured surface again and knead about 3 minutes (adding as little flour as possible) until the dough is smooth, not sticky.

Divide the dough into baseball-size pieces. On a floured surface, roll each ball into a rope ½ inch to ¾ inch thick by 8 to 12 inches long. Cut the gnocchi ropes into 1-inch-long pieces. Poke a depression into the side of each of the gnocchi pieces with your finger or thumb. Sprinkle the gnocchi very lightly with flour and allow to rest for 5 minutes. The gnocchi can now be frozen, by tossing in a plastic bag, or cooked fresh.

In a large pot of boiling water, cook about 20 of the gnocchi for 3 to 5 minutes, or until each one rises to the top. With a slotted spoon, remove those that rise, drain, and keep warm while cooking remaining gnocchi. Serve hot with Marinara Sauce.

PER SERVING (with Marinara Sauce):   Saturated Fat: 0.5 gm
Total Fat: 0.5 gm   Cholesterol: 0 mg   Sodium: 24 mg   Calories: 243

Choosing the Right Sauce for the Right Pasta

There are hundreds of pasta shapes and sizes and, according to Italian tradition, some go better with certain sauces than others. Here's a general rule of thumb.

With sauces such as marinara or pomodoro, or light seafood sauces, use the thin pastas such as spaghetti, vermicelli, capellini, bucatini (a thick hollow spaghetti), perciatelli (also hollow but not as thick as bucatini), or even linguine (a flat, narrow strand).

Thick, complicated sauces that include meat, vegetables, or chicken are generally best with short pastas such as quill-shaped penne, tube-shaped rigatoni and ziti, or any smaller shape with twists or holes, like fusilli or gemellis (twins), which are small double spirals. Farfalle, which we call butterflies or bow ties, medium-size conchiglie (shells), and ruoti (wheels) are also good with the more complicated sauces. These shapes allow the chunky sauces to cling to more surfaces.

Creamy sauces cling best to the noodle or ribbon-shaped pastas such as linguine, fettuccine, and pappardelle.

Tiny pastas that are generally excellent in soups and stews rather than sauced are orzo, acini di pepe, and semi di melone (melon seeds). Some not so classic shapes have been appearing in homemade soups lately too— stars, animals, alphabet letters, dinosaurs, miniature shells, tiny round balls, baseball bats, footballs, even flat pumpkins and Christmas trees. They are available in specialty food stores.

Now that I've stated these rules, let me say that I don't follow them, often pouring a complicated sauce over something as fine as capellini and I love a marinara sauce with mushrooms and green peppers over ziti or penne. It depends on my mood and what's available in my cupboard. Follow your own tastes and experiment with mixing shapes and sauces. I even use odds and ends of pasta together. Be sure to allow for different cooking times.

Fusilli Mushroom Marinara

Fusilli, shells, wheels, ziti, or penne make a fine mouthful to hold this robust sauce. It's a time to try any new shape or size.

1 large onion, coarsely chopped

2 cloves garlic, minced

½ pound portobello or button mushrooms, sliced ¼ inch thick

½ pound cultivated mushrooms, sliced ½ inch thick

2 to 3 cups diced cherry tomatoes or 4 to 6 tomatoes, diced

½ cup sliced fennel

1 teaspoon dried oregano

2 tablespoons chopped fresh basil

¼ teaspoon fennel seed

1 16-ounce can low-sodium whole tomatoes, chopped, juice reserved

¼ teaspoon crushed red pepper

Salt (optional)

¼ teaspoon freshly ground black pepper

Olive oil spray

1 tablespoon cornstarch (optional)

16 ounces fusilli

In a large nonstick skillet over medium heat, heat 3 tablespoons water, the onion, garlic, mushrooms, cherry tomatoes, fennel, oregano, basil, and fennel seed. Cover and cook, adding more water if the mixture becomes dry, for about 10 minutes, and stir occasionally to break up the cherry tomatoes. Stir in the canned tomatoes, crushed red pepper, and salt, if using, and pepper and spray lightly with olive oil. Cover and cook, stirring occasionally, for 5 to 7 minutes.

If the sauce is too thin, mix 1 tablespoon cornstarch with the reserved tomato juice. Increase the heat to high, and add the cornstarch mixture, stirring until thickened.

Meanwhile, in a large pot of boiling water, cook the pasta; drain and remove to a warm serving bowl. Spoon the sauce over the pasta and serve immediately.

PER SERVING: Saturated Fat: Trace   Total Fat: 2 gm
Cholesterol: 0 mg   Sodium: 28 mg   Calories: 340

Vermicelli with Tomato, Olive, and Caper Sauce

This light sauce and pasta is a classic Italian mix of some of the best flavors of the country. Substitute your favorite olive for my green ones if you wish. I use a food processor when I want to make the sauce in a snap.

1 medium onion, coarsely chopped	⅓ cup pitted green olives, cut in half or coarsely chopped
3 cloves garlic, finely chopped or minced	2 tablespoons capers
1 green bell pepper, diced, seeds reserved	2 tablespoons red wine
1 red bell pepper, diced, seeds reserved	1 tablespoon dried oregano
3 ripe tomatoes, coarsely chopped	2 tablespoons fresh basil
½ cup low-sodium tomato juice	Pinch sugar
1 cup low-sodium, defatted chicken stock	Salt (optional)
16 ounces vermicelli	2 tablespoons cornstarch
	¼ cup low-sodium tomato juice
	2 tablespoons chopped watercress

In a large nonstick skillet, combine the onion, garlic, peppers and seeds, tomatoes, tomato juice, and stock and cook over medium heat, stirring occasionally, for 15 to 20 minutes.

Meanwhile, in a large pot of boiling water, cook the pasta until firm; drain and keep warm.

To the sauce, add the olives, capers, wine, oregano, basil, sugar, salt, if using, and stir to combine. Reduce the heat to low and cook, covered, for another 5 minutes. In a small bowl, whisk the cornstarch into the low-sodium tomato juice. Increase the heat to high and stir the cornstarch mixture; cook about 3 minutes until the sauce is thickened. Spoon the sauce over the pasta, sprinkle with watercress, and serve immediately.

PER SERVING: Saturated Fat: 0.5 gm   Total Fat: 4 gm
Cholesterol: 1 mg   Sodium: 300 mg   Calories: 516

Ziti with Prosciutto and Tomatoes

Authentic prosciutto is available in Italian markets, specialty food stores, and some supermarkets. Imported prosciutto di Parma comes from prosciutto's region of origin and will add great character to this dish. However, the American brands are just fine. Be sure to defat the ham completely and use the ripest tomatoes you can find for the best flavor.

16 ounces ziti (short-cut) pasta
Olive oil spray
3 cloves garlic, minced
6 scallions, cut diagonally in
   1-inch lengths
1 pound (about 3 large) very ripe
   tomatoes, coarsely chopped, plus
   1 cup crushed fresh tomato
3 ounces lean prosciutto, thinly
   sliced, completely defatted and
   cut into thin strips
⅛ teaspoon crushed red pepper

⅛ teaspoon coarsely ground black
   pepper
⅓ cup grated nonfat or low-fat
   mozzarella cheese
2 tablespoons nonfat Parmesan
   cheese
½ cup chopped fresh basil plus
   4 whole fresh basil leaves, for
   garnish
4 small slices red bell pepper, for
   garnish

In a large pot of boiling water, cook the ziti until firm; drain and keep warm in the heated pot.

Meanwhile, lightly spray a large nonstick skillet with oil and place over medium-high heat. Add the garlic, scallions, several tablespoons water, and cook, stirring, for 3 minutes until soft but not browned. Add the chopped tomatoes, prosciutto, crushed red pepper, and black pepper and cook, stirring, for an additional 5 minutes. Add the crushed tomato and cook, stirring, 4 minutes until hot. Reduce the heat to medium and add the ziti, mozzarella, Parmesan, and chopped basil; toss until well combined and allow to heat through 1 minute. Serve immediately, garnished with basil leaves and red bell pepper.

PER SERVING: Saturated Fat: 1 gm   Total Fat: 4 gm
Cholesterol: 18 mg   Sodium: 751 mg   Calories: 542

Pasta with Tomatoes, Peppers, Spinach, and Kalamata Olives

Serves 6

This is a lively country-style Mediterranean-style dish worthy of an imported pasta like orecchiette, but you may substitute small shells or even gnocchi. Shop for pitted Kalamata olives if you want to prepare this dish in 15 minutes. The pale green and mild peperoncini are available in most supermarkets. Cheese can be slivered instead of grated in the large-size holes of your shredder or using a potato peeler on the edges of the cheese.

16 ounces orecchiette (little ears)
5 ripe tomatoes, coarsely chopped
1 large onion, coarsely chopped
3 cloves garlic, chopped
1 leafy rib celery, chopped
2 teaspoons dried oregano
4 sprigs fresh basil (about 15
  leaves with stems), chopped
12 pitted Kalamata olives, halved
½ cup chopped peperoncini,
  drained

Pinch sugar
¼ teaspoon crushed red pepper
Salt (optional)
¼ cup low-sodium tomato juice
2 tablespoons cornstarch
½ teaspoon dried tarragon
½ pound spinach leaves, torn
2 tablespoons slivered Romano
  cheese
Freshly ground black pepper

In a large pot of boiling water, cook the orecchiette until firm; drain and keep warm in the heated pot.

Meanwhile, in a food processor, coarsely chop the tomatoes; drain and set aside.

In a large nonstick skillet over medium–high heat, add enough water to measure ¼ inch. Add the onion, garlic, celery, oregano, and basil and cook, stirring, about 5 minutes until the onion is softened. Reduce the heat and add the tomatoes (not the juice); cook, covered, stirring occasionally, for 5 minutes. Stir in the olives, peperoncini, sugar, crushed red pepper, salt, if using, and cook, covered, adding more water if necessary, for another 3 minutes.

Meanwhile, in a small bowl, whisk the tomato juice with the cornstarch until blended. Increase the heat and tip the skillet to pool the liquid. Add the tomato juice and stir for 1 minute. Reduce the heat and distribute the thickened liquid in the skillet. Stir in the tarragon and add the spinach on top; cook, covered, for 2 minutes until the spinach is wilted. Spoon the sauce on the pasta, sprinkle with Romano cheese and pepper generously, and serve hot.

■ PER SERVING: Saturated Fat: 0.5 gm Total Fat: 3 gm ■
Cholesterol: 2 mg Sodium: 366 mg Calories: 358

■

GRAINS, RICE, AND BEANS

■■   ■■

G rains grew wild for thousands of years before man walked the
   Earth. When our ancestors arrived, they sustained themselves on
the seed berries in the stalks of barley, rice, and wheat. They ground the
kernels into coarse flour or softened them in water.

Nomadic peoples timed their wandering food hunts to the wild harvests. In very early China, tribes drew near and camped at the edge of a
field on the days just before the barley was ready for picking. Then some
eleven thousand years ago, someone figured out that it would be a lot
easier to grow your own than to wander about in search of ripening grain.
So he or she planted a field, thereby inventing grain farming. By 6700
B.C., our ancestors were cooking grain cereals, crude biscuits, and flat
breads.

Though grains have always been a staple in human societies, certain
varieties have come in and gone out of fashion over the centuries. For the
Egyptians, barley was the grain of choice. They believed it to have mystical
medicinal powers, and jars of barley kernels were buried with pharaohs as
it was believed they would need them for their journey to the afterlife.
There is also evidence that barley beer fueled the pyramid builders.

In early China, barley as well as the soy bean were revered for their
adaptability and long growing seasons. These days, rice is the staple grain
throughout Asia.

More of the Earth's surface is given to growing wheat than to any other
crop. There are, in fact, thirty thousand varieties of wheat, with only a
hardy few grown for mass consumption.

Corn, on the other hand, comes in only eight thousand varieties. Actually, corn and the other great grain from South America, quinoa (pronounced "keen-wa"), seem to have been cultivated a little later in history, about 3500 B.C.

Beans, or legumes, are the second most available plant food after grains and have been growing on the planet about as long. Lentils, a pulse, and peas first appeared in the Mediterranean, Middle East, and Asia around the same time as barley, wheat, and rice—about 7000 B.C. The garbanzo bean (chickpea) came a thousand years later, and on the other side of the globe in 6000 B.C., the Inca were growing limas and beans while Asians were growing and using soy beans.

The bean was held in such high regard for its virtues of taste and nutrition in the early days of Rome that certain Roman families named themselves after the bean. The Lentulus family (after the lentil), Fabius (after the fava), the Piso family after the pea, and Cicero after the chickpea.

▓ Grain Basics ▓

Grains are readily available, inexpensive, and an excellent source of carbohydrates.

Barley The most popular form is the hulled pearl variety. The thick bran layer has been removed in milling and the pearl cooks up light and fluffy to an irresistibly chewy texture. Yes, some nutrients are lost through milling, but even so, one cup cooked pearl barley is packed with vitamins and minerals.

Cornmeal and polenta Both are ground from dried corn kernels. Cornmeal and polenta are slightly less nutritious than other grains. For this reason it is traditionally combined with other sources of protein and carbohydrates. Varieties include white, yellow, and even blue cornmeal. In boxes or bags, stone ground or enriched, fine or coarse ground, canned or cooked, polenta and cornmeal are available in all supermarkets and specialty food stores.

Quinoa The small pale quinoa seed is not much bigger than millet and has a fresh grasslike aroma. Most brands available here are no longer imported from the Peruvian Andes but are grown high in the Rocky Mountains or the Cascades in Washington State. Quinoa tends to be costly and is most often available in health-food stores and specialty markets.

Wheat From whole wheat berries to flour, wheat comes in many forms. When soaked and cooked, wheat berries have a nutty flavor and make a chewy addition to salads and soups. Bulgur is precooked cracked wheat that has been steamed and dried. It is high in vitamins, proteins, and carbohydrates and is deliciously tender in cereals, salads, and side dishes.

BUYING AND STORING Purchase all grains in closed containers to maximize their long shelf life; store in a jar with a tight-fitting lid in a cool, dry place. Technically, grains should keep a long time, but a good rule of thumb is 6 to 9 months.

COOKING Each kernel, even after milling off tough layers of husk and bran, is still as hard as a nut. Cooking in water softens the grain, making it deliciously edible.

Follow the package or recipe directions for each variety. If you cook the grain in water, bring the water to a boil, then add the grain, stirring so the grain doesn't stick together. Reduce the heat and continue cooking for the length of time on the package.

Barley, like most hulled grains, cooks in triple the amount of water to the amount of grain for about 40 minutes.

Cornmeal and cracked wheat (bulgur) cook in triple the amount of water to the amount of grain in about 20 minutes.

Quinoa cooks in double the amount of water to grain for about 15 minutes.

▪▪ Rice Basics ▪▪

In all its forms—long grain, short grain, glutinous—rice may be the most adaptive of all the grains. It's good hot or cold; as a simple side dish; as a stuffing; or, when mixed with other foods, it absorbs savory or sweet flavors to create wonderfully satisfying main dishes and desserts.

Like barley, rice grows protected by an inedible husk, and under the husk is a thin layer of bran. Brown rice retains the bran layer for extra nutrients and texture. When the bran layer is milled off, the grain becomes the familiar white rice, which cooks up faster, lighter, and less chewy than brown rice.

There are a great number of rices available today. I suggest you experiment. Mix rices that come in many colors and sizes with some aromatic basmati brown rice.

BUYING AND STORING Rice comes in three grain sizes—long, medium, and short. Long-grain rice is good in main dishes and salads as the grains remain separated during cooking. Short- and medium-grain rice tend to stick together when cooked.

All rice should be stored in a cool, dry place at room temperature. Store in a glass or plastic container with a tight-fitting lid.

COOKING For best nutritional advantage, cook rice in just the amount of liquid that will be fully absorbed. Follow the package or recipe directions exactly. You can also add quadruple the liquid to the rice and pour off the excess when the rice is cooked. One cup of regular rice makes about 3 cups cooked; 1 cup brown rice makes 3 to 4 cups cooked. Or you can also add quadruple the liquid to the rice and pour off the excess when the rice is cooked.

▦ Bean Basics ▦

Legumes, or beans, are technically seeds that have been removed from their pods and dried. They are richer in protein and carbohydrates than grains. They are negligible in fat and, like all fruits and vegetables, contain no cholesterol. All beans contain flavor and texture and have as much versatility and use as pasta or rice. Use beans in salads, soups, chili, rice, dips, and pasta dishes. They are excellent hot or cold.

BUYING AND STORING The varieties I use most often are black beans, limas, garbanzos, kidney beans, lentils (really a pulse, or seed), black-eyed peas (a bean), pinto beans, and navy beans. But I use many other exotic kinds too. Beans are inexpensive, so you can experiment with scarlet runners, roans, madeiras, Christmas, and any of the dozens of varieties. They all use similar preparations, except lupinis (which need to soak for 12 days, change the water each day). Buy them in clean bags or boxes and store them in airtight containers in a cool, dry place. Canned varieties are terrific; I use them all the time. Although they tend to be higher in sodium and softer than the firm-textured bean cooked from scratch, they are a good choice when time and convenience are important.

COOKING Wash dried beans carefully to remove dirt and pebbles that may be left from the harvesting and packaging process.

Do not presoak dried beans before cooking. I find that presoaking creates the very problem (gas) it is meant to eliminate. As the beans soak they ferment and the fermentation is what I find to be gas inducing. Unsoaked beans, when cooked and eaten right away, have texture, are flavorful, and do not produce as many gastrointestinal problems.

Barley Pilaf

Serves 6 as a side dish

The spicy-sweet flavors of this pilaf are reminiscent of Middle Eastern cuisine, but the toothsome barley adds a comforting quality that makes this dish very American! This is excellent served hot or cold with chicken, turkey, game hen, or duck. Add small amounts of meat or poultry to make this side dish a satisfying entrée.

1 cup pearl barley
1 bay leaf
Salt (optional)
Freshly ground black pepper
1 medium onion, minced
½ cup raisins
⅓ cup chopped dried apricots
⅓ cup chopped pitted dates
2 tablespoons tahini

3 tablespoons fresh lemon juice
½ teaspoon cumin
½ cup thinly sliced scallion tops, for garnish
¼ cup toasted sunflower seeds or almond slices, toast for 10 minutes in a 350°F. oven
½ cup chopped Major Grey's mango chutney

In a large saucepan over high heat, heat the barley, bay leaf, 4 cups water, salt, if using, and pepper to boiling; reduce the heat and simmer for 20 to 40 minutes, or until the barley begins to soften. Add the onion and cook an additional 8 to 10 minutes, until the barley is tender and most of the water is absorbed. Stir in the raisins, apricots, dates, tahini, lemon juice, and cumin. Turn off the heat, cover, and let stand for 10 minutes to plump the fruit. Stir well.

Garnish with the scallions and the sunflower seeds and serve hot or cold with chutney.

PER SERVING: Saturated Fat: 1 gm   Total Fat: 6 gm
Cholesterol: 0 mg   Sodium: 60 mg   Calories: 310

Saffron Couscous with Seven Vegetables

In Morocco, where seven is a lucky number, this vegetable dish is made like a vegetarian stew. Saffron lends a pungency and beautiful color to the stew. It is available in some supermarkets, specialty food stores, and in Indian and Middle Eastern markets.

1 10-ounce box couscous prepared according to package directions

1 medium onion, diced

6 medium carrots, diced

½ rutabaga, peeled and diced

½ cup diced green cabbage

½ teaspoon powdered saffron, or 20 threads, crushed

1 medium zucchini, diced

1 small eggplant, diced, salted, and drained

3 plum tomatoes, diced

½ cup golden raisins

3 cloves garlic, minced

Salt (optional)

Freshly ground black pepper

2½ tablespoons cornstarch

1¾ cups vegetable stock

In a nonstick 5-quart sauce pot or Dutch oven over high heat, heat 1 inch water to boiling. Add the onion, carrots, rutabaga, cabbage, and saffron and reduce the heat to medium; cover and cook for 6 minutes. Check the water and add more to maintain ½ to 1 inch. Stir in the zucchini and eggplant; cover and cook over low heat for about 8 minutes. Stir in the tomatoes, raisins, garlic, salt, if using, and pepper. Cover and cook over low heat about 5 more minutes.

Meanwhile, in a small bowl, whisk the cornstarch into the stock. Add the stock to the vegetables and cook, stirring until thickened. Mound the couscous on a large platter and make a well in the center. Fill the well with the vegetables and serve immediately.

PER SERVING: Saturated Fat: Trace   Total Fat: 0.5 gm
Cholesterol: 0 mg   Sodium: 38 mg   Calories: 227

Polenta Strata

An Italian specialty much like lasagna, this dish replaces lasagna noodles with thin layers of polenta. Make the polenta one day in advance and refrigerate it so that it is firm. Use your favorite tomato sauce or my simple Marinara Sauce (page 168).

POLENTA:

Olive oil spray

6 cups low-sodium, defatted chicken or vegetable stock or water

2 cups cornmeal

Salt (optional)

Freshly ground black pepper

VEGETABLE LAYER:

12 ounces mushrooms, mix of buttons and shiitakes with stems removed, sliced

10 ounces fresh spinach, stems removed and coarsely chopped

1 teaspoon fresh chopped basil

CREAMY LAYER:

2 cups nonfat cottage cheese, drained for 10 minutes in a cheesecloth-lined strainer

2 cloves garlic, minced

1 egg white

1 cup fresh bread crumbs

2 scallions, thinly sliced

4 medium plum tomatoes, sliced

1½ cups low-sodium tomato sauce

¼ cup chopped parsley

Line an 11-inch by 14-inch baking sheet with foil and lightly spray with olive oil. In a 4-quart microwave-safe casserole dish, combine the stock, cornmeal, salt, if using, and pepper and stir. Cook at high for 15 to 20 minutes, stirring every 5 minutes, covered, in a large nonstick saucepan over medium heat, stirring occasionally, for about 20 minutes. The mixture should be thick enough for a spoon to stand up straight when inserted in the middle. Spread the ½-inch-thick polenta in an even layer on the baking sheet. Cover with plastic wrap and refrigerate for 6 hours or overnight, until firm.

Preheat the oven to 350°F.

(continued)

Lightly spray a 7-inch by 11-inch baking pan with olive oil and set aside. In a large nonstick skillet lightly sprayed with olive oil over high heat, sauté the mushrooms for 3 minutes. Add the spinach, cover, and reduce the heat to medium high and cook, stirring once, until the spinach is just wilted. Stir in the basil and set aside.

In a food processor or blender, puree the cottage cheese for 3 minutes or until smooth. Add the garlic, egg white, bread crumbs, and scallions and pulse until just blended.

To assemble, cut the polenta in half lengthwise. Place ½ in the bottom of the lasagna pan. Spread half the vegetable mixture evenly over the polenta, arrange the tomatoes on top of the vegetable layer, followed by ½ cup of the tomato sauce and top with half the cheese mixture. Repeat with the remaining polenta, vegetable mixture, and cheese mixture. Spread the remaining 1 cup tomato sauce over the top. Bake for 35 to 40 minutes until bubbly. Let the polenta cool for 15 minutes, then cut into squares. Sprinkle with chopped parsley and serve passing additional heated tomato sauce.

PER SERVING: Saturated Fat: Trace   Total Fat: 2 gm
Cholesterol: 6 mg   Sodium: 318 mg   Calories: 220

Polenta and Peppers
Serves 6

Polenta is fast becoming a standard selection on restaurant menus these days because the simple taste and texture of cornmeal provides a perfect base for other flavors. In this side dish, it is a soothing complement to hot and spicy ingredients.

Vegetable oil spray

2 cloves garlic, minced

½ medium onion, thinly sliced

1 green bell pepper, sliced

1 red bell pepper, sliced

1 yellow bell pepper, sliced

1 poblano, ancho, or chili pepper, seeded and thinly sliced

½ pound mushrooms, thinly sliced

1 teaspoon chopped fresh oregano or ¼ teaspoon dried

Salt (optional)

Freshly ground black pepper

½ cup flour

½ teaspoon salt (optional)

1 teaspoon baking powder

1½ cups cornmeal

½ cup egg substitute

2 cups nonfat milk

2 tablespoons crumbled goat cheese or blue cheese

Preheat the oven to 350°F.

In a medium nonstick skillet lightly sprayed with vegetable oil, over high heat, add 3 tablespoons water, garlic, onion, peppers, mushrooms, oregano, salt, if using, and pepper. Lightly spray the mixture with vegetable oil and cook for about 5 minutes, stirring occasionally. Remove from the heat and set aside.

Meanwhile, in a large bowl, combine the flour, ½ teaspoon salt, if using, baking powder, and cornmeal and mix well. Add the eggs and milk and stir until thick and smooth. Lightly spray a large nonstick ovenproof skillet with vegetable oil. Pour the batter into the skillet, spreading it evenly with a rubber spatula. Place the skillet over low heat and cook, covered, stirring occasionally, for 10 minutes. Remove the skillet from the stove and spread the pepper mixture on top of the polenta, then sprinkle with the cheese. Bake, uncovered, for 10 minutes.

Turn the oven to broil and place the polenta under the broiler until golden brown. Slice into wedges and serve immediately.

■■   PER SERVING: Saturated Fat: 1 gm   Total Fat: 3 gm   ■■
Cholesterol: 4 mg   Sodium: 184 mg   Calories: 232

Quinoa Italian Style

Quinoa has a sweet, mellow flavor and has been called the super grain because it contains more protein than any other. These beadlike grains can transform a simple rice dish into something special. Quinoa is available in health-food stores and most supermarkets.

Vegetable oil spray

1 large onion, minced

2 cloves garlic, minced

½ pound extra-lean ground top round

2 8-ounce cans low-sodium tomato sauce

1 16-ounce can low-sodium crushed tomatoes or 3 tomatoes chopped

Salt (optional)

2 teaspoons oregano

3 teaspoons chopped fresh basil

½ teaspoon sugar

3 cups quinoa cooked according to package directions

8 ounces nonfat ricotta cheese

4 ounces nonfat mozzarella cheese

2 tablespoons grated nonfat Parmesan cheese

Preheat the oven to 350°F.

In a large nonstick skillet lightly sprayed with vegetable oil, over medium-high heat, cook the onion and garlic until translucent, adding water by the teaspoon if the mixture becomes dry. Stir in the ground meat, 1 can tomato sauce, tomatoes, salt, if using, oregano, basil, and sugar and simmer until all ingredients are just hot.

In an 8-inch casserole dish, layer the meat sauce, the quinoa, and the remaining can tomato sauce. Spread the ricotta evenly over the sauce and sprinkle with the mozzarella. Sprinkle on the Parmesan and bake for 35 minutes.

PER SERVING: Saturated Fat: 1 gm   Total Fat: 6 gm
Cholesterol: 25 mg   Sodium: 228 mg   Calories: 363

Tabbouleh

A Middle Eastern dish, tabbouleh combines protein-rich bulgur wheat with vegetables, fresh parsely, and mint. It is traditional to serve it at room temperature mounded on lettuce leaves and garnished with mint sprigs. Bulgur is available in most supermarkets and in health-food stores.

1 cup bulgur (cracked wheat)	¼ cup fresh lemon juice
3 tomatoes, diced and placed in a colander to drain	½ teaspoon cumin
½ cup chopped parsley	½ teaspoon allspice
1 medium cucumber, peeled if waxed and diced	½ teaspoon salt (optional)
	¼ to ½ teaspoon freshly ground black pepper
3 scallions, chopped	1 head Boston or romaine lettuce
3 tablespoons chopped fresh mint leaves	¼ cup pine nuts (optional)
	Mint sprigs, for garnish

In a colander, rinse the bulgur thoroughly with cold water and drain. In a large bowl, combine the bulgur with 2 cups cold water and stir once. Let stand for 30 minutes to 1 hour and drain. Stir in the tomatoes, parsley, cucumber, scallions, mint, lemon juice, cumin, allspice, salt, if using, and pepper and mix well. Cover and let stand at least 1 hour. If you prefer it chilled, refrigerate for 1 hour.

To serve, mound the tabbouleh on a lettuce-lined plate, sprinkle with pine nuts, and arrange the mint sprigs on top. Serve cold or at room temperature.

PER SERVING: Saturated Fat: Trace   Total Fat: 1 gm
Cholesterol: 0 mg   Sodium: 15 mg   Calories: 108

Basmati Rice with Shrimp and Shiitake Mushrooms

Originally grown only in the foothills of the Himalayas, and an East Indian favorite, aromatic basmati is available in most supermarkets. Unlike most rice varieties such as short-grained white rice, basmati is enhanced by aging.

Olive oil spray
1 medium onion, coarsely chopped
1½ cups basmati rice
3 cups low-sodium, defatted
   chicken stock
1 12-ounce package frozen winter
   squash, thawed, or 1¼ cups
   cooked butternut or acorn
   squash, pureed

¼ teaspoon nutmeg
Salt (optional)
¾ pound medium shrimp, shelled
   and deveined
1 cup shiitake mushrooms, sliced
¼ cup chopped parsley

In a 2-quart nonstick Dutch oven or medium skillet lightly sprayed with olive oil, over medium-high heat, combine the onion and rice and lightly spray with olive oil. Cook, stirring, for 4 to 5 minutes. Add the stock, increase the heat to high, and bring to a boil. Reduce the heat to medium, cover, and cook 10 minutes. Stir in the squash, nutmeg, and salt, if using. Reduce the heat to medium low, cover, and cook for 5 minutes. Check to make sure the rice is not sticking. Layer the shrimp and sliced mushrooms on top of the rice, cover, and cook for 4 minutes, or until the shrimp are bright pink. Remove a few shrimp and mushrooms and set aside for the garnish, then stir the rice to mix well.

Spoon the rice onto a serving platter and garnish with the reserved shrimp and mushrooms. Sprinkle with parsley and serve immediately.

PER SERVING: Saturated Fat: 1 gm   Total Fat: 5 gm
Cholesterol: 160 mg   Sodium: 449 mg   Calories: 466

Fried Rice

Fried rice is notoriously high in fat, but my version duplicates the authentic taste of fried rice without fat, frying, or using any egg yolks. Serve it as a main course with Chinese Eggplant with Garlic Sauce (page 136).

1 cup shredded cabbage

1 cup cooked white or brown rice

4 scallions, chopped

2 tablespoons low-sodium soy sauce

1 tablespoon minced coriander leaves

1 tablespoon chopped parsley

Vegetable oil spray

1½ cups egg substitute or 3 egg whites

½ cup frozen peas, thawed

2 tablespoons chopped chives, for garnish

In a large nonstick skillet over medium heat, cook the cabbage in 1 cup water for several minutes, stirring occasionally, adding water when necessary, until cooked, allowing the water to nearly evaporate at the end. Lower the heat and stir in the cooked rice and cook covered for 4 minutes, stirring. Add the scallions, soy sauce, coriander, and parsley, and cook for 3 minutes, adding a small amount of water if necessary.

You can heat the eggs separately in a nonstick skillet lightly sprayed with oil, over medium-high heat. Dice them before adding to the rice, stirring well, or make a well in the center of the rice mixture and pour in the eggs. Reduce the heat to very low, cover, and cook for 2 to 3 minutes, until the eggs are cooked. With a knifepoint and eggs still in the well, chop the eggs into small ¼-inch bits. Add the peas and stir to mix eggs and peas well. Garnish with the chopped chives and serve immediately.

PER SERVING: Saturated Fat: 0 gm Total Fat: Trace
Cholesterol: 0 mg Sodium: 244 mg Calories: 71

Risotto and Summer Vegetables

Risotto is an Italian rice dish made with Arborio rice, a short-grain glutinous rice available in most fine food markets. The secret is to add about ¼ cup of liquid over medium heat, incorporating it into the rice, and each 5 minutes, you add more liquid (you can also microwave risotto, removing and stirring every 4 minutes, for 16 minutes' total microwaving). Risotto doesn't refrigerate well as it gets soggy and puffy. You can vary the vegetables, using peas, corn, asparagus, carrots, fresh tomatoes, or mushrooms. The recipe calls for defatted Chicken Stock (see pages 48 and 52). It takes 25 to 35 minutes to make risotto.

1 cup Arborio rice

3 cups low-sodium, defatted chicken stock

1 (8-ounce) medium-size zucchini, cut lengthwise in half, sliced ¼-inch thick

1 (8-ounce) yellow, medium-size summer squash, cut lengthwise in half, sliced ¼-inch thick

2 pattypan squashes, cut in half and sliced ¼-inch thick (if available or use ¼ pound asparagus, green beans, snow peas, or other vegetable)

6 scallions, cut into 1-inch pieces

4 shallots, chopped, or 1 onion, chopped

2 cloves garlic, minced

½ cup dry white wine (optional)

10 cherry tomatoes, thinly sliced

5 (about ¼ cup) red or yellow rehydrated sun-dried tomatoes, cut into ¼-inch strips

2 tablespoons chopped watercress

4 tablespoons grated nonfat Parmesan

Salt (optional)

Pepper

In a very large, nonstick skillet on medium–high heat, add the rice, pour in ¼ cup stock, and stir until the rice absorbs it, adjusting the heat to medium to make sure the liquid doesn't just evaporate but is absorbed by the rice. Cook for about 15 minutes, stirring, adding ¼ to ½ cup more stock as needed. Add the zucchini, summer squash, pattypan squash, scallions, shallots, and garlic and continue adding the stock ¼ cup at a time and stirring until all but ½ cup of the stock is used. The rice should be tender but firm and not mushy. Add the wine, if using, stirring lightly to incorporate, heat for 2 or 3 minutes, and add the cherry and sun-dried tomatoes, watercress, and Parmesan. Cover for 2 minutes and serve hot.

■■   PER SERVING: Saturated Fat: 0 gm   Total Fat: 0.5 gm   ■■
Cholesterol: 2 mg   Sodium: 106 mg   Calories: 140

Rice Pilaf

■■   *Serves 4*   ■■

In traditional pilaf recipes, rice is usually sautéed in oil or butter, then simmered in stock. I use just enough vegetable oil spray to coat the rice, which saves on fat calories without sacrificing flavor. If you're in a hurry, use white or brown rice, but white cooks faster——unless you find a quick-cooking brown rice.

Vegetable oil or butter-flavored
  spray
1 cup brown or white rice
2½ cups low-sodium defatted
  chicken stock
1 medium onion, chopped

8 ounces mushrooms, finely
  chopped
1 scallion or shallot, diced
Salt (optional)
2 tablespoons grated nonfat
  Parmesan

In a large nonstick saucepan lightly sprayed with oil, add the rice and lightly spray again while stirring the rice. Turn up the heat and cook for 1 minute. Add the stock, onion, and mushrooms, turn the heat to high, and bring to a boil. Reduce the heat, cover, and simmer for 20 to 40 minutes, or until rice is tender. Stir in the scallion, salt, if using, and Parmesan cheese and serve immediately.

■■   PER SERVING: Saturated Fat: Trace   Total Fat: 2 gm   ■■
Cholesterol: 6 mg   Sodium: 79 mg   Calories: 224

Rice with Sun-Dried Tomatoes

Serves 4

This is a fabulous way to use leftover cooked rice. Use sun-dried tomatoes packed in oil for best flavor and texture.

2 teaspoons oil from jar of sun-
dried tomatoes
2 cups cooked white rice
½ cup sun-dried tomatoes, packed
in oil, diced

¼ cup chopped parsley
Salt (optional)
Freshly ground black pepper

In a large nonstick skillet over medium heat, heat the oil. Add the rice and stir until heated through. Add the tomatoes and parsley and stir to mix well. Add salt, if using, and pepper to taste and serve immediately.

PER SERVING: Saturated Fat: 0.5 gm Total Fat: 3 gm
Cholesterol: 0 mg Sodium: 145 mg Calories: 172

Saffron Rice

Serves 4

One of the world's most prized spices, saffron lends a brilliant orange yellow glow to this dish. Saffron rice is excellent served with Caribbean Rum Chicken with Pineapple (page 244). This is ready in 25 minutes.

Olive oil spray
1 yellow onion, finely chopped
¾ cup short-grain rice
¼ to ½ teaspoon powdered
saffron or 20 threads crushed

¼ teaspoon turmeric
Salt (optional)
1½ cups low-sodium, defatted
chicken stock or water

In a nonstick skillet lightly sprayed with olive oil, over medium-high heat, cook the onion, lightly spraying with olive oil once while stirring, for about 3 minutes until brown. Stir in the rice, once again lightly spraying. Add the saffron, turmeric, and salt, if using, and stir well. Cook, stirring, for 3 minutes. Add the stock, reduce the heat to medium low, cover, and simmer, for 15 to 20 minutes, or until the rice is tender.

■■   PER SERVING: Saturated Fat: 0 gm   Total Fat: Trace   ■■
Cholesterol: 2 mg   Sodium: 10 mg   Calories: 153

Spanish Rice

■■ *Serves 6* ■■

This colorful and spicy dish is traditionally made with white rice. If using canned tomatoes, squeeze the whole tomatoes into the mixture with clean fingers so the chunks are large (or cut into 1-inch pieces). Garnish with a little grated nonfat cheese.

½ onion, chopped
½ green bell pepper, chopped,
    seeds reserved
½ red bell pepper, chopped, seeds
    reserved
1 clove garlic, minced
1 28-ounce can low-sodium
    tomatoes (or 3 fresh), juices
    reserved

½ cup low-sodium tomato juice
1½ cups short-grain white rice
1 teaspoon sugar
1½ teaspoons chili powder
Freshly ground black pepper
¼ to ½ teaspoon chopped seeded
    jalapeño or Tabasco

In a large nonstick skillet in ½ inch water over medium heat, steam the onion, peppers, seeds, and garlic, adding small amounts of water to keep the mixture moist, until tender. Add the tomatoes to the mixture, breaking them up with your fingers. If using canned tomatoes, stir in the reserved tomato juices, rice, sugar, chili powder, pepper, and jalapeño. Cover and cook over low heat for 20 to 25 minutes, stirring occasionally, until the liquid is absorbed.

■■   PER SERVING: Saturated Fat: Trace   Total Fat: 1 gm   ■■
Cholesterol: 0 mg   Sodium: 27 mg   Calories: 223

Wild Rice with Quinoa, Pecans, and Orange Zest

Serves 4

This is an aromatic, flavorful rendition of wild rice that can be used as a main dish garnished by sprinkling with scallions, currants, mandarin oranges, or perhaps covered with a wine-flavored white sauce or as a stuffing base for poultry. The quinoa can be optional (just add a quarter cup more wild rice if you leave it out), but it is very nice in the mixture. During one testing, too much pepper was accidentally added to this recipe, and so many liked it that way that we have kept the rather large amount. Feel free to reduce it.

2½ cups low-sodium, defatted
   chicken stock or water
½ pound fresh mushrooms, sliced
½ cup chopped sweet onion
Olive oil spray
¾ cup wild rice, washed
1 to 2 tablespoons orange zest
   (each tablespoon takes 1
   orange)

½ cup chopped pecans
¼ cup quinoa, washed
½ cup fresh orange juice
Salt (optional)
½ to ¾ teaspoon pepper
3 or 4 longish strips of orange
   zest, for garnish
4 whole pecan halves, for garnish

In a large nonstick saucepan, simmer a few tablespoons of the stock over medium heat. Add the mushrooms and onions, and spray the vegetables lightly with olive oil and heat for 5 minutes, stirring occasionally. Add the remaining stock, wild rice, a tablespoon of the zest and a tablespoon or two of the pecans. Bring to a boil, and turn down the heat to low and simmer for 40 minutes. Add the quinoa and orange juice, the remaining orange zest and nuts and simmer, uncovered, over medium-low heat another 15 minutes. Stir in the salt, if using, and liberally pepper the top; cover and let sit for 5 minutes (on or off very low heat, depending upon the moisture content), and serve hot on individual plates or in a casserole dish garnished with the orange zest and whole pecans.

■■   PER SERVING: Saturated Fat: 1 gm   Total Fat: 13 gm   ■■
Cholesterol: 3 mg   Sodium: 22 mg   Calories: 311

■■

Beans and Rice

■■   *Serves 4*   ■■

This version gets its smoky rich flavor from the ham stock. Serve this with Jalapeño Relish (page 295) or harissa.

4 cups defatted ham stock
1½ cups dried pinto beans
1 cup white or brown rice
Salt (optional)

Freshly ground black pepper
1 onion, finely chopped (optional)
1 cup Salsa Cruda (page 279)

In a large sauce pot over high heat, heat the ham stock to boiling. Add the beans and reduce the heat to low; cover and cook for 1 to 1½ hours. Add the rice, additional water if necessary, and cover and cook for ½ hour. Check the liquid content during the cooking once or twice to be sure it isn't too dry. Add more if necessary. Add salt, if using, and pepper to taste. Serve immediately with onion and salsa on the side.

■■   PER SERVING: Saturated Fat: 0.5 gm   Total Fat: 3 gm   ■■
Cholesterol: 5 mg   Sodium: 190 mg   Calories: 495

Camp Town Beans with Pork

Lean pork adds character and flavor to this old-fashioned American favorite. The marmalade, a substitute for the traditional heavy molasses, lends a subtle sweetness to this savory dish. I use canned beans to save time.

Olive oil spray

8 ounces extra-lean pork, cubed

1 large red or green bell pepper, diced

1 onion, coarsely chopped

1 pound mushrooms, thickly sliced

2 8-ounce cans low-sodium peeled tomatoes, coarsely chopped

1 15-ounce can pinto or kidney beans, drained

1 15-ounce can garbanzo beans (chickpeas), drained

⅓ cup orange marmalade

1 tablespoon cider vinegar

½ teaspoon cumin

1 teaspoon chili powder

3 drops Tabasco

Salt (optional)

Freshly ground black pepper

In a large soup pot lightly sprayed with olive oil over medium-high heat, cook the pork on all sides until browned. Add the pepper, onion, mushrooms, and a few tablespoons water, and cook until softened, about 6 minutes, stirring occasionally. Add more water if necessary if the mixture becomes too dry. Add the tomatoes, beans, marmalade, vinegar, cumin, chili powder, Tabasco, salt, if using, and pepper. Cook, stirring, until hot and bubbly, about 4 minutes. Serve immediately.

PER SERVING: Saturated Fat: 1 gm   Total Fat: 3 gm

Cholesterol: 20 gm   Sodium: 274 mg   Calories: 277

Confetti Bourbon Beans

This hearty southern-style soup, gently spiked with bourbon, is ready to eat in less than an hour. Use small pearl barley to ensure quick cooking time. For the confetti look, garnish with diced green, red, and yellow peppers.

1 6-ounce can low-sodium tomato
  paste
1 bay leaf
½ cup small pearl barley
4 cups low-sodium defatted
  chicken or vegetable stock
1 cup canned pinto beans, drained
1 cup canned kidney beans,
  drained

1 cup canned butter beans,
  drained
1 teaspoon Old Bay seasoning
2 teaspoons Worcestershire
¼ cup bourbon
Salt (optional)
Tabasco (optional)
Freshly ground black pepper
¾ cup mixture diced green, red,
  and yellow bell peppers

In a large saucepan over high heat, heat the tomato paste, bay leaf, barley, and stock to boiling. Reduce the heat, cover, and simmer for 35 to 40 minutes, until the barley is cooked. Add the beans, additional water to thin if necessary, Old Bay seasoning, Worcestershire, and bourbon. Cook for 2 minutes, season with salt, if using, Tabasco, and pepper to taste, and serve immediately.

PER SERVING: Saturated Fat: Trace   Total Fat: 1 gm
Cholesterol: 3 mg   Sodium: 354 mg   Calories: 237

Vegetarian Chili

The secret to the success of this chili is to use the freshest ingredients possible and to prepare the vegetables exactly as I do. For a darker, richer chili, simmer for up to 2 hours.

2 large yellow onions, coarsely chopped

4 cloves garlic, minced

1 green bell pepper, seeds reserved, cut into 1-inch square pieces

2 fresh tomatoes, peeled, and coarsely chopped

1 teaspoon brown or white sugar

1 6-ounce can low-sodium tomato paste

1 8-ounce can low-sodium tomato sauce

1 8-ounce can low-sodium whole tomatoes

2 to 4 tablespoons chili powder

1 to 1½ tablespoons cumin

1 to 1½ tablespoons basil

1 to 1½ teaspoons oregano

½ to 1 teaspoon chopped seeded jalapeño or several drops Tabasco

1 tablespoon vinegar (optional)

1 teaspoon salt (optional)

¼ teaspoon freshly ground black pepper

1 26-ounce can dark kidney beans, well drained

In a large nonstick skillet over medium heat, cook the onions, garlic, bell pepper, seeds, in a few tablespoons water, for 8 minutes stirring often. Add water as necessary to keep the vegetables steaming.

Add the fresh tomatoes to the skillet and continue to cook, stirring, for several minutes more, until all the vegetables are soft and the onions are translucent. Add water, if necessary, to keep the vegetables steaming. Transfer the vegetables to a large soup pot and keep warm over low heat.

Meanwhile, in a medium bowl, whisk together the sugar, tomato paste, tomato sauce, and the juice from the canned whole tomatoes and add to the vegetables in the skillet. Increase the heat to medium and squeeze the canned tomatoes through your fingers into the sauce, breaking them into large chunks. Add the chili powder, cumin, basil, oregano, jalapeño, vinegar, salt, if using, and pepper; cover and cook for about 5 minutes, stirring occasionally. Add the beans and cook for 10 minutes, or until the beans are heated through. Serve immediately.

▚ PER SERVING: Saturated Fat: Trace Total Fat: 2 gm ▚
Cholesterol: 0 mg Sodium: 208 mg Calories: 164

▚

Black Beans and Rice

Serve this dish the way it is served throughout the Caribbean: black beans in one bowl, rice in a second, and chopped sweet onions in a third. Let everyone fill his own bowl with the rice first, then beans and onions, a dash of hot sauce and a squeeze of fresh lime juice.

4 cups defatted ham stock	¼ to ½ teaspoon finely chopped
1½ cups black beans	seeded jalapeño pepper
1 onion, finely chopped	Salt (optional)
1 carrot, finely shredded	Freshly ground black pepper
1 leafy rib celery, finely shredded	¼ cup sherry (optional)
1 tomato, finely chopped	6 cups cooked rice, 1 cup for each
3 cloves garlic, minced	serving
¼ teaspoon thyme	3 onions, chopped
¼ teaspoon turmeric (optional)	1 avocado, sliced
1 teaspoon cumin	3 limes or lemons, cut in wedges
1 bay leaf	Hot sauce or Tabasco

In a large pot over medium-high heat, combine the stock, beans, onion, carrot, celery, tomato, garlic, herbs and spices, and jalapeño for 5 minutes. Lower the heat, cover, and simmer for 2½ to 3 hours, adding water when needed until the beans are soft but not mushy. Set an immersion, or hand, blender into the pot and puree about half the beans. Alternatively, transfer half the beans to a food processor, puree, and return to the pot. Add the sherry, serve hot with the rice accompanied with the onions, avocado slices on the beans. Limes on one side, ¾ cup chopped onions on the other, and hot sauce are for passing.

PER SERVING: Saturated Fat: 1 gm   Total Fat: 7 gm
Cholesterol: 3 mg   Sodium: 109 mg   Calories: 607

FISH AND SHELLFISH

■■   ■■

The estimated 5.5 billion people on Earth consume about 100 million tons of fish and shellfish each year. Of that, Americans each eat about 15 pounds every year. After grains, fish has been the second most important food in human history, and among all animal foods (well, not counting insects) it is the most abundantly available on the planet.

Carved and chiseled images of fish and shellfish on the walls of cave dwellings tell us how crucial fish was in the daily lives of our prehistoric ancestors. Later civilizations, too, painted homages to fish on pottery, carved them in decorative bas-reliefs, and chiseled depictions on the walls of tombs and temples.

The Egyptians actually may have been the first aquafarmers, raising their favorite fish in ponds to have them readily available. This good idea has been repeated throughout history: Fourteenth-century English lords kept moats filled with fresh fish.

The Assyrians, who dominated the known Mideastern world in 2300 B.C., prepared fifty different species of fish for eating. The Roman rulers who followed were enthusiastic fish eaters, too. One favorite was tender sole prepared from a flounder they called *solea Jovi* (Jupiter's sandal). The dictator Claudius Appius (who built the Appian Way) was known for his addiction to daily treats of salted, sun-dried anchovies. And the Roman thinker and writer Pliny was the first to consider oysters an aphrodisiac. Thanks to him, most of the world still associates the sweet mollusk with sensuality.

This is not surprising, since our vast coastlines, lakes, and river systems have supplied us with hundreds of species that vary from the Pacific albacore and mountain rainbow trout to the Atlantic salmon and Chesapeake Bay blue crab.

However, statistics also show that Americans are more likely to order fish in restaurants than to prepare it at home. Whether this is a result of confusion over the overwhelming variety of fish available today or the belief that fish is difficult to prepare, the recipes I've included here will convince you that fish is, indeed, a snap to cook at home. What's more, it will become a standard part of your healthful eating plan.

■ Fish and Shellfish Basics ■

FATS AND CHOLESTEROL Choosing the fish or shellfish you like is a matter of personal taste.

With about 75 to 85 milligrams of cholesterol in 3½ ounces, fish (except for halibut, which can be as low as 35 milligrams) and shellfish, such as crab, shrimp, and lobster—having about 125 milligrams, depending on where it comes from—compare almost exactly with the same amount of lamb, chicken, or pork. However, shellfish contains the lowest amount of saturated fat of any animal food. Most fish contains under 2 grams of saturated fat per 3½ ounces.

The saturated and total fat contents for fish vary according to the fish. But because the amounts of fats are so low in the first place, a 100-percent increase from a lean fish—which has 1 gram of saturated fat—to a fatty fish—which has 2 grams—is relatively little. Because saturated fat has greater artery-clogging capability than poly- and monounsaturated fat, fish is a good choice for a healthful menu plan.

BUYING Thanks to a five-billion-dollar-a-year aquaculture industry, there are larger, more tender, sweeter, leaner, and because of breeding, clean water, and medication, more disease-resistant fish and shellfish in the marketplace today. Most of the catfish and rainbow trout you find at the fish counter are from fish farms, and some of the salmon, oysters, scallops, clams, mussels, crab, and lobster are farm raised as well.

On the question of purity, let me say that no fish is chemical free these days. The farmed fish, like other farmed animals, have been grown with the aid of therapeutic drugs, and freshwater and saltwater fish come with the normal pollutants of our times—traces of mercury and pesticides. However, the Federal Drug Administration says that of all food-borne illness, those related to seafood comprise only one quarter of 1 percent of the total.

What do you look for when buying fish? Freshness is key. Buy fish the day of or the day before you intend to cook it. Buy from a reputable fish market or supermarket. Get to know your fishmonger and don't be afraid to ask him or her the origins of their fish.

The freshest fish (97 percent of which were frozen at sea or during processing) should smell sweet not "fishy." A whole fish has scales that are shiny and intact; the eyes are clear and full, not sunken; the gills are bright red in color. If you can buy whole fish and have it filleted at the fish store, do so because most cuts of fish on display deteriorate rapidly and are subject to bacteria. If you are limited, as most of us are, to supermarket fish, pay attention to the dates on the labels and try to buy as fresh as possible.

If you buy frozen, thaw the fish in the package overnight in the refrigerator. When thawed, blot the fish with paper towel before cooking.

The freshest shellfish is alive. Live lobster will keep at home in a cool place or the refrigerator about 12 hours; live crab will keep 24 to 36 hours in a cool place or the refrigerator at home.

If you're buying fresh-cooked whole shellfish such as blue crabs, it should be heavy for its size and bright pink or red in color. Fresh lobster will have its tail tucked under.

Fresh shrimp raw or cooked is pink and sweet smelling.

Fresh mollusks—oysters, clams, scallops, and mussels—are firmly closed and sweet smelling. Raw and in the shell they will keep 24 to 36 hours in a cool place or the refrigerator at home. Scallops need to be used within twenty-four hours since you don't know how long the market has had them. Many feel oysters and clams should no longer be eaten raw.

COOKING Cooking fish seems to intimidate even the most adventurous home cook. Usually, less is more when it comes to cooking fish or shellfish. Do not overcook or the tender texture can become rubbery and a sweet-tasting fish becomes bland.

To cook fish, a general guideline is to cook the fish 10 minutes per inch of thickness, 5 minutes on either side. For example, a 1-inch-thick piece of tuna should cook 5 minutes per side. A 1½-inch salmon steak should cook about 7 minutes per side for a total of 14 minutes.

Fish is cooked when it begins to flake and turns opaque. Remove it from the heat immediately as it will continue to cook for several minutes.

Shellfish are cooked according to weight and overall size rather than thickness. The moment of doneness is usually a visual cue. Lobster may take 6 minutes. Remember they keep on cooking after leaving the pot, so allow for it. Crab and shrimp will turn pink after about 3 minutes (depending on weight) of steaming.

Mollusks, including clams, oysters, scallops, and mussels, will simply open during steaming or grilling. Discard those that have not opened when most others have.

Leftover cooked fish and shellfish will keep refrigerated for 1 or 2 days.

Leanest and Fattiest Fish

■ Leanest ■

(less than 5 gm fat per 3½-ounce portion)

Abalone	Ling
Cod	Orange roughy
Cusk	Pink snapper
Dolphinfish, or mahi-mahi	Red snapper
Flounder	Rockfish
Haddock	Sole
Halibut	Yellowfin tuna

■ Fattiest ■

(more than 5 gm fat per 3½-ounce portion)

Anchovy	Lake trout
Bluefin tuna	Mackerel
Bluefish	Pompano
Butter	Sable
Carp	Sardine
Catfish	Shad
Chinook salmon	Sock-eye salmon
Coho salmon	Swordfish
Herring	White

Poached Catfish with
Lemon-Rosemary Mignonette

Serves 4

Raised for the most part on fish farms, catfish has a firm texture and subtle flavor comparable to orange roughy, scrod, and red snapper. Serve this dish with vegetables or Wild Rice with Quinoa, Pecans, and Orange Zest (page 202).

1 pound catfish or tilapia fillets

1 teaspoon raspberry or cider
   vinegar

2 teaspoons fresh lemon juice

Salt (optional)

Freshly ground black pepper

Lemon or lime wedges, for garnish

LEMON-ROSEMARY
MIGNONETTE:

2 tablespoons raspberry or cider
   vinegar

2 tablespoons fresh lemon juice

¾ cup finely chopped fennel

3 scallions, minced

½ cup Madeira

½ teaspoon freshly chopped
   rosemary or ¼ teaspoon dried

Place the fish in a medium shallow baking dish. Drizzle with vinegar and lemon juice. Sprinkle with salt, if using, and pepper. Let it sit in the refrigerator for 30 minutes.

Meanwhile, prepare the mignonette: In a small bowl, combine the vinegar, lemon juice, fennel, scallions, Madeira, 1½ tablespoons water, and rosemary; stir and set aside.

Place the fish in a single layer in a microwave-safe dish and cover with waxed paper or plastic wrap laid loosely on top. Microwave at high for 7 to 8 minutes, rotating after 3 minutes. Or, in a large nonstick skillet, add the liquid, an immersible rack, if possible; if not, lay the fish in the liquid, cover, and over medium-low heat, heat for 10 minutes, watching to be sure the fish doesn't burn. Serve immediately with the sauce on the side.

PER SERVING: Saturated Fat: 2 gm   Total Fat: 7 gm
Cholesterol: 59 mg   Sodium: 85 mg   Calories: 172

White Fish Fillets
and Vegetable Bundles

Inside each foil-wrapped packet is delicately steamed white fish and a colorful array of tender-cooked carrots, peas, and red peppers. This is a dinnertime showpiece. For special occasions, I use parchment hearts instead of foil packets. Serve this with your favorite rice.

4 14-inch by 16-inch pieces heavy aluminum foil or 2 lengths of 32-inch-wide parchment paper, cut into 4 14-inch-tall heart-shape pieces
Vegetable oil spray
2 large carrots, julienned
1½ pounds fresh sugar snap peas or green beans
1 large red bell pepper, cut into matchstick-size strips, seeds reserved

4 scallions, thinly sliced
1 cup fat-free Tangy Honey-Mustard Dressing (page 124) plus extra to coat the fish fillets
12 ounces mild white fish, such as flounder, grouper, orange roughy, sole, or red snapper, cut into 2-inch by 5-inch strips
Salt (optional)
Freshly ground black pepper

Preheat the oven to 400°F.

Spray the foil with vegetable oil. In a large bowl, add the carrots, peas, peppers, scallions, and ¼ cup salad dressing and toss to coat. Place one fourth of the vegetables on each piece of foil (or parchment) packet, place one fourth of the fish on the vegetables, drizzle the remaining dressing over the fish. Sprinkle lightly with salt, if using, and pepper. Fold the other half of the foil over the fish. Fold the edges 2 or 3 times to seal the packets. Place on a baking sheet and bake for 15 to 20 minutes. Remove the packets, remove the contents from the foil, taking care to open the packet away from you, and place on individual serving plates. Serve hot.

PER SERVING: Saturated Fat: Trace   Total Fat: 2 gm
Cholesterol: 42 mg   Sodium: 319 mg   Calories: 187

Classic Sole Meunière

Purists say that Dover sole, imported fresh from England, is the only "real" sole. It is thicker and has a stronger flavor than sole from our waters. Regardless of which kind you are able to buy, this easy, classic rendition is pure and simple and brings out the delicate sole (or flounder) flavor.

½ to ¾ cup white wine
½ teaspoon cornstarch
2 teaspoons butter
2 8-ounce sole fillets, cut in half

2 to 3 tablespoons fresh lemon
    juice
4 tablespoons chopped parsley

In a small bowl, whisk together the white wine and cornstarch until blended. In a large nonstick skillet over medium–high heat, heat the butter until melted. Add the fillets and cook about 30 seconds per side, or until lightly browned. Add the lemon juice, wine mixture, and 2 tablespoons parsley. Cook for 3 to 4 more minutes, occasionally spooning the sauce over the fish, until the fish is opaque and the sauce thickens. Sprinkle with the remaining parsley and serve immediately.

PER SERVING: Saturated Fat: 1 gm   Total Fat: 3 gm
Cholesterol: 61 mg   Sodium: 109 mg   Calories: 137

Flounder Pecan

Lightly toasted pecans add taste, texture, and a touch of elegance to this main course. I serve this with broccoli steamed with a little orange juice in water and baked potatoes.

3 tablespoons finely chopped
   pecans
Butter-flavored spray or vegetable
   oil spray
1 pound flounder fillet or 4
   4-ounce fillets

2 tablespoons fresh lemon juice
½ teaspoon paprika
2 tablespoons chopped parsley

Preheat the broiler. In a 9-inch by 13-inch baking pan, spread the pecans and lightly spray them with oil. Place under the broiler for 2 minutes, stirring twice, until golden, making sure they don't scorch.

Lightly spray the fillets with oil and arrange in a single layer over the pecans. Pour the lemon juice over the fillets and sprinkle with paprika. Broil 3 to 4 minutes until the thickest part of the fillet is opaque. Remove the fillets to individual plates or a large serving platter and sprinkle with parsley. Serve immediately.

PER SERVING: Saturated Fat: 1 gm   Total Fat: 5 gm
Cholesterol: 56 mg   Sodium: 87 mg   Calories: 136

Halibut with Watercress Sauce

Halibut is lowest in fat of all fish. It's mild white meat tends to be somewhat drier than many, making it an excellent partner for this creamy piquant sauce. Garnish with watercress sprigs and sliced almonds.

2 cups fish stock
10 scallions, chopped
2 green bell peppers, seeded and
  chopped
2 bunches fresh watercress, stems
  removed and a few sprigs
  reserved, for garnish

4 anchovy fillets, rinsed and
  patted dry
Freshly ground white pepper
1½ cups yogurt cheese
Olive oil spray
4 4-ounce boned halibut steaks
2 tablespoons sliced almonds, for
  garnish (optional)

In a saucepan over high heat, heat the stock to boiling. Add the scallions and peppers and cook for 2 minutes. Add the watercress and cook for 30 seconds. Remove the saucepan from the heat and add the anchovies and pepper. Using an immersion, or hand, blender or a food processor, puree the mixture until smooth. Gently whisk in the yogurt and set aside.

In a nonstick skillet lightly sprayed with oil, over medium-high heat, cook the fish for 3 to 5 minutes until brown. Turn and cook for 3 to 5 minutes more until brown and opaque. To serve, ladle a pool of sauce onto individual plates and arrange the fish in the middle. Garnish with watercress sprigs and almonds and serve immediately.

PER SERVING: Saturated Fat: 0.5 gm   Total Fat: 4 gm
Cholesterol: 46 mg   Sodium: 389 mg   Calories: 278

Halibut with Sherry

Garnishes of mandarin oranges or fresh tangerines enhance this delicate and very low-fat mellow-flavored entrée. Flounder or sole, even orange roughy and monkfish, can be substituted for the halibut.

4 scallions, chopped
1 very small clove garlic, minced
*½ to 1 cup low-sodium, defatted
   fish stock*
*1½ pounds boned halibut, cut
   into 4 serving pieces*

⅓ cup nonfat sour cream
2 tablespoons cornstarch
3 tablespoons cream sherry

In a nonstick skillet over medium heat, combine half the scallions with the garlic and a few tablespoons stock or water and cook, adding more water to keep the vegetables moist, for about 4 minutes. Add the fish, several more tablespoons stock, and cook the fish for 3 minutes on each side, or until opaque. Transfer the fish to a warm platter and cover with foil to keep warm. Stir the sour cream and remaining stock into the skillet but don't boil. Meanwhile, mix the cornstarch with the sherry. Add it to the skillet and stir over medium heat (still without boiling) until the sauce thickens, about 30 seconds. (If the sauce accidentally curdles, process for 3 to 4 minutes.) Spoon over the fish and sprinkle with remaining scallions and serve immediately.

PER SERVING: Saturated Fat: 0.5 gm   Total Fat: 4 gm
Cholesterol: 59 mg   Sodium: 121 mg   Calories: 253

Healthful Fish Cookery

As with all healthful cooking techniques, avoiding the use of oil, creams, butter, etc., is key.

Baking is one of the easiest methods of cooking fish. Place the fish in a baking dish, adding liquid, such as water or wine, mushrooms, onions, carrots, or other vegetables, and cover loosely with foil. Bake in a pre-heated 350°F. oven. Baking works well for kippers, herring, cod, and other salty fish as well as the firmer fish, such as monkfish, lobster, and crab.

Broiling can dry out delicate fish, so save this method for robust rich fatty fish, such as salmon and tuna. If broiling smaller pieces, skewer them first or wrap them in foil. Lightly spray the fish with olive oil, brush with lemon juice, and place 3 inches from the heat. When broiling fillets with skin, cook the cut side first. Thinner fillets don't need to be turned.

Grilling is wonderful for large whole fish, such as baby salmon, salmon or tuna steaks, and kabobs of moist meaty fish cubes. For kabobs of scallops, swordfish, oysters, shrimp, or even pieces of tuna steak, use wooden skewers soaked in water.

Dry frying is a low-fat way of pan searing the fish for a quick cooking crisp effect. Spray a nonstick skillet or rub the fish with ½ teaspoon oil, butter, or margarine. Cook with herbs and spices, even a few teaspoons of wine or juice.

Steaming fish or shellfish in a simple vegetable steamer, fish steamer, or on any improvised rack over simmering liquid helps keep the meat of the fish or shellfish moist and juicy. Wrapping the fish in foil or leaves of cabbage, spinach, or lettuce ensures moistness and flavor. You may even lay the fish on thick beds of herbs but be sure you like those herbs.

Poaching, like steaming, can produce a very juicy piece of fish. Ideally, place the whole fish or fish pieces on a rack, but it isn't necessary, and immerse in simmering liquid and cook until fish is opaque. If poached too long, the fish, like poached chicken, will harden. After poaching, drain the fish on paper towel. Fish can be poached in wine, lemon juice and water, vegetable juice, or low-sodium chicken, fish, or vegetable stock.

Monkfish with Mustard Sauce

The tender-sweet meat of the tail of the monkfish is widely appreciated in America, southern Europe, and England. This dish takes less than 10 minutes to prepare. Other fish such as scrod, flounder, sole, and halibut can be substituted.

Olive oil spray
1 pound monkfish, cut into 4
    pieces
¼ cup nonfat sour cream

1 tablespoon nonfat milk
1½ tablespoons Dijon mustard
2 tablespoons chopped chives

In a nonstick skillet sprayed with olive oil, over medium heat, cook the fish for 3 minutes on each side and transfer to a platter. Combine the sour cream, milk, and mustard in the skillet, mix well, and cook until hot. Spoon the sauce over the fish, sprinkle with chives, and serve immediately.

PER SERVING: Saturated Fat: 0 gm   Total Fat: 2 gm
Cholesterol: 31 mg   Sodium: 176 mg   Calories: 110

Honeyed Salmon on a Bed of Herbed Zucchini

Pink fillets of salmon bedded on a mix of fresh herbs and zucchini come to the table in only 25 minutes. Substitute cayenne for paprika if you want more heat.

3 tablespoons honey
2 medium zucchini, trimmed, cut
   in half lengthwise
Salt (optional)
Freshly ground black pepper
2 teaspoons chopped fresh mint,
   plus 1 teaspoon, for garnish

2 teaspoons chopped fresh basil,
   plus 1 teaspoon, for garnish
1 tablespoon balsamic or cider
   vinegar
4 5-ounce salmon fillets, about
   1 inch thick, skin removed
Paprika

Remove the broiler pan. Preheat the broiler. Line the broiler pan with foil.

In a small microwave-safe bowl, melt the honey in the microwave at high for 10 seconds. Alternatively, in a saucepan over medium heat, heat the honey for 3 to 5 minutes.

Lightly brush the zucchini with the honey and place on the broiler pan. Sprinkle with salt, if using, and pepper, place the broiler pan 2 inches from the heat, and broil for 5 to 7 minutes until brown and bubbly. Remove the zucchini to a cutting board. When cool enough to handle, cut into very thin slices crosswise. In a medium bowl, combine the zucchini, mint, basil, and vinegar and toss. Cover to keep warm.

Place the salmon fillets on the same baking sheet and lightly brush with honey. Sprinkle with salt, if using, pepper, and paprika and broil for 5 to 6 minutes until golden brown. Turn the fillets over, brush with honey, sprinkle with salt, if using, and pepper and broil for 5 minutes until brown and firm to the touch.

To serve, place a bed of zucchini on individual plates and top with a fillet. Garnish with mint and basil and serve immediately.

PER SERVING: Saturated Fat: 1 gm   Total Fat: 10 gm
Cholesterol: 82 mg   Sodium: 68 mg   Calories: 274

Orange Roughy St. Tropez

This entrée, replete with the fragrance of thyme, is vibrant with the colors and flavors of the Mediterranean. Orange roughy is a firm and mild white fish available in some supermarkets and in specialty markets. Snapper, halibut, scrod, sea bass, and grouper are appropriate here, too.

Olive oil spray
4 4-ounce orange roughy fillets,
    ½ inch thick
1 small crookneck or yellow
    squash, cut into ½-inch cubes
1 small zucchini, cut into ½-inch
    cubes
1 red bell pepper, cut into ½-inch
    cubes, seeds reserved
1 small eggplant, cut into ½-inch
    cubes

2 teaspoons chopped fresh thyme
    or 1 teaspoon dried
2 to 4 tablespoons fresh lemon
    juice
2 tablespoons chopped almonds
Salt (optional)
Freshly ground black pepper
4 sprigs parsley, for garnish
1 lemon, sliced into wedges, for
    garnish

In a large nonstick skillet lightly sprayed with oil, over medium–high heat, heat the oil until hot. Add the fillets, lightly spray them with oil, and cook for about 4 to 5 minutes per side, until brown. Transfer the fillets to a plate and cover with foil to keep warm.

In the same skillet, combine the squash, zucchini, pepper, and eggplant. Lightly spray with oil and cook, stirring, for 6 to 8 minutes until the vegetables are cooked through but crisp. Add the thyme and stir. Gently return the fish to the pan and cook for 2 minutes, or until the fish is heated through. Remove the fish to a warm serving platter or individual plates and surround with the vegetables. Drizzle the lemon juice over the fish and sprinkle with almonds. Sprinkle with salt, if using, and pepper and seeds, garnish with parsley and lemon wedges.

PER SERVING: Saturated Fat: Trace   Total Fat: 3 gm
     Cholesterol: 25 mg   Sodium: 84 mg   Calories: 158

Glazed Grilled Salmon Fillets

These tender fillets are coated in a dazzling honey glaze finish. Serve with a colorful assortment of grilled red peppers, yellow squash, and zucchini.

Vegetable oil spray or 1 teaspoon canola oil	3 tablespoons low-sodium soy sauce
4 4-ounce center cut salmon fillets, skin removed	⅓ cup honey
3 cloves garlic, minced	3 tablespoons fresh lime juice
	Lime wedges, for garnish

Preheat a covered gas grill or start a charcoal fire. When the coals are glowing red, spray the grill rack with oil and set it about 3 inches from the heat.

Place the salmon fillets in a shallow dish. In a small bowl, mix the garlic, soy sauce, honey, and lime juice, and pour over the salmon. Place a large piece of plastic wrap directly on the salmon, and marinate, unrefrigerated, for 15 minutes. Turn the salmon once or twice.

Transfer the salmon to the grill and cook for 5 to 6 minutes, basting with the marinade. Turn the salmon over and grill for 5 to 6 minutes, basting again. Serve immediately with lime wedges.

NOTE: The fish can also be broiled by placing the salmon fillets on a foil-lined broiling pan sprayed lightly with oil, 3 inches from the heat, and broiling 5 to 6 minutes per side.

PER SERVING: Saturated Fat: 1 gm   Total Fat: 8 gm
Cholesterol: 65 mg   Sodium: 503 mg   Calories: 265

Poached Salmon Steaks

You don't have to run out and buy a fancy fish poacher to make this dish successfully. Any large nonstick skillet will do. Garnish with parsley sprigs, lemon slices, or a few shakes of paprika.

1 cup white wine
¼ cup fresh lemon or lime juice
2 teaspoons Dijon mustard
½ cup finely chopped onion or
   shallots

4 4-ounce salmon steaks, less than
   1 inch thick
2 teaspoons capers
1½ tablespoons cornstarch
   (optional)

In a large nonstick skillet, big enough for the 4 steaks, combine the wine, lemon juice, mustard, and onion and bring to boiling. Reduce the heat to low and simmer for 10 minutes, until reduced. Add the steaks to the skillet, cover, and simmer gently for 3 to 4 minutes. Turn the steaks over and cook for 4 to 5 minutes, until opaque. Add the capers and stir. For a thicker sauce, whisk the cornstarch and ¼ cup water together in a small bowl until blended. Add to the skillet and stir until sauce thickens. Serve immediately.

PER SERVING: Saturated Fat: 1 gm   Total Fat: 8 gm
Cholesterol: 65 mg   Sodium: 130 mg   Calories: 222

Grilled Salmon

This succulent whole fish marinates for several hours before being grilled. The marinade is so versatile that you can make double the recipe and use it to marinate vegetables before grilling. Any sweet or spicy rice dish and a large green salad make good accompaniments.

MARINADE:
½ cup low-sodium soy sauce
1 tablespoon sugar
2 teaspoons freshly grated ginger
2 teaspoons fresh lemon juice
1 clove garlic, minced
2 tablespoons sake or sherry

Whole salmon, 3 to 8 pounds,
   cleaned, scaled, head and tail
   removed

Salt (optional)
1 lemon, sliced
1 small onion, sliced
1 cup chopped parsley
4 feet aluminum foil
Lime slices, for garnish

In a small bowl, whisk together the soy sauce, sugar, ginger, lemon juice, garlic, and sherry and pour into a large baking dish. Add the fish and turn until well coated. Cover and refrigerate, for 6 hours, turning often.

Preheat the grill. Place the fish on one half of the foil. Sprinkle inside and out with salt, if using, tuck the lemon and onion in the cavity, then sprinkle with parsley. Fold the other half of the foil loosely over the fish. Grill for 25 to 40 minutes, depending on the size of the fish. Turn once and check after 20 minutes for doneness. Garnish with slices of lime and serve hot.

PER SERVING: Saturated Fat: 1 gm   Total Fat: 8 gm
Cholesterol: 70 mg   Sodium: 360 mg   Calories: 197

Grilled Tuna with White Beans and Artichoke Hearts

Tender-moist tuna is prepared in the classic French style with plenty of savory flavors and garden fresh ingredients. Buy albacore, yellowfin, or bluefin tuna for best results.

4 4-ounce tuna steaks, 1-inch
   thick
1 lemon, seeded and quartered
Salt (optional)
Freshly ground black pepper
Olive oil spray
1 small onion, diced
2 cloves garlic, minced
1 small yellow pepper, seeded and
   diced
2 medium plum tomatoes, diced

1 16-ounce jar marinated
   artichoke hearts, 1 tablespoon
   oil reserved, drained and
   coarsely chopped
1 15-ounce can cannellini beans,
   drained and rinsed
½ cup finely diced tomatoes,
   for garnish
Lime wedges, for garnish
4 green sprigs watercress,
   for garnish

Preheat the grill. Place the tuna in a shallow baking dish and squeeze the juice from the lemon on each steak. Sprinkle with salt, if using, and pepper on both sides, cover, and set aside.

In a medium nonstick skillet lightly sprayed with oil, over medium-high heat, cook the onion, spraying again with oil, for 4 minutes. Add several teaspoons water and cook, stirring and adding more water if necessary. Add the garlic and pepper and cook for 2 more minutes, until the pepper begins to soften. Add the tomatoes, artichoke hearts, reserved oil, and the beans and cook for 3 minutes until mixture is hot. Remove from heat and add salt, if using, and pepper to taste. Cover loosely to keep warm.

Place the tuna on a medium-hot grill and cook 4 to 5 minutes per side, until nearly opaque. Place equal portions of the bean sauce on individual plates, and arrange the tuna steak on top. Garnish with a spoonful of diced tomatoes, lime wedges, and a sprig of watercress.

NOTE: The fish can also be broiled by placing the tuna steaks in a broiling pan 2 inches from the heat. Broil until nearly opaque, about 3 to 4 minutes per side.

■■ PER SERVING: Saturated Fat: 2 gm   Total Fat: 12 gm ■■
Cholesterol: 45 mg   Sodium: 590 mg   Calories: 356

Tuna Steaks with Orange Soy Sauce and Red Grapes

■■ *Serves 4* ■■

These tuna steaks are cooked quickly, with grapes and fresh grape juice and an orange soy sauce for a refreshing taste and a handsome, spritely presentation. This dish takes about 10 minutes.

1 pound (40 to 50) red seedless
  grapes
1 teaspoon olive oil
1 tablespoon fresh orange juice
1 tablespoon fresh lemon juice

2 tablespoons white wine
4 4-ounce tuna steaks, ½ inch
  thick
1 to 2 cups orange soy sauce

Cut the grapes in half and place half of them in a nonstick skillet. With a flat utensil, mash the grapes in the skillet until ½ cup juice releases from them. Remove the grapes and discard. Place the skillet over medium-high heat and add the olive oil, juices, and wine. Add the tuna steaks, cooking until opaque, about 2 to 3 minutes per side; remove to a serving platter and keep warm. In a medium saucepan, heat the remaining grapes and the orange soy sauce to boiling. Pour the sauce over the fish or serve it on the side.

■■ PER SERVING: Saturated Fat: 2 gm   Total Fat: 7 gm ■■
Cholesterol: 45 mg   Sodium: 56 mg   Calories: 229

Campfire Trout

Crispy on the outside, tender and mild on the inside, these delicate fillets are quick to prepare and taste delicious on their own or with many varieties of sauces. Buy the fillets rather than dealing with the tedious tiny bones.

2 large cloves garlic, minced
1¼ cups fresh multigrain bread
   crumbs
2 tablespoons finely chopped
   almonds
1 egg white, lightly beaten
2 tablespoons fresh lemon juice

1 tablespoon water
4 4-ounce trout fillets
Salt (optional)
Freshly ground black pepper
Vegetable oil spray dusted with
   flour (Baker's Joy)
Lemon wedges, for garnish

On a large plate, mix the garlic, bread crumbs, and almonds.

In a medium baking pan, combine the egg white, lemon juice, and water and mix well. Place the fillets in the pan, turn to coat, and add salt, if using, and pepper.

Coat both sides of each fillet with the crumb mixture, pressing the crumbs gently onto the fish. Spray each fillet lightly with the vegetable coating dusted with flour. In a large nonstick skillet over medium-high heat, cook the trout 3 to 4 minutes per side. If the crumbs become brown very quickly, reduce the heat to medium. Serve immediately with lemon wedges or Creamy Horseradish-Cucumber Sauce (page 290).

PER SERVING: Saturated Fat: 1 gm   Total Fat: 7 gm
Cholesterol: 95 mg   Sodium: 152 mg   Calories: 189

Trout Almandine

Trout almandine is a classic method of preparation that has been enjoyed for hundreds of years throughout Europe. I like to use unpeeled almonds sliced wafer thin in this dish because the color of the almond skin adds not only visual appeal but also extra flavor. Other mild white fish, such as turbot, sole, and monkfish, can be substituted for the trout.

1 teaspoon margarine or butter
4 4-ounce trout fillets
3 tablespoons fresh lemon juice

SAUCE:
½ cup white wine
½ cup low-sodium, defatted
  chicken stock

1 tablespoon plus 1 teaspoon
  cornstarch
1 tablespoon currant jelly
¼ cup thinly sliced almonds,
  toasted
1 tablespoon chopped parsley

In a large nonstick skillet over medium–high heat, heat the margarine until bubbling. Add the trout and the lemon juice and cook 1 to 2 minutes per side. Place the trout on a warmed platter and cover with foil to keep them warm while making the sauce.

To the same skillet, add the wine and stock and whisk in the cornstarch and jelly. Turn up the heat to medium, heat, and continue to whisk for 2 to 4 minutes, or until thickened. Return the trout to the pan and heat for 1 minute until warmed through. Arrange trout on a serving platter, spoon the sauce over the trout, and sprinkle with the almonds and parsley.

PER SERVING: Saturated Fat: 2 gm   Total Fat: 8 gm
Cholesterol: 93 mg   Sodium: 83 mg   Calories: 208

Shrimp with Pistachios
and Pita Bread

Redolent of orange and red peppers, this is a hearty meal in itself. Don't be dismayed by the long list of ingredients or the somewhat tricky timing of the preparations. This is simple to put together and is ready for the table in only 25 minutes.

2 6-inch pitas

Olive or vegetable oil spray

½ teaspoon Cajun spice mix

½ pound linguine

6 asparagus spears

½ red bell pepper, cut in strips,
   seeds reserved

½ yellow or orange bell pepper or
   1 banana pepper, cut in strips,
   seeds reserved

8 large shrimp, peeled and
   deveined

1 teaspoon minced seeded jalapeño

¾ cup dry vermouth (optional)

¾ tablespoon cornstarch

2 tablespoons frozen orange juice
   concentrate

½ cup evaporated skimmed milk
   or nonfat liquid creamer

2 scallions, thinly sliced on the
   diagonal

2 tablespoons chopped basil

2 tablespoons unsalted shelled
   green pistachios, coarsely
   chopped

Preheat the oven to 300°F.

Cut the pita into 4 wedges and place them on a baking sheet. Lightly spray with oil, sprinkle lightly with Cajun spice, and bake for 15 minutes.

In an extra-large pot of boiling water, cook the linguine for 7 minutes. Meanwhile, set a curved-bottom fine mesh sieve, colander, or vegetable steamer on top of the pot. Place the asparagus, peppers, and seeds in the steamer and steam the vegetables as the pasta cooks for 5 minutes. Remove the vegetables to a warmed shallow dish, cover with foil, and keep warm. Drain the linguine.

Lightly spray a medium skillet with oil and place over high heat until hot. Add the shrimp, spray lightly with oil, and cook for 2 to 3 minutes, until it is just pink. Remove the shrimp to a plate, cover with foil, and keep warm. Reduce the heat to medium high and add the jalapeño. Spray lightly with oil and cook, stirring (adding a teaspoon water if necessary to keep moist), and cook for 1 to 2 minutes.

In a small bowl, whisk together the vermouth, cornstarch, orange juice concentrate, and milk. Add the mixture to the skillet and cook, whisking constantly, for 1 minute. Reduce the heat and simmer for 3 minutes until thickened. Stir in the scallions and the basil and cook, stirring, for 1 minute. Add the shrimp and cook for 1 minute until warmed through.

Divide the pasta among individual dinner plates, and twirl with a fork to form nests. Tuck the steamed peppers into the nests. Spoon the shrimp and sauce over the pasta. Sprinkle with pistachios. Lay the asparagus alongside the nests and the pita bread and serve hot.

PER SERVING: Saturated Fat: 1 gm   Total Fat: 8 gm
Cholesterol: 157 mg   Sodium: 735 mg   Calories: 564

Barbecued Sea Scallops
and Southern-Style Grits

This dish combines the soft texture of scallops with grits for an interesting mixture. Buy sea scallops no more than one day in advance and keep them refrigerated. They should be pale and glistening.

Vegetable oil spray
1 14-ounce can low-sodium
   defatted chicken stock
¾ cup uncooked white or yellow
   grits (or polenta)
Salt (optional)
3 tablespoons grated nonfat
   Parmesan cheese

12 ounces sea scallops, blotted dry
   with paper towel
¼ cup thick lite barbecue sauce,
   1 tablespoon reserved
1 teaspoon fresh lime juice

Position an oven rack 2 inches below the heating unit.

Preheat the oven to 500°F.

Spray a baking sheet with vegetable oil and set aside.

Place 2½ cups stock and the grits in a 1½-quart nonstick saucepan, combine stock with 1⅝ cups water, salt, if using, and stir to mix over medium-high heat for 3 to 4 minutes. Lower the heat, cover, and cook for about 20 minutes, stirring every 5 minutes, until thick and creamy. Add more water if grits become too thick. Stir in the Parmesan cheese, cover, and keep warm.

Place the scallops about 2 inches apart on a baking sheet. Brush all but 1 tablespoon of the barbecue sauce on top of the scallops and bake 5 to 7 minutes, or until firm to the touch. Spoon a generous dollop of the grits on individual plates, and top with the scallops. Brush with the reserved 1 tablespoon barbecue sauce and sprinkle with lime juice.

PER SERVING: Saturated Fat: 0.5 gm   Total Fat: 3 gm
Cholesterol: 37 mg   Sodium: 560 mg   Calories: 256

POULTRY

The chicken is at least five thousand years old—its wild ancestors originated in the jungles of Southeast Asia. By 2000 B.C., the bird had been domesticated throughout much of India, not so much for its meat but for its eggs. In fact, it might have been taboo to eat the meat. By the time the Romans ruled their massive empire, the bird was commonplace at their feasts. The Romans enjoyed chicken prepared in many ways, including roasted in wine. After the fall of the empire, the chicken continued to thrive, primarily as a farm animal and egg producer.

During the same stretch of centuries, the turkey (which almost made our national bird) was flying wild in Central and North Americas. It was eventually domesticated by the Aztec around 3000 B.C. Around A.D. 1530, the Spanish explorers brought the turkey back to Europe where the big bird was quickly domesticated.

Before World War II, there was no mass marketing of chickens, and a chicken dinner was a rare treat, unless you had your own chicken shed. One of President Herbert Hoover's campaign promises in 1927 was "On every Sunday, a chicken in every pot." It might have won him the election, but the chicken promise was more like a dream destined to wait twenty years to come true.

The dream did come true when, in 1945, America started hopping with one of the many new postwar small business crazes—chicken ranches and hatcheries. By 1950, chicken was readily available in butcher shops and grocery stores.

Turkey may be America's special occasion bird, but chicken, whether it's stewed, fried, fricasseed, grilled, pouched, barbecued, roasted, or simmered to become soup, has become the number-one preferred dinner meat. And it's no wonder: Chicken is versatile, delicious hot or cold; can be dressed up or down; lends itself to any style of cooking—southern, Asian, Middle Eastern, or French. It can also be—if correctly prepared—an ideal centerpiece for a low-fat meal.

■ Chicken Basics ■

BUYING There is hardly a plain chicken out there anymore. There are tenders, nuggets, fillets, cutlets, half chickens, parts, and whole chickens if you're interested. The whole ones come free range, organic, kosher, or old-fashioned fryers, broilers, and stewers.

Buy as fresh as possible whatever poultry is best suited for your recipe. A 3½-pound chicken will serve three to four people. Try to keep each serving size to one portion, or one chicken part such as one leg, one defatted thigh, or one (half) breast. Chicken, even defatted, can be very fat.

For tasty, tender chicken, buy with the skin, fat, and bones intact, instead of buying the more expensive skinless and deboned breasts and thighs. The reason for this is that even though it appears to be wrapped tightly in plastic, that clear packaging is actually porous, which allows air to dry the chicken. A layer of fat and skin will do what it's intended to do—protect the chicken from drying and losing flavor. If you remove the skin and fat just before you prepare the chicken, you will enjoy a less expensive yet very moist and flavorful chicken.

FAT AND CHOLESTEROL The cholesterol content of chicken is less important than the saturated fat content, because it is primarily the saturated fat that raises blood cholesterol. The good news is that chicken contains about the same amount of cholesterol (75 milligrams in 3½ ounces) as does salmon or swordfish. The bad news is that nearly all chickens raised in America contain far too much saturated fat. A mass-produced 3-pound chicken can exude more than 1 cup of saturated fat when roasted.

Free-range chickens have far less fat, but organic are just as fatty. Only when chicken (including organic) is defatted and skinned before it is cooked and eaten does it come close to the saturated fat content of salmon, lean beef, or lean pork. To enjoy chicken on a healthful eating plan, you must remove the fat before cooking and I remove the skin then, too. Here are some tips on how to do so:

Ask your meat cutter to skin the chicken (it costs nothing). At home, use scissors, knives, and paper towel to remove the rest of the fat.

To remove the skin and fat yourself from a whole chicken:

Cut the fatty little tail off and cut the wing ends off to the second joint. Pull out all visible clumps of fat.

At the opening of the large cavity, slip your hand under the breast skin, lift, and pull up toward the neck end, using paper towel if you have to, to get a good grip.

Pull the skin up and over the neck end, wings, and legs. Use kitchen shears and a small knife to cut the fat off the edges of the thigh, back, and breast.

▪▪ Turkey Basics ▪▪

BUYING For everyday eating the fresh turkey tenderloins and fillets (bought with skins that are removed before cooking) are the best choice. With careful cooking, they remain tender and moist.

For special occasions, commercial, organic, free-range, and kosher birds are available frozen or fresh killed. I prefer fresh-killed free-range turkey for a moist bird without added fat but they must almost be steamed. That is, oven baked in a bag or tightly crimped foil. The fresh-killed wild turkeys available in fancy food markets have an intense flavor and are exceptionally low in fat.

Ground turkey is not always a good choice as many companies grind the fat as well as the muscle meat producing a mix that is very fatty. Look for brands that advertise 97 percent or 98 percent fat free. For true fat-free ground turkey, buy a fresh turkey breast and have the meat cutter remove the skin and fat and grind it for you. Or take it home and grind it yourself in a food processor.

FAT AND CHOLESTEROL Most commercially raised turkey contains too much fat. The fat is slightly less saturated in turkey than in chicken, which is why it is often recommended. If one could remove the skin as with chicken, it would help cut down more on fat, but turkey dries out excessively without the protection of the fatty skin during roasting. To make matters worse, many whole turkeys are pumped full of whopping amounts of fat, some highly saturated coconut oils and those can't be removed. Turkey fillets can cook up easily and are tender.

Duck, Game Hens, and Quail Basics

FAT AND CHOLESTEROL The wild duck that comes home in the hunter's sack is almost free of all fat. Commercially raised duck, on the other hand, has a tremendous amount of fat. However, most of the duck fat is directly under the skin and can be removed in much the same way as you remove the fat and skin from chicken. It is a much tougher pull, however, so you may want the meat cutter to do it for you.

The small Rock Cornish game hen is a hybrid of white Plymouth Rock and Cornish chickens. They weigh up to 2½ pounds when they are ready for eating. They, too, are high in fat, but can be defatted as easily as chicken.

Wild quail is a tiny bird that is almost fat free, but farm-raised quail is fat. The meat is moist and delicately flavored. These can be baked, grilled, dry fried (panfried with a spritz of olive oil), and roasted.

COOKING POULTRY Be sure there is no pink or bloody meat. All poultry can be put back in the oven or microwave for continued cooking. Be aware that microwave ovens differ in cooking speed depending upon size and power of the machine. We've given a range based on extensive testing, but your food may need slightly less or more time.

Health and Safety

All poultry is extremely perishable and in handling it, be sure to take precautions against the spread of bacteria by not cross-contaminating the cutting board, knives, or basting brushes. Any item, including your hands, that have touched raw poultry need to be washed before touching any other food. Salmonella should be imagined to be on every bird. Salmonella can't be washed off a chicken but must be cooked out, so be sure poultry is never eaten pink.

Refrigerate the poultry as soon after purchase as possible. Make sure it and all its juices are contained. Don't allow it to drip onto other foods in the refrigerator. Use it within one or two days after purchase. If it smells bad when you open the package, discard it and inform the meat manager.

If the bird is frozen, defrost it in the refrigerator, never at room temperature, in order to ensure the least stress on the tender meat.

Wash your hands after handling poultry.

Wash the chicken well and, afterward, wash the sink, colander, and anything the wash water might have touched.

Really pay attention, any surface—platter, countertop, utensils, knives—that touched raw poultry should be washed thoroughly with hot water and soap. Keep a separate glass, wood, or plastic cutting board just for poultry and scrub it with hot water and soap. Put plastic and glass boards in the dishwasher.

Cook poultry using a thermometer for roasting—160°F. is safe. If the meat near the bone is still red or pink, cook it some more.

Refrigerate cooked poultry even if it's still hot or warm; don't let it sit at room temperature more than an hour or two. You may also freeze leftovers.

Beth Mendelson's
Chicken Fricassee

■■ *Serves 6* ■■

From my dear friend Beth, who has a knack for making great meals and great friendships seem effortless. After simmering, the chicken is so flavorful and tender, it nearly falls from the bone. Serve with rice or couscous and a steamed green vegetable or two.

2 large onions, coarsely chopped
8 cloves garlic, minced
½ pound mushrooms, sliced
2 carrots, sliced ½ inch thick
1 cup low-sodium, defatted
*   chicken stock*
2 tablespoons orange juice
*   concentrate*

2 teaspoons fresh lemon juice
2½-pound chicken, skinned,
*   defatted, and cut up and wing*
*   tips and tail removed*
½ teaspoon dried tarragon
Salt (optional)
½ cup plain nonfat yogurt

In a large nonstick skillet in ¼ cup water over medium-high heat, cook the onions, garlic, mushrooms, and carrots for 5 minutes, stirring occasionally. Add the stock, orange juice concentrate, lemon juice, chicken, tarragon, and salt, if using. Reduce the heat, cover, and simmer about 40 minutes, until the chicken is very tender. Garnish with a tablespoon of yogurt and serve hot.

■■ PER SERVING: Saturated Fat: 2 gm Total Fat: 7 gm ■■
Cholesterol: 90 mg Sodium: 114 mg Calories: 249

Roast Chicken with Rosemary and Thyme

This incredibly simple dish tastes so good, takes so little time, and looks so enticing that I use it in television demonstrations, in my cooking classes, and whenever I want a quick meal for myself or friends. You must use an oven bag to ensure a juicy outcome. The fresh herbs are aromatic and the spice mixture gives the bird a speckly look while adding incredible flavor.

2½-pound chicken, skinned,
  defatted, and wing tips and tail
  removed
2 tablespoons spice mixture, such
  as Mrs. Dash, Spike, or other
  colorful herb or spice mixture

2 sprigs fresh rosemary
1 sprig fresh thyme

Sprinkle the chicken inside and out with the spice mixture. Place the rosemary and thyme inside the chicken. Place the chicken in an oven bag, tie, and, using a knife, cut a slit into the top. Place the bag in a microwave-safe casserole and cook at high for 12 to 16 minutes (or bake in a preheated 350°F. oven for 25 minutes), turning once after 7 minutes carefully. If any part of the chicken is pink, return (covered) to the microwave oven for 4 or 5 minutes, or the oven for 10 minutes. Remove the chicken from the bag, discard the herbs, and serve hot.

PER SERVING: Saturated Fat: 2 gm   Total Fat: 6 gm
Cholesterol: 90 mg   Sodium: 83 mg   Calories: 179

Indonesian-Style Chicken
in a Parcel

■■   *Serves 6*   ■■

Inspired by a fiery recipe of Madhur Jaffrey's, a renowned cook and cookbook writer of Indonesian, Malasian, and East Indian cuisine and a guest on my TV show, this dish makes the assembling of a few unusual ingredients well worth the effort. Plum sauce and lemon grass are available in Asian markets. Although banana leaves make the dish authentic, you may use foil for baking without sacrificing flavor (I once asked a maître d' to give me the banana leaves from a fancy buffet table and he did. The next day I fixed this chicken: Serve the chicken whole with fresh vegetables, steamed rice, and Mango Salsa (page 283). Serve hot, slice at the table, and pass the sauce.

MARINADE:

3 tablespoons fresh lime juice
2 tablespoons dark brown sugar
½ teaspoon salt (optional)
½ teaspoon ground turmeric
⅛ teaspoon ground (cayenne) red
   pepper

2½-pound chicken, skinned,
   defatted, and wing tips and tail
   removed
2 tablespoons sliced or chopped
   lemon grass
½ teaspoon crushed red pepper
1 red bell pepper, seeded and
   quartered
4 shallots
1 1-inch piece fresh ginger, peeled
   and halved
3 cloves garlic

2 tablespoons fresh lime juice
6 honey-roasted cashews

STUFFING:

1 cup (3 ounces) packaged poultry
   stuffing or herbed bread crumbs
1 onion, chopped
½ cup raisins
1 large ripe banana, diced

WRAPPING:

4 large banana leaves or several
   sheets of aluminum foil cut into
   2-foot lengths
1 large oven baking bag

SAUCE:

Defatted chicken drippings
2 tablespoons cornstarch
1 cup orange juice
2 tablespoons fresh lime juice
¼ cup plum sauce

In a large bowl or gallon-size sealable plastic bag, mix the lime juice, sugar, salt, if using, turmeric, and cayenne.

Cut two deep slits lengthwise in each chicken breast, thigh, and leg. Place the chicken in the bowl or bag and rub the marinade into the slits and over the entire surface of the chicken. Marinate for 1 hour in the refrigerator, turning the bird once or twice.

Preheat the oven to 350°F.

In a measuring cup or bowl, combine the lemon grass, crushed red pepper, and about ¼ cup water and let stand for 30 minutes. In a food processor, combine the red pepper, shallots, ginger, garlic, lime juice, and cashews and process until the mixture becomes a paste. Add the lemon grass mixture and its soaking liquid, and process again until smooth.

In a nonstick skillet over medium-high heat, cook the red pepper mixture, stirring, for 15 minutes, adding spoonfuls of water as necessary to thin, so it is the consistency of cooked, moist oatmeal.

In a large bowl, combine the poultry stuffing, onion, raisins, banana, and stir in enough water to make the mixture moist but not runny. Stir in the red pepper mixture and mix lightly but thoroughly.

Place the chicken on the banana leaves or large sheets of foil. Pack the stuffing into the chicken cavity firmly. Wrap the chicken in the leaves and tie the leaves around the chicken with clean heavy string or wrap in foil; place in an oven bag, tie the end of the bag, and vent the top with a knife by making a slit or two. Slit the bottom of the bag on both ends so that juices can drip out. Place the chicken on a rack in a roasting pan in an ovenproof glass or metal roasting pan so that cooking fats will drip down. Bake for 1 hour or microwave in an ovenproof bag placed in a microwave-safe bowl (no leaves or foil) for 20 minutes, turning after 10 minutes.

Carefully pour off the juices and reserve. Remove the chicken to a platter; remove the string; and trim the leaves with a scissors so they don't extend beyond the edge of the platter. If using foil, remove completely. (You can tuck other fresh leaves, even flowers, under the bird if you used foil.)

Defat the reserved drippings in a defatting cup. In a small bowl, whisk together the cornstarch and orange juice. In a small saucepan over high heat, cook the defatted drippings, cornstarch mixture, lime juice, and plum sauce, whisking constantly, until thickened. Pour into a gravy boat.

PER SERVING (with 3 ounces stuffing):   Saturated Fat: 2 gm
Total Fat: 8 gm   Cholesterol: 90 mg   Sodium: 457 mg
Calories: 383

Baked "Fried" Chicken

The secret to this crispy, tender, and moist chicken is to use homemade bread crumbs rather than the store-bought variety. Toast the bread if you are out of day-old or dry bread.

6 to 8 slices toasted bread, or
    enough to make 1½ cups finely
    ground bread crumbs
½ cup loosely packed parsley
    leaves
2 tablespoons freshly grated nonfat
    Parmesan cheese
½ teaspoon thyme
½ teaspoon marjoram

½ teaspoon salt (optional)
¼ teaspoon freshly ground black
    pepper
2 egg whites
¼ cup nonfat milk
1 large garlic clove, minced
2½-pound chicken, skinned,
    defatted, and cut up, wing tips
    and tail removed

Preheat the oven to 350°F.

Line a 9-inch by 13-inch roasting pan with foil.

In a food processor, process half the bread slices to make bread crumbs; remove to a shallow bowl or pie plate. Repeat with the remaining bread.

In the same food processor, finely chop the parsley. To the bread crumbs, add the parsley, Parmesan cheese, thyme, marjoram, salt, if using, and pepper, and stir to mix well.

In a shallow bowl, whisk the egg whites, milk, and garlic until frothy. Dip the chicken into the egg mixture, then roll in the crumbs, coating each piece well. Arrange chicken pieces in the prepared roasting pan and bake for 35 to 45 minutes, or until the chicken is tender and cooked through. Serve hot or cold.

PER SERVING: Saturated Fat: 2 gm   Total Fat: 7 gm
Cholesterol: 91 mg   Sodium: 205 mg   Calories: 230

Szechwan Sweet and Sour Chicken

It looks complicated, but this colorful dish takes just 20 minutes to prepare. It can be made with cooked leftover chicken as well as fresh, but do not substitute fresh for canned pineapple as the sauce will not thicken properly.

Vegetable oil spray
2½-pound chicken, skinned, defatted, and cut into 6 pieces, wing tips and tail removed
½ teaspoon cayenne pepper
¼ teaspoon five-spice powder
1 large onion, coarsely chopped
2 cloves garlic, minced
6 large mushrooms, sliced ¼-inch thick
1 green bell pepper, seeded and cut into 1-inch pieces
½ red bell pepper, seeded and cut into 1-inch pieces
½ yellow bell pepper, seeded and cut into 1-inch pieces
2 carrots, diagonally sliced ¼-inch thick
1 tablespoon grated fresh ginger

2 to 4 tablespoons low-sodium soy sauce
⅔ cup low-sodium, defatted chicken stock
½ cup (4 ounces) canned (not fresh) pineapple chunks, drained and juice reserved
1 8-ounce can sliced water chestnuts, drained

SAUCE:
½ cup low-sodium, defatted chicken stock
2 teaspoons cider vinegar
2 teaspoons brown sugar
2 tablespoons cornstarch
½ cup chopped scallions, for garnish
½ teaspoon toasted sesame seeds, for garnish

In a large nonstick skillet lightly sprayed with vegetable oil, over medium-high heat, cook the chicken 4 minutes or until brown. Add the cayenne and five-spice powder, and turn the chicken several times. Remove to a plate and keep warm.

Into the same skillet, add the onion, garlic, mushrooms, bell peppers, carrots, ginger, soy sauce, and 2 tablespoons stock. Reduce the heat to medium and cook, stirring and adding remaining stock if necessary, for about 12 to 15 minutes until vegetables are tender. Add the chicken to the vegetable mixture; stir in the pineapple and water chestnuts, cover, and cook over medium-low heat for 15 minutes.

In a small bowl, whisk together the reserved pineapple juice, stock, vinegar, sugar, and the cornstarch. Tip the pan till the liquid puddles and add the cornstarch mixture to the pooled liquid. Cook and stir for about 30 seconds, until the sauce thickens, lowering the pan and mixing the sauce throughout. Remove chicken to a serving platter and spoon on the sauce and vegetables. Sprinkle with scallions and sesame seeds and serve immediately.

PER SERVING: Saturated Fat: 2 gm   Total Fat: 7 gm
Cholesterol: 90 mg   Sodium: 303 mg   Calories: 281

Caribbean Rum Chicken with Pineapple

Serves 6

This spirited tropical dish is hot, sweet and so good that it is worth the extra effort of gathering this long list of ingredients. Serve it with Saffron Rice (page 200).

2½-pound chicken, skinned,
    defatted, and cut up, wing tips
    and tail removed
Salt (optional)
Freshly ground black pepper
1 onion, chopped
½ cup lime juice plus ¼ cup fresh
    lime juice
Olive oil spray
¾ cup golden or dark raisins
½ teaspoon Tabasco
1 tablespoon honey

¼ cup dark rum
2 tomatoes, finely chopped
6 scallions, chopped
½ teaspoon salt (optional)
2 tablespoons cornstarch
2 tablespoons low-sodium soy
    sauce
1½ cups cubed fresh or canned
    pineapple
2 scallions, chopped, for garnish
1 orange, thinly sliced, for garnish
1 lime, thinly sliced, for garnish

Rub the chicken with salt, if using, and pepper. In a gallon-size sealable plastic bag, combine the onion and ½ cup lime juice; add the chicken and marinate in the refrigerator for at least 1 hour or overnight.

Spray a large nonstick skillet with olive oil and set over medium-high heat until hot. Add the chicken pieces, the marinade, and cook until brown (which occurs quickly when there is no skin and the pan is very hot). Spoon the marinade over the chicken pieces and reduce the heat to low. Cover and simmer for 10 minutes, turning often.

Stir the raisins, Tabasco, honey, rum, tomatoes, scallions, and ¼ cup lime juice and salt, if using, into the skillet. Cover and cook for another 10 to 15 minutes, or until done. In a small bowl, whisk together the cornstarch and soy sauce. Remove the chicken to a warm platter and cover to keep warm. Increase the heat to high, and stir the cornstarch mixture into the liquid, whisking or stirring until it thickens. Reduce the heat and stir in the pineapple and cook until warmed through, about 2 minutes. Pour the sauce over the chicken, garnish with scallions, orange slices, and slices of lime, and serve immediately.

PER SERVING: Saturated Fat: 2 gm   Total Fat: 7 gm

Cholesterol: 89 mg   Sodium: 295 mg   Calories: 342

Chicken Taco Stack

This layered variation on the old taco theme makes a perfect meal for your spicy-food-loving friends or family. Baked flour tortillas rather than the customary fried corn shells make this a low-fat dish. Make Salsa Cruda (page 279) or use your favorite brand. You may want to sprinkle the sliced avocado with lemon or lime just (on all surfaces) to keep it fresh looking.

4 6-inch flour tortillas
6 ounces skinned and boned
   chicken breasts
1 teaspoon ground cumin
Salt (optional)
Vegetable oil spray
2 large scallions, thinly sliced
2 medium fresh tomatoes, thinly
   sliced

1 cup shredded nonfat or low-fat
   sharp Cheddar cheese
½ avocado, thinly sliced
1½ to 2 cups homemade or jarred
   salsa
1 cup nonfat sour cream
¼ cup pitted black olives, sliced

Preheat the oven to 375°F.

Wrap the tortillas in foil and place in the oven to warm for 10 minutes.

Meanwhile, sprinkle the chicken with cumin and salt, if using. Lightly spray a medium nonstick skillet with vegetable oil and place over medium-high heat. Add the chicken and cook about 3 minutes per side until golden and firm but not dry. Remove and slice into ¼-inch by 1½-inch pieces.

To assemble the taco, place 1 warm flour tortilla on a baking sheet. Top with one third of the sliced chicken, one third of the scallions, one third of the sliced tomato, and one fourth of the cheese. Repeat with 2 more layers and top with a flour tortilla. Sprinkle the top with the remaining cheese. Cover the stack loosely enough with aluminum foil to allow the top cheese to melt. Bake for 15 to 20 minutes.

To serve, arrange the avocado slices on top of the taco in a fan design. Slice the taco into 4 wedges and serve with salsa, sour cream, and olives on the side.

PER SERVING: Saturated Fat: 1 gm   Total Fat: 9 gm
Cholesterol: 32 mg   Sodium: 598 mg   Calories: 333

Lime-Grilled Chicken with Mango-Basil Salsa

This is easy grilled fare replete with fragrant mango, orange, basil, and lime. You may substitute boneless and skinless turkey, duck, or lean pork fillets for the chicken. Mangoes are available year-round in most supermarkets, but the bottled, found in the refrigerated section, are excellent.

2 tablespoons frozen orange juice
2 tablespoons frozen limeade
Salt (optional)
Freshly ground black pepper
4 4-ounce skinned and boned,
  chicken breasts or defatted
  thighs

MANGO-BASIL SALSA:
2 ripe mangoes, peeled, pitted,
  and diced

½ red bell pepper, diced, seeds
  reserved
½ cup fresh orange juice
Juice of 2 limes
¼ cup finely chopped basil
Salt (optional)
Freshly ground black pepper
Vegetable oil spray or 1 teaspoon
  canola oil

In a nonreactive baking dish or medium sealable plastic bag, combine the orange juice, limeade, salt, if using, and pepper. Add the chicken, cover or seal, and marinate for 2 hours in the refrigerator.

In a medium bowl or medium sealable plastic bag, combine the mangoes, bell pepper, orange juice, lime juice, basil, salt, if using, and pepper. Cover or seal and refrigerate for 2 hours.

Preheat the grill. Spray or brush the rack with oil and place about 3 inches from the heat. Grill the chicken about 7 minutes per side until brown and firm to the touch. Spoon the salsa on top and serve.

PER SERVING: Saturated Fat: 1 gm   Total Fat: 4 gm
Cholesterol: 84 mg   Sodium: 77 mg   Calories: 284

Mango-Sauced Chicken Breast

Serves 4

This tangy entrée comes together in just a few minutes. Mango is the star ingredient here, papaya and lemon, apricots, or pineapple can be substituted. The bottled version, found in the refrigerator section, will do fine if you can't find fresh mango. Couscous or rice makes an excellent side dish.

4 4-ounce skinned and boned
  chicken breasts
⅓ cup all-purpose flour
1 teaspoon curry powder
Salt (optional)
1 teaspoon cumin
Vegetable oil spray

MANGO SAUCE:

1 cup mango or apricot nectar
1 to 2 tablespoons fresh lime juice
2 teaspoons cornstarch
1 tablespoon low-sodium soy sauce
1 teaspoon freshly grated ginger
1 ripe mango peeled, pitted, and
  diced (or 1 cup diced bottled
  mango)

Place the chicken breasts between 2 sheets of plastic wrap and lightly pound with the flat side of a mallet or heavy skillet, until ½ inch thick. In a sealable plastic bag or on a large plate, combine the flour, curry powder, salt, if using, and cumin until well blended.

Lightly spray a large nonstick skillet with oil and set over medium heat. Dredge the chicken in the flour mixture until well coated and arrange in the skillet; cook for about 6 minutes per side, or until golden and the chicken is cooked. Remove to a platter and cover with foil to keep warm.

In a medium saucepan, combine the mango nectar, lime juice, and cornstarch. Whisk in the soy sauce, ginger, and mango, stirring for 3 minutes until thick.)

Place the chicken on individual serving plates and top with the sauce.

PER SERVING: Saturated Fat: 1 gm   Total Fat: 4 gm
    Cholesterol: 84 mg   Sodium: 227 mg   Calories: 284

Pecan-Crusted Turkey Fillets
with Pear-Cranberry Relish

Pecans work particularly well with turkey, chicken, duck, and pork, and here they add rich taste and texture to the delicate fillet. This thin cut of breast meat requires very little cooking; be careful as overcooking will produce rubbery turkey.

Vegetable oil spray

½ cup Tangy Honey-Mustard Dressing (page 124) plus 2 tablespoons reserved

1½ cups corn-bread stuffing mix, finely crushed

⅓ cup finely chopped pecans

4 4-ounce turkey fillets or cutlets

PEAR-CRANBERRY RELISH:

1 cup whole-berry cranberry sauce

1 large ripe Bosc pear, peeled, cored, and diced

1 scallion, finely chopped

2 teaspoons freshly grated ginger

2 tablespoons Tangy Honey-Mustard Dressing (page 124)

Preheat the oven to 450°F.

Lightly spray a baking pan with oil.

Pour ½ cup of the honey-mustard dressing on a large plate. On another large plate, mix together the stuffing and pecans.

Place the fillets between 2 sheets of plastic wrap and lightly pound with the flat side of a mallet or a heavy skillet until ¼ inch thick. Dip the turkey into the honey-mustard dressing to coat thoroughly. Then dredge the turkey in the corn-bread-pecan mixture until well coated, pressing crumbs gently to adhere. Place the turkey fillets on the baking sheet, and bake for 8 to 10 minutes, turning once after 4 or 5 minutes.

In a small bowl, mix together the cranberry sauce, pear, scallion, ginger, and 2 tablespoons of the honey-mustard dressing. Pour into a serving bowl and serve with the turkey.

PER SERVING: Saturated Fat: 2 gm   Total Fat: 11 gm
Cholesterol: 57 mg   Sodium: 647 mg   Calories: 486

Turkey Shanghai

This is a quick stir-fry meal. The turkey and vegetables are cooked over very high heat with very little fat. Make sure all the ingredients are cut the same size for even cooking. Ramen noodles are fast-cooking curly noodles found in nearly all food markets and in the Asian or ethnic section. You can add a Thai spice, cayenne, or Tabasco for heat.

GLAZE:
1 cup orange juice
3 tablespoons low-sodium soy
   sauce
2 teaspoons cornstarch

Vegetable oil spray
16 ounces skinned and boned
   turkey breast, cut into ½-inch-
   thick strips
2 carrots, shredded

1 red bell pepper, seeded and
   thinly sliced
8 ounces string beans, trimmed
   and cut on the diagonal into
   2-inch lengths
2 cloves garlic, minced
1 teaspoon fresh minced ginger
⅓ cup finely sliced scallions
8 ounces (2 packages) cooked
   noodles

In a small bowl, combine the orange juice and soy sauce, and whisk in the cornstarch until the cornstarch dissolves.

Lightly spray a large nonstick skillet or wok with oil and place over high heat until hot. Add the turkey strips and stir-fry 3 to 4 minutes, or until lightly browned. Add a few teaspoons water if the turkey is browning too quickly. Remove to a plate and cover to keep warm.

Lightly spray the same skillet with oil and set over high heat. Add the carrots, bell pepper, and string beans, and stir-fry for 3 to 4 minutes. Add the garlic, ginger, and scallions, and stir-fry for an additional 2 minutes, adding water if necessary to keep the vegetables steaming. Stir in the orange juice mixture. Add the turkey to the skillet or wok and stir about 1 minute, until heated through and the glaze has thickened. Serve over individual portions of cooked noodles.

PER SERVING: Saturated Fat: 1 gm   Total Fat: 4 gm
Cholesterol: 93 mg   Sodium: 1867 mg   Calories: 358

Turkey Fillets with Capers, Raisins, and Pine Nuts

Full of piquant flavors and contrasting textures, this dish is also so easy to prepare that it may become your signature dish. If you don't have Baker's Joy, spray with vegetable oil and dust with all-purpose flour.

4 4-ounce turkey fillets or cutlets	1 tablespoon cornstarch
Salt (optional)	½ cup golden or dark raisins
Freshly ground black pepper	2 teaspoons capers
Baker's Joy spray	⅓ cup low-sodium, toasted pine
½ cup dry white wine	nuts, for garnish
⅔ cup low-sodium, defatted	Lemon wedges, for garnish
chicken stock or water	

Place the fillets between 2 sheets of plastic wrap and lightly pound with the flat side of a mallet or a heavy skillet until ¼ inch thick. Sprinkle with salt, if using, and pepper.

Place a large nonstick skillet over medium–high heat. Lightly spray each side of the turkey with Baker's Joy. Cook for 1 to 2 minutes until brown on each side. Remove the turkey fillets to a platter and cover to keep warm.

In a small bowl, combine the wine and stock and whisk in the cornstarch until the cornstarch dissolves. Into the same skillet over medium–high heat, add the raisins, capers, and cornstarch mixture and cook until slightly thickened; whisking continuously. Reduce the heat to medium, and add the turkey; cook for 1 minute until heated through. Spoon the sauce over the turkey and serve, garnished with toasted pine nuts and lemon wedges.

PER SERVING: Saturated Fat: 2 gm   Total Fat: 9 gm
Cholesterol: 57 mg   Sodium: 67 mg   Calories: 279

Treasure-Filled Turkey
Burgers in Pita Pockets

■■ *Serves 2* ■■

These are no ordinary turkey burgers. There is a flavor treasure hidden at the center of each one. You may bury your own treasure as well, substituting precooked mushrooms and onions, or ½ teaspoon grated string cheese, and canned whole cranberries, or just a teaspoon of chopped onions and corn or carrots, or a small cube of feta.

8 ounces ground turkey breast	*1 tablespoon finely minced onion*
4 teaspoons grated nonfat	*1 teaspoon honey mustard*
Parmesan cheese	*3 to 4 drops Tabasco*
1 teaspoon chopped capers	*2 pitas cut in half*

Divide the turkey into four equal parts and round each into a patty. On two of the patties, sprinkle 1 teaspoon each Parmesan cheese.

In a small bowl, mix together the capers, onion, honey mustard, and Tabasco. Spoon half of the mixture on top of the Parmesan cheese, being careful to keep it near the center of the burger. Place the remaining patties on top of the filled patties, pressing them firmly together around the edges to enclose the filling. Burgers may be cooked on a stove-top grill, seared or dry-fried in a hot, heavy skillet, lightly sprayed with oil, broiled or grilled over charcoal (all should be well done). For broiling or grilling indoors or out, allow at least 8 minutes for well-done burgers.

■■ PER SERVING: Saturated Fat: 1 gm Total Fat: 3 gm ■■
Cholesterol: 57 mg Sodium: 462 mg Calories: 314

Circassian Cornish Game Hens

Circassia is a region in the northern Caucasus of what was formerly Russia where poultry cooked with onions, carrots, garlic, and, occasionally walnuts, is common. This aromatic showpiece is perfect for a country-style cold buffet, special occasion, or a romantic dinner for 2 (just halve the recipe) of cold chicken, potato salad, and fruit. It can be made the day ahead and it can be served hot with rice, pasta, or potatoes.

1 yellow onion, thinly sliced
1 carrot, thinly sliced
1 leafy rib celery, thinly sliced
2 cloves garlic, minced
2 bay leaves
5 whole black peppercorns
3 whole cloves
½ teaspoon salt (optional)
2 12- to 14-ounce Cornish game
   hens, skinned, defatted, and
   split in half

1 cup toasted walnuts
2 slices hard or dry white bread,
   torn into ½-inch pieces
½ teaspoon paprika, for garnish
Lemon wedges, for garnish
Sprigs of watercress or parsley, for
   garnish

In a large nonstick Dutch oven, over high heat combine the onion, carrot, celery, and garlic. Place the bay leaves, peppercorns, and cloves in a cheesecloth sack, add salt, if using, and 2 cups water and bring to boiling. Add the hens and just enough water to cover; reduce the heat to low, cover, and simmer for 15 minutes, skimming frequently to remove foam. Remove the hens and set aside to cool. Remove the bay leaves, peppercorns, and cloves from the broth and discard. Defat the broth, and bring to a boil; reduce the heat to medium, and cook for about 10 to 15 minutes.

In the food processor, finely chop the walnuts. Add the bread and process for 10 seconds. Gradually, add the broth and vegetables from the skillet and process until the sauce becomes light in color and is the consistency of thick gravy.

(continued)

Cut and pull the meat from the bones and cut into bite-size chunks. Cover the bottom of a serving platter with the meat pieces and top with the walnut sauce. Cover with plastic wrap or aluminum foil and refrigerate for about 1 hour or longer. Garnish with paprika, lemon wedges, and sprigs of watercress or parsley and serve cold or hot.

■■ PER SERVING: Saturated Fat: 4 gm   Total Fat: 25 gm   ■■
Cholesterol: 74 mg   Sodium: 364 mg   Calories: 418

■■

Roast Quail with Grapes

■■   *Serves 4*   ■■

These tiny birds can be for special occasions such as a wedding or holiday. The recipe can easily be halved, doubled, tripled, or served at a banquet for fifty or more. The birds, all placed together on a decorated platter, look festive and enticing. The recipe is deceptively simple. Quail may be skewered and roasted on a spit, grilled, or, as in this recipe, baked. Allow two birds per person if domestic, four if wild. It isn't usually necessary to skin wild quail, but most quail marketed today through specialty food shops have been raised on game bird farms and can be fat, making skinning and defatting a must.

2½ cups green seedless grapes, chopped
½ onion, coarsely chopped
½ leafy rib celery, chopped
½ apple, cored and coarsely chopped
1 cup herbed bread crumbs
8 quail, tails discarded

GLAZE:
1 tablespoon Worcestershire
Juice of 1 orange
1 teaspoon canola oil

SAUCE:
1 cup Madeira
3 shallots, minced
½ pound fresh mushrooms, finely chopped
2 tablespoons cornstarch
1 cup orange juice
1 teaspoon fresh lemon juice
1 teaspoon sugar

Preheat the oven to 400°F.

In a small bowl, combine ½ cup grapes, onion, celery, apple, and bread crumbs and stuff each quail with the mixture until very tightly packed, filling falling out. In the same bowl, mix together the Worcestershire, orange juice, and oil and rub the birds with the glaze.

Place the quail in a deep baking dish, pouring any remaining glaze over the birds. Reduce the heat to 325°F. and roast for 20 to 25 minutes.

Meanwhile, in a large nonstick skillet over medium-high heat, heat the wine. Add the shallots and mushrooms and cook, stirring, for about 10 minutes, or until tender. Add the remaining grapes and cook until heated through. In a small bowl, whisk together the cornstarch, orange juice, lemon juice, and sugar. Add to the skillet and cook over medium heat, whisking continuously, for about 30 seconds, or until the sauce is thick.

Remove the quail to a serving platter and pour some of the sauce over the top. Serve with the remaining sauce passed in a sauce boat.

■■   PER SERVING: Saturated Fat: 3 gm   Total Fat: 11 gm   ■■
Cholesterol: 129 mg   Sodium: 850 mg   Calories: 564

Duck with Berry Sauce

This dish is perfect for a special occasion or holiday dinner. Chicken breasts, turkey fillets, and lean pork can be substituted for the duck.

4 4-ounce skinned and boned
   duck breasts
½ teaspoon salt (optional)
Freshly ground black pepper
Vegetable oil spray
1 small onion, chopped
2 leafy ribs celery, diced
1 cup cranberry juice
¼ cup Madeira or sweet sherry
   (optional)

2 tablespoons fresh lemon juice
2 teaspoons lemon zest
1 tablespoon cornstarch
2 cups fresh blueberries or
   raspberries, 2 tablespoons
   reserved, for garnish
⅛ teaspoon cinnamon
Sprigs of parsley, for garnish

Sprinkle the duck breasts with salt, if using, and pepper. Spray a large nonstick skillet with oil and place over medium-high heat until hot. Arrange the duck in the center and the onion and celery around the sides. Sear the duck for 2 to 3 minutes on each side while stir-frying the vegetables. Add the cranberry juice and Madeira and reduce the heat to medium low; cover and simmer for 5 minutes, or until the duck is cooked. With a slotted spoon, remove the duck to a platter and cover to keep warm. With an immersion, or hand, blender, puree the onion and celery, continuing to cook the sauce.

In a small bowl, whisk together the lemon juice, lemon zest, and cornstarch. Add mixture to the skillet and cook, whisking constantly, until thickened. Add all but the 2 tablespoons blueberries and the cinnamon to the skillet and cook for 1 to 2 minutes. Add the duck and cook about 1 minute until heated through.

Remove the duck from the skillet, place on a carving board, and cut diagonally across the grain into ⅛-inch-thick slices. Fan each breast on a platter or individual serving plates and spoon the sauce on top. Garnish with remaining berries and parsley and serve hot.

PER SERVING: Saturated Fat: 1 gm   Total Fat: 3 gm
Cholesterol: 69 mg   Sodium: 81 mg   Calories: 242

MEAT

M an's earliest ancestors were hunter-gatherers who lived on a
fairly steady diet of grains, nuts, and vegetables accompanied
only occasionally by animal meat.

During the Middle Ages, after a variety of animals—cows, pigs, sheep—
had been domesticated, meat became central to the European diet. That
tendency reversed, so that by the nineteenth century in Europe meat
accounted for no more than 10 to 20 percent of total foods consumed.

Americans have always had an overabundance of meat. From the time
the Pilgrims arrived, wild game and livestock have been plentiful. But it
was not until the 1800s, when cattle production was a thriving business,
that meat became central to the American diet. In fact, meat consumption
between 1830 and 1840 reached an all-time high of about 178 pounds
per person each year. As phenomenal as that figure seems, it was actually
matched in the 1960s. Since 1980, however, when meat consumption
dropped to 150 pounds per person per year, meat has been pushed to the
side of the plate, replaced by grains, vegetables, fish, and poultry.

Most people want meat in their diets, but in a healthful way. Any meat
cut can be used. With fatty cuts, make into stock and defat. Lean cuts or
ground meat can be fashioned into traditional Filet Mignon au Poivre
(page 262), Beef Stroganoff (page 261), Old-fashioned Meat Loaf (page
266), and Hamburgers (page 265) to Beef Marengo on Toasted French
Bread (page 264) and Stuffed Flank Steak Kirov (page 263). These recipes
will keep the meat you want low fat and high in taste.

Separating the Fat from the Lean

When selecting meat, let your eyes guide you. If the meat is marbled with visible fat, then it's loaded with fat. If it has a consistent texture of even-colored meat, then it is probably lean. The meats given below include chicken and turkey.

▪ The Leanest Meats ▪

(less than 5 gm fat per 3½-ounce portion)

Buffalo
Chicken breast, defatted
Deer/venison
Ham, 3 percent fat
Hot dogs, 3 percent fat

Pork tenderlion, trimmed
Top round, trimmed
Turkey breast, defatted
Veal leg, trimmed

▪ The Moderately Lean Meats ▪

(5½ to 10 gm fat per 3½-ounce portion)

Beef tenderloin, visibly
  lean
Canadian bacon
Filet mignon, visibly lean
  and trimmed
Ham, lean
Hamburger, 10 percent
  fat
Leg of lamb, lean

Pork chops, visibly lean
  and trimmed
Pork roast, lean
Rabbit
Turkey with skin
Veal chops, visibly lean
  and trimmed
Veal roast, lean

▪ The Moderately Fat Meats ▪

(10½ to 15 gm fat per 3½-ounce portion)

Chicken with skin
Pork chops
Pork rast

Veal roast
Turkey with
  skin

■■ The Exceptionally Fat Meats ■■

(15½ to 25 gm fat per 3½-ounce portion)

Baby beef ribs   Lamb roast
Chicken or turkey   Pork chops
    sausage   Veal cutlet
Hamburger, 20 percent
    fat

■■ The Fattiest Meats ■■

(more than 25½ gm fat per 3½-ounce portion)

Bacon   Hot dogs, regular
Beef brisket   Pork ribs
Beef short ribs   Salt pork
Hamburger, regular   Sausage

■■ Meat Basics ■■

Red meat, if trimmed and lean, can be low in saturated fat. Make sure the meat you choose is lean, the serving size no more than 3½ ounces cooked, you eat it only occasionally, and you balance it with lots of vegetables, fruit, and grains.

BUYING When buying beef, lamb, or pork, purchase lean cuts with the least amount of visible fat. The cuts that are generally (depending on the animal) the leanest are: flank steak (which also delivers the best flavor for the money), leg roast, round steak, round tip, rump roast, skirt steak, tenderloin, top loin, top round, top sirloin, ham (defatted), pork tender-loin, and Canadian bacon.

Trim any visible fat before cooking.

One secret to enhancing meat flavor is to cook it either a very long time, which caramelizes it and deepens the taste, or cook it a very short time to seal in flavor.

Marinating meat for several hours imparts different flavors and can tenderize the meat. Dry rubs, mixtures of ground spices and herbs, rubbed in just before cooking, add pungency and flavor without giving the meat a grainy or pebbly surface as some marinades can do.

When buying packaged hamburger, don't rely on the word "lean" on the label. Buy only meat that is between 93 percent and 97 percent fat free. Better yet, pick out a lean top round and ask the meat cutter to trim it and grind it for you. Be very clear you want *all* fat removed or they will leave some, mistakenly believing fat is essential. If you're making hamburgers with the ground meat, add back a tablespoon of the lower saturated fat canola oil and bread crumbs to each pound so the meat holds together.

When buying processed meats, such as bologna, sausage, salami, and hot dogs, buy only those that are 97 percent fat free or more.

FAT AND CHOLESTEROL Many health-conscious people have switched to eating more poultry and less red meat because they feel it has less cholesterol and saturated fat than red meat. The difference in the amount of cholesterol and saturated fat between 3½ ounces of skinned, defatted chicken and the same amount of lean beef is only slight. Both contain about 80 to 85 milligrams of cholesterol. Lean lamb contains only slightly more; 3½ ounces of lean, trimmed beef or pork contain 1½ to 2 grams saturated fat as compared to 1 gram saturated fat in the same amount of lean and skinned chicken.

COOKING Even with a lean cut of meat, cook it thoroughly (not rare) to a tender and flavorful finish as well as cooking out any fat. The best methods for this are boiling, broiling, grilling, dry frying in a ridged pan and roasting on a spit or in the oven. The fat must drip down and away from the meat during cooking.

For meat loaf, which is usually very high in fat because it is hamburger cooked in its juices, use a double-inset pan with holes in the inner pan. The fat will drip out of the loaf and into the second pan during cooking. If you don't have a double-inset pan, place marbles or pebbles in the bottom of a loaf pan and then line the bottom and sides of the inner pan with two layers of heavy-duty foil. Poke holes in the bottom layer of foil. Fill the pan with the meat-loaf mixture and bake as usual.

For panfrying, use a pan with ridges on the bottom and lightly spray to eliminate sticking.

Stir-frying is an excellent method as long as you cook the meat quickly in liquid other than copious amounts of oil, such as low-sodium soy sauce, wine, juice, fat-free stock, a light vegetable spray, or even water.

Beef Stroganoff

Count Paul Stroganoff, the nineteenth-century Russian diplomat for whom this dish was named, would smile with approval of this stroganoff. Use the leanest beef tenderloin you can find. Serving stroganoff over rice is traditional, but I prefer noodles, such as linguine or pappardelle.

1 large onion, cut into ½-inch slices
2 cloves garlic, minced
12 ounces mushrooms, thickly sliced
¾ pound lean beef tenderloin, trimmed of fat and cut into ½-inch by 2-inch strips
Salt (optional)

3 tablespoons flour
1 cup low-sodium, defatted beef stock
1 cup nonfat sour cream
12 ounces nonegg noodles or nonegg linguine, cooked
Freshly ground black pepper
Chopped parsley, for garnish
Chopped chives, for garnish

In a large nonstick skillet in ¼ inch water, over medium heat, steam the onion, garlic, and mushrooms, stirring often, for about 4 minutes until they are partially cooked (adding more water if needed). Drain the vegetables and return them to the skillet. Stir in the beef and salt, if using, and cook over medium–high heat for 2 or 3 minutes, stirring occasionally.

In a small bowl, whisk together the flour and stock until smooth. Reduce the heat to medium, stir the stock mixture into the meat mixture and cook, stirring, about 3 minutes until thickened. Reduce the heat to low, add the sour cream and cook, stirring, until warmed through. Spoon the meat over the cooked pasta, and sprinkle with pepper, parsley, and chives. Serve immediately.

PER SERVING: Saturated Fat: 3 gm   Total Fat: 8 gm
Cholesterol: 57 mg   Sodium: 111 mg   Calories: 460

Filet Mignon au Poivre

This elegant dish is perfect for company or, when you divide the recipe in half, a romantic dinner for two. Serve it with potatoes, green vegetables, salad, and a fruit tart for a spectacular repast.

½ cup whole green or black peppercorns (black for a stronger flavor)

1 teaspoon salt (optional)

1 tablespoon canola oil

1 scant tablespoon melted butter or margarine

1 teaspoon Worcestershire

2 tablespoons brandy or cognac (optional)

Butter-flavored or vegetable oil spray

4 3½-ounce lean filets mignons

½ cup chopped parsley, for garnish

Place the peppercorns in a heavy plastic bag. With a rolling pin or the bottom of a heavy skillet, coarsely crush the peppercorns. Add the salt, if using, to the crushed pepper, then firmly press both sides of the meat into the pepper until both sides are covered with pepper.

In a small bowl, combine the oil, butter, Worcestershire, and brandy and set aside. In a large nonstick skillet lightly sprayed with oil, over high heat, brown the filets on both sides. Reduce the heat to medium high and cook about 5 minutes on each side, until medium or medium well in the center (check with a knife). Remove the meat to a warmed platter, cover with foil to keep warm.

To the same skillet, add the brandy mixture, and cook for 1 to 2 minutes, deglazing the pan with a spatula. Pour the sauce onto individual plates and top with a filet. Sprinkle with parsley and serve immediately.

PER SERVING: Saturated Fat: 4 gm   Total Fat: 13 gm   Cholesterol: 79 mg   Sodium: 81 mg   Calories: 230

Stuffed Flank Steak Kirov

A flavorful country-style Russian dish of meat and cabbage, this steak is rolled with fresh cabbage and spices, then baked and sliced. A food processor can chop the cabbage. Use strong white kitchen string for securing the roll. The roll does not close. Oftentime you'll have more veggies than meat——just add to top: Don't worry if the veggies overflow.

½ cup all-purpose flour
1½ pounds flank steak, all visible
    fat removed and pounded flat
Vegetable oil spray
½ cup Dijon mustard
1 cup thinly sliced carrots
¼ cup chopped low-sodium dill
    pickles

1 small red or white cabbage,
    finely chopped
½ red bell pepper, chopped
1 large onion, finely chopped
½ cup chopped parsley
2 teaspoons fresh thyme
½ teaspoon dried oregano
½ cup red wine (optional)

Preheat the oven to 350°F.

Rub the flour on both sides of the steak. In a large nonstick skillet lightly sprayed with oil, over medium-high heat, brown the steak on both sides. The meat will shrink during cooking, and as it shrinks, remove it from the skillet and pound it flat, then return it to the skillet to cook until brown.

On a counter, place 3 1-foot lengths of string, side by side, about 1 inch apart, and place the browned meat across the string. Spread the meat with mustard, then spread evenly with the carrots, pickles, cabbage, bell pepper, onion, parsley, thyme, and oregano. Roll the meat gently and tie the string around the roll to hold it in place. Place the roll in a deep nonstick baking dish and pour the wine into the dish. Cover the pan with foil and bake for 45 minutes. Remove the roll carefully from the pan and cut into 1½-inch slices. Remove the string and serve immediately, spooning the vegetables that have fallen out of the roll over the top.

PER SERVING: Saturated Fat: 3 gm   Total Fat: 9 gm
Cholesterol: 46 mg   Sodium: 462 mg   Calories: 232

Beef Marengo on Toasted French Bread

After his victory at the Battle of Marengo, Napoleon requested (and got) this dish. Since then, tradition dictates that chicken or veal be used in authentic Marengo, but a lean cut of beef works equally well. Seared gently and simmered with fresh vegetables, it is usually served heaped on crusty French bread, but try it with rice or pasta if you like. This is nearly a meal.

2 tablespoons all-purpose flour

7 ounces beef round, cut in
½-inch cubes

Olive oil spray

8 ounces mushrooms

1 pound pearl onions, fresh,
jarred, or frozen, cut in half if
larger than a marble

1 28-ounce can low-sodium plum
tomatoes, coarsely chopped,
liquid reserved

2 tablespoons low-sodium tomato
paste

¼ cup red wine

1½ teaspoons finely crumbled
rosemary

¾ teaspoon tarragon

Salt (optional)

Freshly ground black pepper

1 baguette

12 asparagus spears or green
beans, steamed

Preheat the broiler.

On a large plate, spread the flour and toss the meat in it until lightly coated. Lightly spray a large nonstick saucepan with oil and set over medium-high heat until hot. Add the meat and sear for 5 minutes; cook until evenly browned. Add the mushrooms, onions, plum tomatoes and their juice. Meanwhile, in a small bowl, whisk together the tomato paste, wine, and herbs and add to the pan. Bring to a gentle boil and reduce the heat to low, cover, and simmer for 15 minutes, stirring occasionally.

Slice the baguette on the diagonal into ½-inch-thick ovals. Lightly spray the bread with oil on both sides and place on the broiler pan under the broiler until golden brown, and turn to brown on the other side. Remove from the oven and set aside.

Add salt, if using, and pepper to the skillet just before done. Divide the asparagus among individual dinner plates, and arrange 1 or 2 slices of toast on top of the asparagus, and top with the Marengo.

■■ PER WHOLE MEAL: Saturated Fat: 1 gm   Total Fat: 4 gm ■■
Cholesterol: 33 mg   Sodium: 680 mg   Calories: 353

Hamburgers with Fixin's
■■ *Serves 6* ■■

The savory ingredients combined with the meat make these burgers scrumptious. To guarantee that the lean meat cooks up to the familiar firm and juicy texture of all-American hamburgers, I remove the saturated fat from the ground round and add oil that is low in saturated fat so that the meat holds together. You can also add soy extenders such as Harvest Direct.

¾ pound lean top round, trimmed
of all visible fat and ground
2 tablespoons canola oil
1 small onion, chopped
2 leafy ribs celery, chopped
2 tablespoons herbed bread crumbs

1 teaspoon Worcestershire
4 hamburger buns
4 slices tomato
4 slices onion
4 tablespoons nonfat mayonnaise

Preheat the grill or broiler.

Prepare a charcoal grill or preheat the gas grill. Alternatively, turn on the broiler. In a large bowl, mix together the meat, oil, onion, celery, bread crumbs, and Worcestershire and form into 4 patties. Place them on the grill or in the broiler and cook for 7 to 8 minutes per side, until the desired doneness. Serve on a bun and pass the tomato, onion, and mayonnaise.

■■ PER SERVING: Saturated Fat: 1 gm   Total Fat: 9 gm ■■
Cholesterol: 38 mg   Sodium: 466 mg   Calories: 277

Old-fashioned Meat Loaf

This basic meat loaf will please the most discerning meat-loaf lover. I offer a variation here, too, with layers of vegetables in the center of the loaf. Whichever you make, be sure to use the low-fat cooking method for meat loaf (page 260).

1 pound very lean top round or London broil, trimmed of all visible fat and coarsely ground

½ cup Harvest Direct TCP or other soy product granules (optional)

3 tablespoons bread crumbs

1 egg white

1 large onion, chopped

2 leafy ribs celery, chopped

1 teaspoon Worcestershire

½ teaspoon vinegar (optional)

Freshly ground black pepper

¾ cup low-sodium tomato sauce

OPTIONAL LAYERS
FOR VARIATION:

9 carrots, julienned and steamed

½ yellow, red, or green bell pepper, julienned and steamed

1 cup chopped pitted black olives

6 hard-cooked egg whites, cut into slivers

½ pound chopped spinach, parboiled and well drained

Preheat the oven to 375°F.

In a large bowl, mix together the ground round, bread crumbs, egg white, onion, celery, Worcestershire, vinegar, and pepper. Fill a loaf pan with the mixture and spoon the tomato sauce over the top.

If making the variation, press 1 inch of the meat mixture evenly in the bottom of the loaf pan. Layer each of the vegetables on top and cover with remaining meat mixture. Spoon the tomato sauce over the top. Bake for 1 hour. Slice and serve immediately, or refrigerate and serve chilled.

PER SERVING: Saturated Fat: 0.5 gm Total Fat: 2 gm
Cholesterol: 38 mg Sodium: 60 mg Calories: 96

Grilled Lamb
with Eggplant Salad

Succulent grilled lamb and eggplant make an age-old winning taste combination. If you wish, make the salad in advance by baking the vegetables in the oven rather than cooking them on the grill.

To serve, slice the lamb ¼ inch thick and fan out the slices, placing a dollop of eggplant salad on the top.

MARINADE:

1 cup dry red wine

3 tablespoons low-sodium soy
   sauce

3 tablespoons Worcestershire

6 cloves garlic, minced

Salt (optional)

Freshly ground black pepper

2 pounds lean lamb shoulder,
   boned and all visible fat
   removed

EGGPLANT SALAD:

Olive oil spray

1 medium eggplant, cut in ½-inch
   lengthwise slices

1 large onion, cut in ½-inch slices

4 medium plum tomatoes, diced

¼ cup chopped fresh basil

2 cloves garlic, minced

1 tablespoon balsamic or cider
   vinegar

1 tablespoon chopped fresh mint

Several basil or mint leaves, for
   garnish

In a 1-gallon sealable plastic bag, combine the wine, soy sauce, Worcestershire, garlic, salt, if using, and pepper. Add the lamb and gently shake until well coated. Place the bag in a shallow baking dish and marinate in the refrigerator for at least 2 hours but no more than 4.

Preheat the grill. Lightly spray the eggplant and onion with oil, and grill until lightly browned on all sides. When cool enough to handle, chop the eggplant and onion into bite-size pieces. In a medium bowl, stir together the eggplant mixture, tomatoes, basil, garlic, vinegar, and mint; set aside.

Before heating, lightly spray the grill with oil and grill the lamb for about 5 minutes per side until brown. Move the lamb to the edge of the grill, away from the coals, and cover the grill (or tent the lamb with foil) and cook 15 to 20 minutes more, turning once, or until lamb is cooked to medium well. Let the lamb rest 5 minutes before slicing thinly. Garnish with fresh basil or mint leaves and serve hot or cold with the eggplant salad.

NOTE: This recipe can also be broiled. Lightly spray a broiler grill rack and place over a flat baking sheet. Place the lamb on the rack and broil 2 inches from the heat unit for 15 to 20 minutes, turning every 5 minutes.

PER SERVING: Saturated Fat: 2 gm   Total Fat: 6 gm
Cholesterol: 65 mg   Sodium: 140 mg   Calories: 176

Skewered Lamb and Ratatouille

Serves 4

This is a quick and simple rendition of a classic French ratatouille. Lamb is the perfect meaty compliment to these fresh garden vegetables. The wilted spinach doused with the basting sauce adds savory contrast.

BASTING SAUCE:

6 tablespoons balsamic or cider
   vinegar
4 cloves garlic, finely minced
4 teaspoons finely chopped fresh
   rosemary or 1 teaspoon dried,
   crumbled
Salt (optional)
Freshly ground black pepper

SKEWERS:

½ pound lean lamb, cubed
8 cherry tomatoes, or 2 medium
   tomatoes, cut into 1-inch pieces

2 small zucchini, coarsely chopped
1 medium eggplant, coarsely
   chopped
8 small red bliss potatoes (not
   larger than 2 inches in
   diameter) scrubbed and
   microwaved for about 2 minutes
   to soften, or boiled 15 minutes
   in a 350°F. oven
Olive oil or vegetable oil spray
1 pound fresh spinach

In a medium bowl, mix together the vinegar, garlic, rosemary, salt, if using, and pepper. Pour half the mixture into a small baking dish or medium sealable plastic bag. Add the lamb, tossing to coat well, and marinate in the refrigerator for 1 hour. Reserve the remaining marinade.

Prepare a grill or preheat the broiler. On eight skewers, alternate threading the lamb, tomatoes, zucchini, eggplant, and potatoes, and spray lightly with olive oil. Brush all but 1 tablespoon of the sauce on the skewered lamb and vegetables. Place the skewers on the grill, or under the broiler, 2 inches from the heat unit, and cook for about 10 to 15 minutes, turning to brown evenly.

Meanwhile, prepare the spinach. In a large nonstick saucepan over medium heat, heat 1 or 2 tablespoons of water, add the spinach, cover, and cook, just until the spinach has begun to wilt. Remove from the heat, add the reserved 1 tablespoon basting sauce, and toss. Remove the spinach to individual serving plates and arrange the skewers over the spinach.

PER SERVING: Saturated Fat: 1 gm   Total Fat: 5 gm
Cholesterol: 40 mg   Sodium: 135 mg   Calories: 240

Lamb Couscous with Tomatoes

This Moroccan specialty is a meal in itself. A flavorful mix of vegetables, spices, and lamb sits atop the couscous, tiny granules of semolina flour. Although it is a grain, couscous cooks in minutes and is a type of pasta; rice can be substituted for the couscous. Find it in most supermarkets or in Middle Eastern markets. Although lamb makes the dish authentic, you may substitute 3 ounces of cooked chicken or turkey.

2 cups couscous, cooked according to package directions, or rice	LAMB:
1 cup water or low-sodium, defatted chicken stock	Olive oil spray
	½ pound very lean lamb, diced
1 onion, coarsely chopped	½ teaspoon Worcestershire
3 cloves garlic, minced	½ teaspoon garlic powder
1 carrot, diced	½ cup currants or raisins
1½ cups shredded cabbage	½ cup garbanzo beans (chickpeas), drained
¼ teaspoon freshly ground black pepper	½ teaspoon ground turmeric
Pinch cayenne pepper or Cajun spice	1 teaspoon freshly grated ginger
	3 tablespoons chopped parsley
Large pinch powdered saffron	4 medium tomatoes, parboiled, skins and stems removed, and cut into 1½-inch cubes
	2 tablespoons harissa, ½ teaspoon Tabasco, or hot sauce

If the couscous is cold, place it in a small saucepan over medium heat to warm; set aside.

In a large nonstick skillet over medium-high heat, heat the water; add the onion, garlic, carrot, cabbage, pepper, cayenne, and saffron and cook, stirring occasionally, and adding more liquid if the mixture becomes too dry, for about 7 minutes, or until the vegetables are nearly tender.

Meanwhile, in a small nonstick skillet lightly sprayed with olive oil, over high heat, cook the lamb, Worcestershire, and garlic powder until the meat is well browned. Remove from the heat, and cover loosely with foil.

To the large skillet, add the currants, garbanzo beans, turmeric, ginger, and parsley and cook 2 to 3 minutes. Add the couscous to the skillet and heat thoroughly. Mound the couscous mixture on individual plates and top with the diced tomatoes and lamb. Serve with harissa.

PER SERVING: Saturated Fat: 1 gm   Total Fat: 4 gm
Cholesterol: 29 mg   Sodium: 84 mg   Calories: 387

Ham, Asparagus, and Baby Carrot Sauté with Honey-Mustard Sauce

Serves 4

A stir-fry of ham and colorful vegetables, this delicious medley is enhanced by the sweet and spicy touch of honey mustard. Serve it over rice with butternut squash for a hearty feast. Reduced-salt ham is available in some supermarkets.

1½ cups white, brown, or basmati rice

2 tablespoons Dijon mustard

1 tablespoon honey

½ cup nonfat sour cream

Olive oil spray

1 cup fresh baby carrots, julienned

1 pound asparagus, trimmed and cut into 1-inch lengths

½ red bell pepper, julienned

10 ounces low-salt baked ham, julienned

¼ cup parsley, for garnish

In a large nonstick pot over high heat, heat 3 cups water to boiling. Add the rice, reduce the heat, cover, and simmer for 30 minutes or until tender (brown rice will take 40 minutes).

In a small bowl, whisk together the mustard, honey, and sour cream.

In a large nonstick skillet lightly sprayed with oil, over medium–high heat, add ½ cup water, and cook the carrots for 4 minutes until slightly tender. Add the asparagus and bell pepper and cook for 4 minutes. Add the ham to the vegetable skillet and toss with the vegetables, cooking until hot, about 2 minutes. Add the honey-mustard sauce and cook, stirring a few minutes more until the mixture is heated through. Mound the rice on individual serving plates and spoon the ham and sauce mixture on top. Garnish with parsley.

PER SERVING: Saturated Fat: 2 gm Total Fat: 6 gm

Cholesterol: 38 mg Sodium: 1042 mg Calories: 451

Fruity Stuffed Pork Chops

This pineapple and cranberry stuffing makes ordinary pork chops extraordinary. Dried cranberries are available in specialty food stores and even in many supermarkets these days. Dried tart cherries can be substituted. To save time, ask your meat cutter to cut the pockets into the chops.

½ cup jalapeño jelly

Olive oil spray

2 to 3 slices (1 cup cubed) toasted fresh bread

2 scallions, thinly sliced

1 8-ounce can crushed pineapple with juice

⅓ cup dried cranberries or cherries

4 4½-ounce extra-lean pork chops, about ½ to ¾ inch thick, all visible fat removed

Salt (optional)

Freshly ground black pepper

Preheat the broiler with the broiler pan set 2 to 3 inches from the heat unit. In a small microwave-safe container, cook the jalapeño jelly, at high for 1 minute to melt. In a large nonstick skillet lightly sprayed with oil, over medium-high heat, combine the bread cubes, scallions, pineapple and juice, cranberries, a few tablespoons water, and cook for 2 to 3 minutes until the bread cubes are lightly browned and the berries are plump.

With a knife, cut a deep pocket into each chop, slicing parallel to the surface and cutting through to the bone, leaving ½ inch of meat on each side. Lightly salt, if using, and pepper the chops inside and out. Fill each chop with ¼ of the stuffing. Place the chops on a broiler pan and brush with the melted jalapeño jelly. Broil for 3 to 5 minutes. Turn the chops, brush with the remaining jelly, and broil 2 to 4 more minutes. With a knife, cut through the thickest part of one chop and place back under the broiler if still pink or uncooked. When done, serve immediately.

PER SERVING: Saturated Fat: 3 gm   Total Fat: 8 gm
Cholesterol: 80 mg   Sodium: 117 mg   Calories: 390

Pork Chops in Nectarine and Peach Brandy Sauce

The tart fruit and creamy spiked leek sauce give these pork chops a tangy twist. It is an easy preparation. If you substitute peaches or apricots, add 1 teaspoon of lemon juice.

4 3½-ounce center cut, lean
    boneless pork chops, ½-inch
    thick, all visible fat removed
Salt (optional)
Olive oil spray
2 leeks, white part only, sliced in
    half lengthwise, and ¼-inch
    slices crosswise
¾ cup low-sodium defatted
    chicken stock

¼ cup cranberry juice
1½ tablespoons cornstarch
¼ cup peach or apricot brandy
⅓ cup nonfat sour cream
3 nectarines or peaches halved,
    pitted, and cut into ¼-inch
    slices
1 teaspoon chopped parsley

Sprinkle the chops with salt, if using. Lightly spray a large nonstick skillet with oil and set over medium-high heat until very hot. Arrange the pork chops in the skillet and sear 3 minutes on each side. Remove the chops to a warm platter. Reduce the heat to medium, add the leeks and a few teaspoons water, and cook for about 2 minutes. In a small bowl, whisk together the stock, cranberry juice, and cornstarch. Pour the mixture into the skillet, add the peach brandy and the sour cream, and cook, stirring constantly, until slightly thickened. Return the pork chops to the skillet, add the nectarines and spoon the sauce over the chops. Cook for 6 to 8 minutes, or until the pork is cooked through. Serve chops with the sauce and garnished with parsley and serve hot.

PER SERVING: Saturated Fat: 2 gm   Total Fat: 7 gm
Cholesterol: 64 mg   Sodium: 82 mg   Calories: 318

Grilled Pork Tenderloin with Galveston Salve and Sopping Sauce

Serves 4

Highly concentrated blends of herbs and spices, when rubbed into the surface of meat, fish, or poultry, can create intensely flavorful results. Texans call them "salves" and in the Carolinas, they are "rubs." Whatever you call the technique, it produces a taste-filled tenderloin here.

5 cloves garlic	*Vegetable oil spray*
2 tablespoons yellow mustard seed	*1 12-ounce pork tenderloin*
¼ cup fresh lime juice	*Lime wedges, for garnish*
2 teaspoons ground cumin	*Tropical Mango Salsa (page 283)*
Salt (optional)	

Preheat the grill. In a food processor or blender, puree the garlic, mustard seed, lime juice, cumin, and salt, if using, until smooth. The mustard seeds will not be completely crushed.

Pat dry the pork with paper towel, then coat liberally with the salve. Lightly spray the grill with oil and place the tenderloin on the grill. Cover the grill with a lid or tent the pork with foil. Turn the pork every 4 minutes, brushing with any remaining salve only after the first turn. Grill the pork for 16 minutes, or until well done and there is no pink in the center.

Remove the pork from the grill and let rest, covered, for 5 minutes, then carve into ⅜-inch slices. Serve with lime wedges and Tropical Mango Salsa on the side.

NOTE: This recipe can also be broiled. Lightly spray a grilling rack, and place over a flat baking sheet. Place the tenderloin on the rack and broil 2 inches from the heat unit, for 15 to 20 minutes, turning every 5 minutes until done. Baste with the salve after the first turn.

PER SERVING: Saturated Fat: 1 gm   Total Fat: 5 gm
Cholesterol: 54 mg   Sodium: 41 mg   Calories: 151

SALSAS, SAUCES, CONDIMENTS, AND GRAVIES

G iven that early explorers risked life and limb to establish spice trade routes to new parts of the world, it's not surprising that flavor, particularly flavorful sauces, have been essential to good eating since long before the Roman epicureans.

As the world changed, the taste for savory sauces did not. In the twelfth century, the English poet Geoffrey Chaucer wrote, "Woe to the cook whose sauces had no sting . . ." In those days, a successful sauce with sting might have been an elaborate compote of black cherries, bone marrow, ground almonds, crab apples, grapes, gooseberries, raisins, chicken broth, vinegar, wine, oil, egg yolks, quince, parsley, garlic, ramps, and a great number of herbs including sage, thyme, cinnamon, nutmeg, and sorrel. Less complex sauces of the day were simple mixed figs and ale or pureed beans and bacon.

The sauce seemed to evolve from a heavy condiment (which I suspect was used to cover up the taste of slightly tainted food) to the refined clear or opaque, light and velvety sauces that developed in nineteenth-century France. Just after the French Revolution, saucing foods became a fine art, and creating, developing, and serving fine sauce became a culinary way of life and a point of rivalry among Parisian chefs.

A quick scan of supermarket and specialty food store shelves tells the story best: Americans like their condiments and sauces. Aisles are filled with jars of relishes, chili sauces, mayonnaise, ketchup, chutneys, gravies, barbecue sauces, spicy rubs, gourmet caper sauces—even jars of Hollandaise. In fact, more than seventy thousand American brands alone are offered in the United States, which doesn't count the foreign brands of which there are twenty thousand more.

Fortunately, these can be part of a healthful diet if prepared properly. They can be luxuriously indulgent with elegant and smooth, spicy, and thick low-fat sauces. If you are just beginning a healthful eating plan and can't bear the thought of giving up your favorite sauces, look at the recipes that follow for inspiration. You can still enjoy White Sauce (page 292), Meat-Loaf Gravy (page 298), Red-Eye Ham Gravy (page 299), and Curried Apricot Mayonnaise (page 287).

■■ Sauce Secrets ■■

You can indulge in my sauces because I use herb blends and low-fat substitutions instead of butter, cheese, heavy cream, whole milk, and other notoriously high-fat dairy products. The secret to flavor doesn't lie in these fats; rather, it is achieved by the creative blending of substitutions, fresh ingredients, and seasonings.

For surprisingly creamlike tastes and textures in sauces, use pureed non-fat cottage cheese, nonfat sour cream, nonfat cream cheese, nonfat coffee creamers, farmer cheese, skim milk, evaporated skimmed milk, and nonfat dry milk in place of their high-fat counterparts.

Make a roux or white sauce by whisking flour in a very small amount of margarine or canola oil in nonfat milk, or just flour and nonfat milk.

Make barbecue sauce without oil. Rather than tenderizing, oil simply adds excess fat and calories. Skinless chicken and lean meats are tenderized and flavored more successfully when oil is omitted from the sauce or marinade.

To make nonfat gravy, defat meat or poultry stock or drippings using a defatting cup or chill the liquid and remove the congealed layer of fat (page 48). You may also use gravy seasonings if you wish. They are readily available in most markets: liquid smoke, Magi Seasons Gravy Master, Kitchen Bouquet, and Bovril. And a few companies, like Pioneer flour, make nonfat gravy mixes and there are bottled nonfat gravies.

Salsa Cruda

A good salsa takes little longer to make fresh than the total time it takes to buy it, store it, and open the jar, *and* it has a fresher homemade taste. Coarsely chop the vegetables and when using fresh or watery tomatoes, you might want to drain 1 tablespoon of the liquid if you like thick salsa. An interesting addition is ½ cup of canned and drained black beans or black-eyed peas. Serve salsas alongside hot or cold beans, over fish and poultry, or as a spicy dip for tortilla chips and vegetable sticks. Many ingredients can be omitted or increased, such as the garlic and jalapeño. Salsa will keep for a week.

3 very ripe tomatoes, coarsely
   chopped
2 tablespoons chopped onion
2 tablespoons chopped scallion
1 clove garlic, minced
½ teaspoon finely chopped
   jalapeño

2 tablespoons cider vinegar
1 tablespoon fresh lime juice
3 tablespoons fresh lemon juice
2 teaspoons chopped cilantro
1 teaspoon coarsely chopped
   parsley
Lemon or lime slices, for garnish

In a large bowl, combine the tomatoes, onion, scallion, garlic, jalapeño, vinegar, lime juice, lemon juice, cilantro, and parsley and refrigerate for several hours or overnight. Serve cold, garnished with lemon or lime slices.

PER ¼ CUP: Saturated Fat: 0 gm   Total Fat: 0 gm
Cholesterol: 0 mg   Sodium: 4 mg   Calories: 11

Yellow Salsa

The tiny sweet yellow pear tomatoes give this golden salsa an unusually bright color and lively flavor. Use large yellow tomatoes if you can't find pear tomatoes. This is good for dipping vegetables or crisp tortillas, and is a refreshing topping or side for grilled beef, fish, or chicken. Or, add a dollop to your favorite bean soup, meat loaf, or hamburger.

$\frac{1}{4}$ cup chopped cilantro, including
   stems (optional)

2 tablespoons chopped parsley

2 leafy ribs celery, chopped

4 scallions, chopped, including the
   light green but not the dark
   green part

2 tablespoons chopped onion

1 clove garlic, minced

2 tablespoons chopped yellow
   (banana) pepper

$1\frac{1}{2}$ cups diced yellow pear
   tomatoes or yellow cherry
   tomatoes

2 tablespoons fresh lime juice

1 tablespoon fresh orange juice

1 teaspoon cider vinegar

Tabasco to taste

Salt (optional)

In a medium bowl, combine all ingredients, and stir. Cover and refrigerate for at least 30 minutes. Taste to adjust heat and serve cold. The salsa can be stored in the refrigerator for up to 1 week.

PER $\frac{1}{4}$ CUP: Saturated Fat: 0 gm   Total Fat: 0 gm
Cholesterol: 0 mg   Sodium: 13 mg   Calories: 15

Peach Salsa

Adapted from Jean Carper's *The Food Pharmacy Guide to Good Eating*, this recipe is great with grilled poultry or fish, on sandwiches, and cold black bean salad (as Jean served it). Plums can substitute for peaches.

3 unpeeled peaches, pitted and
  diced
2 scallions, sliced (green and white
  parts)
¼ cup diced red bell pepper
¼ cup diced green bell pepper
2 to 3 tablespoons fresh lime juice

¼ cup chopped cilantro
3 tablespoons chopped parsley
½ teaspoon ground cumin
1 tablespoon honey
Minced jalapeño or crushed red
  pepper, to taste

In a medium bowl, combine the peaches, scallions, bell peppers, lime juice, cilantro, parsley, cumin, honey, and jalapeño and stir. Cover and refrigerate for at least 30 minutes or up to 4 days. Serve chilled.

PER ¼ CUP: Saturated Fat: O gm   Total Fat: O gm
Cholesterol: O mg   Sodium: 2 mg   Calories: 27

Tricolor Pepper and Caper Salsa

This versatile savory salsa is a colorful condiment for hearty meats, milder chicken dishes, sandwiches, seafood, or try it with beans and polenta. You can add the sweet, high-fiber pepper seeds if you wish.

Olive oil spray
1 medium onion, quartered and thinly sliced
1 medium green bell pepper, seeded and sliced into ¼-inch strips
1 medium red bell pepper, seeded and sliced into ¼-inch strips

1 medium yellow bell pepper, seeded and sliced into ¼-inch strips
1 teaspoon cider vinegar
2 tablespoons capers
Salt (optional)
Freshly ground black pepper

In a large nonstick skillet lightly sprayed with oil, over medium–high heat, sauté the onion for 4 minutes, reducing the heat if the onion begins to burn. Add the peppers, and sauté for 6 minutes, or until the peppers are barely cooked and brightly colored. Remove from the heat and stir in the vinegar, capers, salt, if using, and pepper. Serve hot.

PER ¼ CUP: Saturated Fat: 0 gm   Total Fat: 0 gm
Cholesterol: 0 mg   Sodium: 9 mg   Calories: 13

Rita Calvert's Tropical Mango Salsa

Rita Calvert, the art director of more than two hundred of my television shows brought this salsa to a production meeting. It won such raves that Rita indulged us with mango salsa at every meeting thereafter. It is a terrific accompaniment for all spicy meats, fish, and poultry. Mango is a highly flavored fruit that adds flavor to many dishes.

1 cup chopped fresh pineapple
1 cup chopped fresh or bottled
   mango
2 cloves garlic, minced
3 scallions, chopped

1 red bell pepper, finely diced
2 tablespoons chopped cilantro
2 tablespoons chopped basil
½ cup fresh lime juice

In a small bowl, combine the pineapple, mango, garlic, scallions, red pepper, cilantro, basil, and lime juice and stir. Cover and refrigerate for 1 hour.

PER ¼ CUP: Saturated Fat: 0 gm   Total Fat: 0 gm
Cholesterol: 0 mg   Sodium: 1 mg   Calories: 22

Black-eyed Pea Salsa

This salsa comes together in minutes and is a spicy dip for chips, a topping for baked potatoes or egg substitute omelettes, and as a sauce for hot or cold poultry, beef, or fish.

1 tablespoon minced pickled seeded
  jalapeño
2 cloves garlic, minced
4 scallions, finely chopped
1 small yellow bell pepper, diced
4 medium plum tomatoes, seeded
  and diced

2 tablespoons fresh lime juice
Salt (optional)
1 15-ounce can black-eyed peas,
  drained and rinsed

In a medium bowl, combine the jalapeño, garlic, scallions, yellow pepper, tomatoes, lime juice, salt, if using, and the black-eyed peas and stir. Cover and refrigerate 30 minutes before serving. Can be made up to a day in advance.

PER ¼ CUP: Saturated Fat: 0 gm   Total Fat: Trace
Cholesterol: 0 mg   Sodium: 96 mg   Calories: 31

Raita

Raita is the thick and creamy sauce that is served with many Indian foods. It provides a cool balance to hot and spicy dishes. It is also excellent with simple fish and chicken dishes or as a condiment with vegetables, rice, and beans. You can pulse in a food processor instead of chopping.

1¼ cups plain nonfat yogurt,
   drained for 5 minutes
1 small burpless cucumber, diced
2 scallions, finely minced
1 teaspoon finely minced or finely
   diced fresh or pickled jalapeño
   slices

3 small plum tomatoes, diced
2 tablespoons finely chopped
   cilantro (optional)
Salt (optional)
Freshly ground black pepper

In a medium bowl, combine the yogurt, cucumber, scallions, jalapeño, tomatoes, cilantro, salt, if using, and pepper and stir. Refrigerate for 1 hour before serving.

PER ¼ CUP: Saturated Fat: 0 gm   Total Fat: 0 gm
Cholesterol: 1 mg   Sodium: 26 mg   Calories: 23

Spicy Chili and Steak Relish

I prefer chili sauce rather than ketchup as a base for some sauces. Chili sauce is less sweet and more interesting, I think. This chunky, spicy steak sauce is best served cold with cold lamb or beef. It will keep in the refrigerator for up to 5 weeks.

1 cup bottled chili sauce or ketchup	¼ cup chopped onions or scallions
⅓ cup chopped green pimento-stuffed olives	1 teaspoon fresh lemon juice
¼ cup chopped peperoncini	Dash Worcestershire
¼ cup pitted chopped black olives (optional)	¼ teaspoon Tabasco

In a medium bowl, combine the chili sauce, green olives, peperoncini, black olives, scallions, lemon juice, Worcestershire, and Tabasco and stir. Refrigerate for 1 hour and serve.

PER ¼ CUP: Saturated Fat: 0 gm   Total Fat: 0 gm
Cholesterol: 0 mg   Sodium: 654 mg   Calories: 43

Tartar Sauce

Makes about 2 cups

Tartar sauce is an all-time favorite with white fish. This is a thick and chunky version that is also good as a sandwich spread. If you like it sweet, use sweet pickles rather than dills.

1 cup nonfat mayonnaise

1/3 cup chopped onions or scallions

1/4 cup finely chopped dill pickles

1/4 cup finely chopped pimento or
roasted red pepper

1/4 cup chopped parsley

1/2 teaspoon dry mustard

1/4 teaspoon cider vinegar

In a medium bowl, combine the mayonnaise, onions, pickles, pimento, parsley, mustard, and vinegar and stir. Refrigerate for 1 hour and serve.

■■   PER 1/4 CUP: Saturated Fat: 0 gm   Total Fat: 0 gm   ■■
Cholesterol: 0 mg   Sodium: 401 mg   Calories: 28

Curried Apricot Mayonnaise

■■ *Makes about 1 cup* ■■

This nonfat adaptation of Betty Rosbottom's recipe from her collection *First Impressions* is an excellent accompaniment for poultry or fish. This is also a wonderful spread for chicken or turkey sandwiches.

1 cup nonfat mayonnaise

1 teaspoon curry powder

2 tablespoons apricot preserves

1 teaspoon finely chopped dried
apricots

1/2 teaspoon fresh lemon juice

In a small bowl, combine the mayonnaise, curry powder, apricot preserves, dried apricots, and lemon juice and stir. Cover and refrigerate for 1 hour. Serve cold.

■■   PER 1/4 CUP: Saturated Fat: 0 gm   Total Fat: 0 gm   ■■
Cholesterol: 0 mg   Sodium: 679 mg   Calories: 70

Dijon Mustard Mayonnaise

Makes about 1 cup

This traditional mustard sauce is a favorite sandwich spread. It can be served with fish, too, and as a dip for vegetables or artichokes.

4 tablespoons prepared mustard, American or Dijon
½ cup nonfat mayonnaise

½ teaspoon dry mustard
¼ to ½ cup nonfat milk

In a small bowl, combine the mustard, mayonnaise, dry mustard, and nonfat milk and stir. Refrigerate for 1 hour and serve.

PER ¼ CUP: Saturated Fat: O gm   Total Fat: I gm
Cholesterol: O mg   Sodium: 541 mg   Calories: 42

Oriental Hot Mustard Sauce

Makes about ½ cup

Much like the hot sauce served with egg rolls in Chinese restaurants, this sauce is for artichokes, steamed vegetables, fish, and shrimp.

¼ cup boiling water
2 tablespoons dry mustard

2 tablespoons brown sugar
2 tablespoons cider vinegar

In a small saucepan, heat water to boiling. Add the mustard, sugar, and vinegar, and cook for 30 seconds or until the sugar melts. Serve hot or warm.

PER ¼ CUP: Saturated Fat: O gm   Total Fat: 3 gm
Cholesterol: O mg   Sodium: 7 mg   Calories: 95

Honey-Mustard Sauce

Makes a little more than ¹⁄₂ cup

This mild sauce is perfect for plating servings of fish. Use a hot Chinese-style mustard for a more spicy version. Heating the ingredients for 3 minutes thins the sauce, but you can thicken it with a tablespoon of cornstarch melted in the wine, added while cooking. The heating burns off the alcohol and gives the sauce a more mellow flavor.

4 tablespoons dry white wine
  (optional)
2 tablespoons fresh lemon juice

2 tablespoons coarse grain mustard
2 tablespoons honey

In a small bowl, combine the wine, lemon juice, mustard, and honey and stir. Refrigerate for 2 hours until chilled or put in pan on low heat for 3 minutes. Serve warm or cold.

PER ¹⁄₄ CUP: Saturated Fat: 0 gm   Total Fat: 1 gm
Cholesterol: 0 mg   Sodium: 381 mg   Calories: 107

Creamy Horseradish-Cucumber Sauce

A zesty, smooth accompaniment for beef, poultry, fish, and pork, this sauce is also a terrific topping for baked potatoes and a good dip for vegetables.

1 cup (8 ounces) burpless
    cucumbers, minced
Salt (optional)
⅓ cup nonfat sour cream

⅔ cup nonfat plain yogurt
2½ teaspoons horseradish
1 teaspoon dill
¼ to 1 teaspoon sugar

Place the cucumber in a strainer. Lightly salt and let drain for 30 minutes. Press gently to remove the excess juices. In a medium bowl, stir together the cucumber with the remaining ingredients. Serve immediately or refrigerate for up to 4 days.

PER ¼ CUP: Saturated Fat: 0 gm   Total Fat: 0 gm
Cholesterol: 0 mg   Sodium: 57 mg   Calories: 20

Cocktail Sauce

Makes about 1 cup

This is a salsa-type ketchup. This is a good cocktail sauce that enlivens shrimp, oysters, lobster, clams, crab, and mussels. The lemonade sweetens it, and it can be omitted. Use either the hot or mild version according to your own tastes.

¾ cup salsa or plain ketchup
2 tablespoons finely chopped
    scallion
2 teaspoons lemonade frozen
    concentrate (optional)

1 teaspoon horseradish
½ teaspoon Tabasco

In a small bowl, combine the salsa, scallion, lemonade concentrate, horse-radish, and Tabasco and stir. Serve immediately or refrigerate for up to 4 days.

■■   PER ¼ CUP: Saturated Fat: 0 gm   Total Fat: 0 gm   ■■
Cholesterol: 0 mg   Sodium: 551 mg   Calories: 54

■■

Bold Barbecue Sauce

■■   *Makes just over 2 cups*   ■■

I use this thick, slightly sweet marinade, basting, and serving sauce that is spicy, rich, and sweetened with fruit jams and brown sugar to baste grilled poultry and meat or as a dipping sauce. If you cook this sauce 5 minutes, it will become thin at first but thicken again as it cools.

½ cup maple syrup or brown sugar	1 clove garlic, minced
1 to 2 tablespoons cider vinegar	1 medium onion, chopped
¼ cup sour cherry or apricot jelly	1 cup chili sauce or ketchup
1 tablespoon Worcestershire	1 tablespoon chili powder
1 tablespoon low-sodium soy sauce	1 tablespoon prepared mustard
	½ teaspoon Tabasco

In a small bowl, combine the syrup, vinegar, jelly, sauces, garlic, onion, chili sauce, chili powder, mustard, Tabasco, and stir. Spoon over the meat during barbecuing or grilling or use as a dip. Serve room temperature or hot or cold.

■■   PER ¼ CUP: Saturated Fat: 0 gm   Total Fat: 0.5 gm   ■■
Cholesterol: 0 mg   Sodium: 594 mg   Calories: 125

White Sauce

An easy and flavorful milk-based white sauce is a must in every cook's repertoire. This one is superb when served over simple vegetables, such as potatoes, corn, peas, and onions. Combine it with ¼ cup of sherry to make a sauce for chicken or with ½ cup of finely chopped dill for a fish sauce. It can also be a base for macaroni and cheese, cream sauces, and gravies. It will keep refrigerated for 3 days.

½ cup nonfat dry milk
1 tablespoon flour
1 tablespoon cornstarch
½ teaspoon salt (optional)

Freshly ground white pepper
1 cup defatted chicken or vegetable
    stock

In a nonstick saucepan over low heat, stir together the milk, flour, cornstarch, salt, if using, and pepper. Slowly whisk in the stock, and cook for about 4 minutes, whisking continuously, until it thickens. Serve immediately.

PER ¼ CUP: Saturated Fat: 0 gm   Total Fat: 0 gm
Cholesterol: 2 mg   Sodium: 42 mg   Calories: 40

Hollandaise Sauce

Use this over vegetables such as asparagus, broccoli, cauliflower, or green beans; as a dip for artichokes; over (substitute) eggs Benedict; and with many other foods. Egg substitutes are pasteurized, so unlike the usual Hollandaise, this is a safe sauce. The sauce will freeze and reheat. Keep up to 2 days.

4 to 6 tablespoons fresh lemon
  juice
1 cup low-sodium, defatted
  chicken stock
1/2 cup egg substitute

1/2 teaspoon flour
1 tablespoon margarine
Salt (optional)
Freshly ground white pepper

In a small nonstick saucepan over high heat, heat the lemon juice and stock to boiling. Reduce the heat to medium low and simmer for 4 minutes. Meanwhile, in a small nonstick saucepan over low heat, whisk together the egg substitute and flour until frothy, about 30 seconds. Gradually whisk the hot broth into the egg mixture, 1 tablespoon at a time, and cook, whisking constantly, for about 4 minutes, until the sauce thickens. Increase the heat to medium low and whisk in the margarine. Add the salt, if using, and pepper and continue whisking a few minutes until the sauce thickens, about 2 minutes.

PER 1/4 CUP: Saturated Fat: 0 gm   Total Fat: 2 gm
Cholesterol: 1 mg   Sodium: 53 mg   Calories: 32

Applesauce

Homemade applesauce is a quick assembly of fresh ingredients microwaved or on a stove and adds tart snap to lean pork tenderloin, duck, potato pancakes. To dress up the sauce, add ¼ cup chopped walnuts during cooking. If you don't have tart apples, add more lemon juice and slightly more sugar. Apples can also be left unpeeled.

6 tart apples, such as Granny
  Smiths or Gravenstein,
  unpeeled, cored, and coarsely
  chopped
⅓ to ½ cup brown sugar or
  maple syrup

½ cup raisins
1 to 4 tablespoons fresh lemon
  juice
Pinch of freshly grated nutmeg
⅛ teaspoon cinnamon

In a microwave-safe container, combine the apples, sugar, raisins, lemon juice, nutmeg, and cinnamon and toss. Cover loosely and cook at high for 20 minutes, stirring once or twice. Alternatively, in a nonstick saucepan over very low heat, cover and cook for 40 minutes, until the apples turn brown and the mixture becomes thick. Serve hot or cold.

PER ¼ CUP: Saturated Fat: 0 gm   Total Fat: 0 gm
Cholesterol: 0 mg   Sodium: 2 mg   Calories: 61

Lil Smith's Cranberry-Orange Sauce

My friend Lillian Pulitzer Smith of New Orleans excels at making fine sauces. Sweet, tangy, and filled with fruit, this one is best over pancakes, lean ham, or pork tenderloin. Use sparingly——a little goes a long way.

2 tablespoons cornstarch
1 cup fresh orange juice

1 cup whole berry cranberry sauce
½ cup grape preserves or jelly

In a small nonstick saucepan over medium heat, whisk the cornstarch into the orange juice until blended. Stir in the cranberry sauce and grape preserves, and cook for several minutes, stirring, until thickened. Serve hot or cold.

■■ PER ¼ CUP: Saturated Fat: 0 gm   Total Fat: 0 gm   ■■
Cholesterol: 0 mg   Sodium: 10 mg   Calories: 92

Jalapeño Relish

■■ *Makes about 3 cups* ■■

While skiing with my niece Susie Fischer McGarry and her husband, Mark, their friend Rick Hager gave me his recipe for this hot relish. Rick stores his for a week before using, but I haven't been able to keep mine around for more than a few minutes. It will keep for 6 weeks in the refrigerator. It is *very* hot.

¾ cup cider vinegar
1 teaspoon salt (optional)
1 cup chopped jalapeño

⅓ cup chopped green bell peppers
⅓ cup chopped yellow bell peppers
1 cup chopped onion

In a nonstick saucepan over medium heat, boil the vinegar and salt, if using, for 5 minutes. Meanwhile, in a bowl, combine the jalapeños, bell peppers, and onion. Pour the hot vinegar over the vegetables and stir. Cover and refrigerate for one week before using.

■■ PER ¼ CUP: Saturated Fat: 0 gm   Total Fat: 0 gm   ■■
Cholesterol: 0 mg   Sodium: 1 mg   Calories: 14

Orange Soy Sauce

Orange soy sauce is excellent over poultry.

1 cup low-sodium, defatted
  chicken stock
3 tablespoons cornstarch
2 tablespoons low-sodium soy
  sauce

1/2 teaspoon grated fresh ginger
2 tablespoons orange juice
  concentrate
1 teaspoon orange zest
Several drops Tabasco

In a medium nonstick saucepan over medium heat, combine the stock, cornstarch, soy sauce, ginger, orange juice concentrate, orange zest, and Tabasco and cook until thickened. Serve immediately.

PER 1/4 CUP: Saturated Fat: 0 gm   Total Fat: 0 gm
Cholesterol: 1 mg   Sodium: 204 mg   Calories: 32

Chicken Gravy

Low-sodium, defatted chicken stock produces a glistening and clear gravy while evaporated skimmed milk produces a creamier, opaque finish. If you have less than 1/2 cup drippings, combine them in a small metal bowl with 1/2 cup hot water or defatted chicken stock and place in the freezer for a few minutes and defat (page 48).

1/2 cup pan drippings, defatted
  (page 48)
1 1/2 cups low-sodium defatted
  chicken stock

2 heaping tablespoons cornstarch
2 tablespoons all-purpose flour

In a large nonstick skillet over medium heat, combine the drippings and 1 cup of the stock and cook until heated through. Meanwhile, in a small bowl, whisk together the cornstarch, flour, and remaining ½ cup stock. Add the cornstarch mixture to the skillet and cook, whisking constantly, about 3 minutes, until mixture thickens. Serve immediately.

■■ PER ¼ CUP: Saturated Fat: 0 gm   Total Fat: 0 gm   ■■
Cholesterol: 1 mg   Sodium: 5 mg   Calories: 22

Turkey Gravy

■■   *Makes about 2 cups*   ■■

Turkey gravy doesn't have to rely on fat to be delicious. If you prefer a creamier version, use evaporated skimmed milk instead of chicken stock. Add ½ cup hot water to the drippings if you don't have enough to make up ½ cup of liquid. To defat, pour the drippings into a metal bowl and place in the freezer for 10 minutes. Remove the layer of congealed fat from the surface (page 48).

½ cup pan drippings, defatted
(page 48)
1½ cups low-sodium, defatted
chicken or turkey stock

2 heaping tablespoons cornstarch
2 tablespoons all-purpose flour

In a medium nonstick skillet over medium heat, combine drippings and 1 cup stock and cook until heated through. In a small bowl, whisk together the cornstarch, flour, and remaining ½ cup stock. Add the cornstarch mixture to the skillet and cook, whisking constantly, about 3 minutes, until the mixture thickens. Serve immediately.

■■ PER ¼ CUP: Saturated Fat: 0 gm   Total Fat: 0 gm   ■■
Cholesterol: 1 mg   Sodium: 5 mg   Calories: 22

Meat-Loaf Gravy

Makes about 2¹/₂ cups

This is a pebbly downhome gravy that incorporates some of the meat loaf in the sauce to lend flavor and texture. Spoon it on hot meat loaf, meat-loaf sandwiches or mashed or baked potatoes. You can defat the gravy or just the meat-loaf drippings by using a defatting cup or by chilling and removing the fat when it congeals at the top (page 48).

Meat-loaf drippings, cooked and
  defatted
2 cups nonfat milk or evaporated
  skimmed milk
1 ¹/₄-inch slice meat loaf, broken
  into pieces

3 tablespoons all-purpose flour
1 teaspoon Worcestershire
Freshly ground black pepper
4 tablespoons ketchup, for garnish
  (optional)

In a large nonstick skillet over medium heat, cook the defatted meat-loaf drippings until heated through. Stir in 1 cup nonfat milk and the crumbled meat loaf, mashing the loaf as it heats. In a small bowl, whisk together the flour, Worcestershire, pepper, and the remaining 1 cup nonfat milk. Add to the skillet, reduce the heat to low, and cook, whisking constantly, about 4 minutes until the mixture thickens. Serve immediately.

PER ¹/₄ CUP: Saturated Fat: 0 gm   Total Fat: Trace
Cholesterol: 5 mg   Sodium: 37 mg   Calories: 36

Beef Gravy

Makes just over 2 cups

Beef gravy can be thick or thin, cream style, or glisteny. The basic recipe is made with water but for a creamier finish, add 1 tablespoon of no fat dry milk at the beginning of cooking, and substitute nonfat milk or evaporated skimmed milk for the water.

1 cup beef drippings, defatted
   (page 48)
1 cup water, nonfat milk, or
   evaporated skimmed milk

1 tablespoon cornstarch
1 tablespoon flour
Freshly ground black pepper

In a medium nonstick skillet over medium heat, heat the drippings. In a small bowl, whisk together the water, cornstarch, flour, and seasonings, and add to the skillet, whisking continuously. Reduce the heat to low and cook for about 3 minutes, until the mixture thickens. Serve immediately.

PER ¼ CUP: Saturated Fat: 0 gm   Total Fat: 0 gm
Cholesterol: 0 mg   Sodium: 2 mg   Calories: 7

Red-Eye Ham Gravy

Makes about 1½ cups

This peppery gravy is usually served with ham, potatoes, grits, and biscuits. I make it in the Louisiana style, using extra-strong coffee.

½ cup (or more) ham dripping to
   make at least 1 cup liquid,
   defatted
2 heaping tablespoons all-purpose
   flour
1 cup low-sodium, defatted
   chicken stock, water, or nonfat
   milk

2 tablespoons defatted ham stock
2 tablespoons strong coffee or to
   taste (optional)
¼ teaspoon freshly ground black
   pepper

In a small nonstick skillet over medium heat, heat the defatted ham drippings. In a small bowl, whisk together the flour, stocks, and coffee until blended and add to the skillet. Cook, stirring constantly, for about 4 minutes until the mixture thickens. Add the pepper and serve immediately.

PER ¼ CUP: Saturated Fat: 0 gm   Total Fat: Trace
Cholesterol: 1 mg   Sodium: 21 mg   Calories: 25

Marinara Romano

Here is a classic marinara sauce for pasta, made as it is made in Rome. I discovered this marinara sauce by following the wonderful aroma coming from the kitchen of my neighbor Mrs. Rena DeVita in Washington, D.C. I leave all the vegetables in the sauce and puree everything together with an immersion, or hand, blender. The sauce takes 15 minutes to prepare, not much longer than it takes to cook the pasta or Gnocchi (page 177).

1 28-ounce can low-sodium tomato sauce	4 to 5 fresh basil leaves
1 large onion, quartered	1 bay leaf
1 carrot, quartered	Salt (optional)
Leafy tops of 4 to 6 ribs celery	Pinch sugar

In a large nonstick saucepan over medium-low heat, heat the tomato sauce, onion, carrot, celery, basil, bay leaf, salt, if using, and sugar and simmer, stirring occasionally, for 15 minutes. Remove the bay leaf and process the vegetables with an immersion, or hand, blender. For a smooth sauce, strain and discard the vegetables.

PER ½ CUP: Saturated Fat: 0 gm   Total Fat: 0.5 gm
Cholesterol: 0 mg   Sodium: 71 mg   Calories: 85

Pasta Sauce Siciliano

This sauce with capers and anchovies is always satisfying whether the pasta is spaghetti, ziti, rigatoni, or vermicelli, and even if you vary the ingredients slightly by perhaps using Greek oregano (which I do——available at fancy food markets), a little more basil or onion, or adding a cup or two of sliced mushrooms or a handful of pitted, sliced black olives. Put the anchovies, capers, parsley, and grated cheese on top just before serving. To make it spicier, sprinkle on some crushed red pepper.

1 onion, chopped

2 cloves garlic, minced

2 tablespoons chopped fresh basil

1 tablespoon chopped fresh oregano

½ teaspoon sugar

½ teaspoon salt (optional)

1 15-ounce can low-sodium whole tomatoes with juice, the tomatoes broken up by hand or very coarsely chopped

1 6-ounce can low-sodium tomato paste

⅛ teaspoon crushed red pepper

1 tablespoon chopped anchovies or 2 whole anchovies (optional)

3 tablespoons capers

¼ cup chopped fresh parsley

2 tablespoons grated nonfat Parmesan cheese

In a large nonstick skillet over medium-high heat, cook the onion and garlic in a few tablespoons of water, for 6 minutes, until tender. Stir in the basil, oregano, sugar, salt, if using, tomatoes and tomato paste, crushed red pepper; cover and simmer, stirring several times to blend the paste, for about 10 minutes.

Spoon the sauce over the pasta and add the anchovies, capers, parsley, and cheese. Serve immediately.

PER ½ CUP: Saturated Fat: 0 gm   Total Fat: 0.5 gm
Cholesterol: 2 mg   Sodium: 85 mg   Calories: 62

DESSERTS

An old English rhyme goes, "A meal aren't complete, that do not end with a sweet." But be sure that the human taste for the sweet goes back further than this eleventh-century rhyme. Our earliest relatives had revenous appetites for the most available sweets of the prehistoric day. Apples, pears, cherries, figs, strawberries, and sweetest of fruits, dates, all grew in abundance very early on.

It was discovered that fruit tasted sweeter if first dried in the sun. In order to satisfy even sweeter tastes, man discovered even sweeter delights than those that grew on trees. A cave painting in Spain, dated 8000 B.C., depicts two brave souls risking their lives climbing up a cliff to raid bee-hives for honey. By 2500 B.C., the Egyptians had figured out how to keep beehives for constant sweet satisfaction, thereby eliminating the risky raids.

Things haven't changed much. We still need something sweet every now and then, and more often than not a piece of fruit just won't do the trick. For many, the idea of changing dessert habits and adapting to a low-fat eating lifestyle can be unnerving. But once you make the commitment, it is pretty simple. Desserts are one of the easiest areas to successfully lower fat.

From the very fancy Grandma Ocean's Chocolate Cake (page 316) to the homey Apple Crisp (page 322), I've included low-fat renditions of high-fat favorites to please the most insatiable sweet tooth.

Ovens vary in temperatures, so cooking times might take longer or shorter, depending on the oven.

Baked desserts can be kept covered in a cool place 2 to 3 days unrefrig-erated (unrefrigerated is preferred as refrigeration changes the texture and dries them out) or tightly covered, 4 to 5 days refrigerated.

■ Ingredients ■

Flour other than the all-purpose white wheat flour I use in most of my recipes can add nutrients, color, texture, and sweetness to your cakes and cookies, but be careful when you substitute. Nonwheat flours, such as soy, rice, or buckwheat, or oat flours, or even whole wheat when all-purpose is called for, can contain less gluten or have coarser properties than you need, producing flat, thick, and heavy cakes or cookies. When you want to add whole wheat flour or oat flour, for instance, substitute one quarter of the total amount of the new flour in the recipe with ¾ all-purpose. If that is successful, try one half and one half. Baking is a chemical process and unlike most other cooking, slight variations can dramatically change a recipe, so make small changes to begin with for health or calorie reasons.

Nonfat or low-fat ice creams and frozen yogurts are a boon to dessert lovers. Three-percent fat ice creams and nonfat yogurts, smooth and satisfying, are a far cry from the grainy low-fat products of a decade ago. Some contain guar gum, locust bean, or carrageen. Although these ingredients sound foreboding, they are all natural products (most derived from seaweed) and are actually good for us.

Nutritional analysis for recipes using ice cream or other frozen dessert products are based on frozen desserts with 3 percent fat content.

Nuts add fiber, nutrients, texture, and flavor to desserts as well as natural (not processed) fat, but don't feel that you must omit them from desserts for health or calorie reasons. Some nuts are lower in saturated fat than others—walnuts, chestnuts, hazelnuts, pistachios, almonds, and pecans being among the lowest. Use more sparingly peanuts, cashews, macadamias, and Brazil nuts; they are among the highest in saturated fat.

Salt lends a depth of taste to many cookies and cakes. Recipes with lemon, lemon zest, rhubarb, tart cherries, apples, plums, or any strong citrus flavor are fine without salt.

Sugar is a simple carbohydrate containing no fat and with 16 calories per teaspoon. Sugar doesn't raise or make cholesterol, unless several pounds are consumed in a day. Sugar does not convert into body fat as readily as edible fat and oil convert into body fat. So unless one has a specific health situation affected by sugar, consuming sugar daily in a couple of sweet desserts, several sweet beverages, or a few candies poses few problems for a healthy eating plan.

Whether it is brown or white, fine, powdered, or crystal rock, honey, maple syrup, molasses, corn syrup, or fruit concentrate, these sweeteners act the same once consumed. Nutritionally speaking, sugar is sugar. Sugars contain few vitamins or minerals and their primary sweet element is sucrose. Those containing the most fructose, such as fine white table sugar, are the sweetest. Those with the least amount of sucrose, such as molasses, are less sweet.

I use refined white and brown sugars, corn syrup, maple syrup, and honey in my recipes. I have not experimented with the substitute baking sugars now available.

▪▪ Low-Fat Dessert Alternatives ▪▪

To reduce fat in white or yellow cakes, cookies, and nut breads: Replace half of the fat (butter, oil, etc.) called for with an equal amount of applesauce, apple butter, pureed fresh apples, peaches, pears, very ripe bananas, or baby pears, apricots, or peaches.

To reduce fat in chocolate cakes, cupcakes, and brownies: Replace half the fat called for with pureed baby prunes, lekvar (prune butter), pureed dark or golden raisins or dates, very ripe bananas, or pureed fresh or drained canned plums.

To reduce the fat even more in chocolate recipes: Use pure cocoa powder, canola oil, a smaller amount of melted chocolate, and perhaps a few teaspoons of strong brewed coffee or espresso to further deepen the chocolate flavor instead of using all melted chocolate.

To enrich the taste of fruit pies and tarts when omitting butter and margarine, lemon boosts the fruit flavors.

To thicken double-crust fruit pies and fruit desserts that bake for 1 hour: Add ¼ cup tapioca granules (softened in ½ cup liquid) to the fruit mixture and omit ¼ of the sugar. Top with the crust and bake as directed.

If baking time is less than 1 hour, as with a one-crust pie or other fruit desserts, use a mixture of 2 tablespoons arrowroot or cornstarch softened in ½ cup cool liquid. Add it to the fruit mixture and bake as directed.

To enhance frozen fruits, such as peaches, melon, or berries in pies (or sorbets or sherbets): Add 1 teaspoon to ¼ cup lemon, lime, or tangerine juice and ¼ teaspoon cinnamon.

To reduce cholesterol and fat in custards, tapiocas, rice and bread puddings: Substitute 2 egg whites for each whole egg or use ¼ cup egg substitute (which is 99 percent egg product) for each whole egg.

For reduced-fat whipped toppings: Whip skim milk; 1–percent milk won't whip (page 335). A product called Whip It helps the whipping stay fluffy. Whip It is a starch, available at supermarkets and from the Oetker Company.

Use nonfat and low-fat packaged dry, refrigerated, and canned frostings, and toppings.

For fat-free creamy toppings, sauces, and fillings: Puree nonfat drained ricotta cheese, nonfat sour cream (for cheesecake), nonfat cottage cheese, pot cheese, or farmer cheese, nonfat cream cheese (thinned with nonfat milk) for several minutes. Add vanilla, citrus zest, brown sugar, white sugar, lemon juice, or other flavors and sweeteners. Then frost or fill the dessert.

Use evaporated skimmed milk instead of regular milk. If you want it really thick, let the unopened can sit undisturbed on the shelf for six months and a thicker "cream" settles on the bottom and can be spooned out for a richer creamlike emulsion. To thicken, whisk in a tablespoon or two of nonfat dry (powdered) milk to evaporated skimmed milk or skim milk to make a thicker cream base. Be aware that evaporated skimmed milk has a caramel taste and the dry milk has a discernible sweet taste. So use them in small amounts or in recipes where that taste will add something.

Buttery Lowered-Fat Piecrust

Makes single 8-inch pie shell

This piecrust is as goofproof—as much as any pastry can be—as it is excellent. It is best to roll the crust thin as it plumps and hardens during baking more than most. This crust benefits from time; that is, it becomes more tender in the hours after baking. The dough need not be refrigerated prior to rolling, and actually seems to work better the warmer it is. It is also more manageable if rolled between two pieces of waxed paper. NOTE: This crust might not roll twice (if you make a mistake) and it gets tough with extra flour. Even with all these caveats, it is an easy low-fat piecrust. You can double the recipe for a double crust or increase it by a third if your pie pan is 10 inches or a deep-dish pie.

1⅓ cups all-purpose flour

½ teaspoon salt (optional)

3 tablespoons canola oil

1 tablespoon melted butter

3 to 4 tablespoons water, nonfat
milk, or buttermilk

Preheat the oven to 375°F. for a prebaked crust (although it isn't necessary to prebake for many pies, such as apple or sour cherry.

In a large bowl, combine the flour and salt. Add the canola oil and butter, add 3 tablespoons milk to the butter (adding more if necessary), add the milk and butter mixture to the flour, and, with a fork, mix the ingredients loosely but well, just until they can be pressed into a ball. Sprinkle the counter surface and rolling pin with flour, roll the pastry between sheets of waxed paper (however you don't need it, it's just easier) into a circle about 2 inches larger than the nonstick pie pan. Using a spatula, lift and lightly roll the crust on the rolling pin (to lift the crust without breaking), move the pie pan under the crust on the pin, and unroll it onto the pie pan (or use the waxed paper to place it on the pie pan). Lightly press the crust into the pan, leaving ¼ inch of crust overlapping the pie pan; cut the excess crust with a scissors, roll under and crisscross the edge crust with a fork.

For a prebaked pie shell, poke the bottom with a fork, cover it with a few clean pebbles or metal precrust weights. Prebake for 8 minutes in a 375°F. oven (before adding the filling). You may wish to protect the edge crust with some strips of foil. If you are making an unbaked pie, such as one filled with a chilled custard and you wish the crust to be completely baked, heat the oven to 450°F. and bake for 12 minutes.

PER SERVING: Saturated Fat: 1 gm   Total Fat: 7 gm

Cholesterol: 4 mg   Sodium: 18 mg   Calories: 142

Mary's Old-fashioned Apple Pie

■■   *Serves 8*   ■■

Filled high with apples, this glorious, homey, fifties' style apple pie is my mother Mary's recipe, who introduced me to tapioca to thicken crust-covered fruit pies. Today, the pie can be topped with a nonfat vanilla ice cream. The apples aren't peeled (mother peeled them). The quick-cooking tapioca keeps the juice thick. The best pie apples are California's Gravenstein and a fancy food market can order them for you in the late fall. The pie can have different kinds of crusts: a loose basket-weave lattice-style, a full top crust, or crust cut-outs of apples and leaves. The basket-weave top has less fat than the full crust because there is half the crust; the crust of apples and leaves cuts it even more. A frosting/ glaze (below) can be drizzled on the top crust (after cooling), for those who want a sweeter pie.

1 recipe Buttery Lowered-Fat
 Piecrust (page 306)
6 to 10 tart apples, Gravenstein
 or Granny Smith, cored and
 thinly sliced
3 tablespoons fresh lemon juice
½ cup light brown (or white)
 sugar
¼ cup sugar
3 tablespoons quick-cooking
 tapioca

½ teaspoon cinnamon
⅛ teaspoon nutmeg
⅛ teaspoon allspice
½ cup raisins (optional)
½ cup chopped walnuts (optional)
1 teaspoon sugar for the top crust

OPTIONAL GLAZE:
½ cup confectioner's sugar
3 to 4 teaspoons evaporated
 skimmed milk

Preheat the oven to 400°F.

Roll out the dough using a 9-inch nonstick pie pan and the technique in Buttery Lowered-Fat Piecrust (page 306). Trim off the overhanging pie dough and use for a lattice design on top of the pie or make little leaf or apple cut-outs. In a large bowl, stir together the apples, lemon juice, brown and white sugar, quick-cooking tapioca, cinnamon, nutmeg, and allspice, raisins, if using, and walnuts.

Spoon the apple mixture, including any juice, into the unbaked pie shell, mounding the apples about 4 inches in the center. Arrange the dough cut-outs on top of the apples. Sprinkle with sugar and bake for 10 minutes at 400°F., reduce the temperature to 350°F. and continue baking for an additional 60 minutes to 1 hour and 15 minutes. Remove to a wire rack to cool.

Meanwhile, if using the glaze, in a small plastic bag, squeeze together the confectioner's sugar and the evaporated skimmed milk to mix well. Cut off the tip of one of the bottom corners of the bag to create a piping bag. When the pie cools, squeeze the bag and drizzle the glaze over the crust and apple filling. The glaze will set and become semihard in an hour.

PER SLICE: Saturated Fat: 1 gm   Total Fat: 7 gm
Cholesterol: 4 mg   Sodium: 24 mg   Calories: 296

Sour Cherry Pie

This luscious, tart, cherry-filled pie can be topped with any of several top crusts such as a lattice or basket weave (directions in the recipe). Or for less crust (and fat), try this: With the small end of a melon baller, cut several flat circles to make crust cherries. With a scissors, cut out dough stems and leaves. Arrange cut-outs on the hot filling. If using a commercial crust (most contain extra fat but are very thin and easy to work with), place the second crust in the oven for 5 to 7 minutes to soften, remove it and flatten by hand, and cut strips, ribbons, or cherries and stems to make the top crust (or use the whole bottom crust for the top crust). This pie is best when made with fresh sour cherries. But if they are hard to find, make them with canned (which is better than no sour cherry pie at all).

1 recipe Buttery Lowered-Fat
   Piecrust (page 306) or
   commercial piecrust
3 tablespoons instant tapioca
2 tablespoons cornstarch
2 tablespoons fresh lemon juice
1/2 cup cranberry juice (or juice
   from canned sour cherries)

2 pounds fresh sour cherries, pitted
   (or 2 1/2 16-ounce cans
   unsweetened, pitted sour
   cherries, 1/2 cup juice reserved)
3/4 cup sugar
1/4 teaspoon cinnamon
1/2 teaspoon grated lemon zest

Preheat the oven to 350°F.

Roll out the dough using a 9-inch nonstick pie pan and the technique in Buttery Lowered-Fat Piecrust (page 306). Trim off the overhanging pie dough and use for a lattice design on top of the pie or for cut-outs. Cover the crust edges with foil. Weight the center with glass marbles or piecrust weights and bake for 10 minutes. Remove to a wire rack to cool and remove piecrust weights when cool enough to handle.

In a large nonstick saucepan over medium-low heat, whisk together the tapioca, cornstarch, lemon, and cranberry (or cherry) juice. Add the cherries, sugar, cinnamon, and lemon zest and, with a rubber spatula, mix well. Bring to a simmer and cook, stirring, about 3 minutes. Spoon the hot filling into the partially baked piecrust. Set aside to cool and arrange lattice or leaf cut-outs on top. Set the pie pan on a cookie sheet and bake for 1 hour and 5 minutes, checking to be sure the edge crust doesn't burn.

Turn off the oven and let the pie continue to cook with the door closed for an additional 15 minutes. Remove to a wire rack to cool or serve hot or warm.

PER SLICE: Saturated Fat: 1 gm   Total Fat: 7 gm
Cholesterol: 4 mg   Sodium: 22 mg   Calories: 295

Orange-Grand Marnier Tart

Serves 12

This glamorous and aromatic dessert is absolutely redolent of orange and strawberry. It is a reduced-fat adaptation of one of Lorenza de Médici's (a cookbook author and television cook) and is an unusually elegant pizza-shaped delight. Choose tangy oranges or tangerines for a more successful dessert.

PIE DOUGH:
2¾ cups unsifted all-purpose flour
   plus ½ cup flour (for working
   the flour above)
¾ cup nonfat milk
5 tablespoons canola oil
1 teaspoon baking powder
¼ teaspoon salt (optional)

TOPPING:
½ cup sugar
½ cup orange marmalade

¼ cup Grand Marnier
4 oranges, unpeeled, sliced
   crosswise, ¼-inch thick, and
   seeded
7 strawberries, stemmed and sliced
   lengthwise
14 raspberries
7 blueberries
Several mint leaves, for garnish

Preheat oven to 450°F.

In a large bowl, combine the 2¾ cups flour, milk, oil, baking powder, and salt, if using. Stir with a fork until a soft dough forms. Shape into a ball, cover with plastic wrap, and set aside.

In a large nonstick skillet over medium–low heat, cook the sugar and orange marmalade, stirring, until thick and bubbly. Reduce the heat to low and carefully add the Grand Marnier and orange slices, stirring gently, until the slices are well coated. Using tongs, remove the slices, one at a time, to a wire rack set over waxed paper to catch any extra syrup to drain. Pour any drained syrup that dripped onto the waxed paper back into the pan and continue heating over very low heat, stirring occasionally.

Lightly dust a 20-inch length of parchment or waxed paper with remaining ½ cup flour. With another sheet of the same size parchment or waxed paper on top, press out the pastry. Using a rolling pin, shape the pastry into a 14-inch circle, about ⅛-inch thick, slightly thinner in the middle than at the very edge. (It doesn't need to be a circle. If you have a cookie sheet, it can be rectangular.) When making this for a large group, it cuts into even pieces more easily when rolled on a rectangular baking sheet, then pushed out onto the edges and corners. Turn it once as you roll it out. Lift the paper to get to the edge of the pastry and curl to form a ½-inch rim. Remove the top piece of paper, lift the paper with the dough and transfer it to the baking sheet, remove the rest of the paper, and flatten gently.

Cover the dough with the orange slices arranged in overlapping concentric circles to cover the entire surface. Bake for 10 minutes. Reduce the heat to 400°F. and bake until the crust is golden, about 20 minutes more. Drizzle or brush the tart with the hot syrup covering every slice. Slice the strawberries and fan them, placing them in groups around the edge of the tart. Place 2 raspberries and 1 blueberry at the base of each fan, and garnish with a sprig of mint in the center and a few more tucked in around the edges. Slice very carefully with a large cleaver or double-handled roller knife (a regular knife tears the pastry). Serve within 3 hours, hot, warm, or at room temperature.

■■   PER SERVING: Saturated Fat: 0.5 gm   Total Fat: 6 gm   ■■
Cholesterol: 0 mg   Sodium: 57 mg   Calories: 278

Peach Tartlets

For these tartlets, use the small nonstick individual tartlet pans with removable bottoms. You can also make a large tart by using a regular tart pan with removable bottom, but I prefer the pretty tartlets for special occasions. Top with low-fat vanilla ice cream and a few fresh berries if you wish.

10 very ripe peaches, peeled,
    pitted, and sliced, juice reserved
    in a bowl
Juice of 2 large limes or lemons
⅔ cup maple syrup (depending
    upon the sweetness of the
    peaches you may want a
    tablespoon or two more or less)

½ teaspoon cinnamon
Pinch freshly grated nutmeg
3 tablespoons instant tapioca
Vegetable oil spray
1 recipe Buttery Lowered-Fat
    Piecrust (page 306)

Preheat the oven to 350°F.

In a large nonstick saucepan over medium-high heat, heat the reserved juice from the peaches, lime juice, syrup, cinnamon, nutmeg, and tapioca to boiling. Reduce the heat, cover, and simmer for 10 minutes, or until the tapioca dissolves. Add the peaches, stirring lightly, and cook for 2 minutes; remove from the heat and set aside.

Meanwhile, lightly spray 6 4-inch tartlet pans with oil. Pinch off 6 Ping-Pong-ball-size pieces of pastry from the Buttery Lowered-Fat Piecrust (page 306) and on a well-floured surface or between sheets of waxed paper, roll out the dough pieces into 6-inch diameter circles (if the tartlet pans are 4 inches) until very thin (⅛ inch). Press each into a tart pan, trimming the edge evenly (dough should be even with the top of the sides of the pan and not rise above). Mound each tart pan very high ¼ to ½ inch above the edge with the peach mixture in the pastry and bake for 45 minutes. Remove to a wire rack to cool. Carefully loosen the bottom and sides of the pans gently by pushing up from the bottom and remove the tarts. Serve warm or at room temperature.

PER TARTLET: Saturated Fat: 2 gm   Total Fat: 9 gm
Cholesterol: 5 mg   Sodium: 27 mg   Calories: 364

Fresh Berry Pastry with Yogurt Cheese Cream

This dessert is as elegant as any you might find in the finest restaurant. You can substitute strawberry or mixed berry concentrate for the peach daiquiri if you wish. Tart and creamy with a crispy crust, this must be served within 15 minutes after it's made.

CRUST:
⅓ cup (about 10 cookies) finely
  crushed low-fat gingersnap
  cookies
2 tablespoons light brown sugar
¾ teaspoon cinnamon
4 sheets phyllo pastry
Vegetable oil spray

FILLING:
1 cup yogurt cheese (made from
  plain nonfat yogurt by hanging
  in a cheesecloth or coffee filter
  for 8 hours)

¼ cup frozen peach daiquiri or
  lemonade concentrate, thawed

GARNISH:
2½ cups mixed fresh berries (or
  seedless grapes, papaya, or
  mango chunks)
4 sprigs fresh mint
¼ cup berries, for garnish

Preheat the oven to 375°F.

In a small bowl, stir together the gingersnap crumbs, brown sugar, and cinnamon. Place 1 sheet of the pastry on a flat surface. Lightly spray with oil and sprinkle with 2 tablespoons of the crumb mixture. Top with another sheet of pastry, spray again, and sprinkle with 2 tablespoons of the crumb mixture. Repeat layer with the 2 remaining sheets of pastry and the remaining crumb mixture, ending with the crumbs on top.

With a scissors, cut the sheets of pastry in half lengthwise, then cut each half into 4 equal squares. Place the squares on an ungreased baking sheet 1 inch apart, and bake for 10 minutes; remove from the oven and set aside to cool.

(continued)

Just before serving, in a small bowl, stir together the yogurt cheese and peach daiquiri concentrate. Place 1 baked pastry square on a flat individual plate. Spoon about ⅕ of the yogurt mixture over the pastry. Top with another pastry square to form a sandwich. Add a teaspoon of the yogurt mixture and garnish with the fruit and a sprig of mint. Serve immediately.

■■   PER SQUARE: Saturated Fat: 0.5 gm   Total Fat: 3 gm   ■■
Cholesterol: 2 mg   Sodium: 254 mg   Calories: 265

Grandma Ocean's Chocolate Cake
■■   *Serves 10*   ■■

My Brighton, Iowa, grandmother, Ocean Dosh Irwin, often enjoyed this fudge-dense cake with black coffee in the evening. This is an elegant dessert with a chocolate cream cheese frosting that benefits from chilling time. You may want to make it ahead. Serve in small (they're rich) slices with whipped nonfat dairy topping or nonfat vanilla ice cream or frozen yogurt, if you wish.

Vegetable oil spray
1 cup espresso or extra-strong
  coffee
½ cup prune baby food or prune
  puree
3 egg whites
2 teaspoons vanilla
1½ cups sifted all-purpose flour
1 cup sugar
1 cup unsweetened cocoa
1½ teaspoons baking powder

½ teaspoon baking soda
¼ teaspoon salt (optional)
1 teaspoon melted butter

FROSTING:
1 8-ounce package low-fat or light
  cream cheese (nonfat will not
  work)
3 tablespoons unsweetened cocoa
2 7-ounce jars marshmallow cream
¼ teaspoon almond extract

Preheat oven to 325°F.

Lightly coat a 9-inch by 5-inch by 3-inch loaf pan with the vegetable spray.

In a large bowl, beat the coffee, prunes, egg whites, and vanilla until well blended in a blender or by hand. Add the flour, sugar, cocoa, baking powder, baking soda, salt, if using, and melted butter and stir until well blended. Pour the batter into the prepared pan. Bake 40 to 45 minutes or until a cake tester or toothpick inserted in the center comes out clean. Remove to a wire rack to cool for 20 minutes; remove the cake from the pan and cool completely. Cut into 3 equal horizontal layers.

For the frosting, in a large bowl, beat the cream cheese and cocoa until smooth by hand or with an electric mixer. Add the marshmallow cream and almond extract and stir until smooth. Refrigerate for 1 hour until firm. Spread the frosting between layers, and frost the top and sides. Cover with a cake cover or a larger inverted loaf pan covered with plastic wrap and refrigerate for at least 1 hour. Serve chilled or at room temperature.

PER SLICE: Saturated Fat: 4 gm   Total Fat: 6 gm
Cholesterol: 17 mg   Sodium: 256 mg   Calories: 373

Gingerbread

Gingerbread dates back to medieval Europe, where gingerbread and ginger-bread men were rewards for jousting and for special treats and gifts to and from fair maidens. Several spices, including fresh ginger, is used to make a pungent, sweet, and delicious gingerbread that is best served warm with a nonfat or low-fat whipped topping or ice cream.

⅓ cup canola or safflower oil
½ cup brown sugar
¼ cup egg substitute
½ cup light molasses
¼ cup honey
1 cup hot water
2 tablespoons grated orange zest
2½ cups sifted all-purpose flour
1½ teaspoons baking soda
¼ teaspoon baking powder
1 teaspoon cinnamon

⅛ teaspoon cardamom
¼ teaspoon cloves
¼ teaspoon allspice
3 teaspoons ground ginger
½ teaspoon finely grated fresh
 ginger
½ teaspoon salt (optional)
Vegetable oil spray with flour
 (Baker's Joy)
Confectioner's sugar

Preheat the oven to 350°F.

In a large bowl, whisk together the oil, sugar, and egg substitute. Add the molasses, honey, water, and orange zest and mix well. Into another bowl, sift together the flour, baking soda, powder, cinnamon, cardamom, cloves, allspice, ground and fresh ginger, and salt, if using. Whisk the oil and sugar mixture, a small amount at a time, into the sifted ingredients until well mixed. Lightly spray an 8-inch-square baking pan with vegetable oil and dust with the flour (or use Baker's Joy). Pour batter into the prepared pan and bake for 50 minutes or until a toothpick inserted in the center comes out clean (baking too long will make a hard cake). Serve hot or cold, with whipped nonfat milk (page 335), nonfat ice cream, or drizzle, when cool, with a sugar frosting glaze (page 308).

PER SERVING: Saturated Fat: 0.5 gm Total Fat: 8 gm
Cholesterol: 0 mg Sodium: 230 mg Calories: 298

Pumpkin and Orange
Swirl Cheesecake

■■ *Serves 10 to 12* ■■

A creamy cheesecake spiced with pumpkin and orange, this dessert can be frozen until you're ready to bake it or frozen after baking. For egg yolk watchers, this cake uses 2 whole eggs as substitutes don't work.

Vegetable oil spray
1¼ cups gingersnap cookie crumbs
  (about 12 cookies)
1 8-ounce package light cream
  cheese, room temperature
1 8-ounce package nonfat cream
  cheese, room temperature
1 15-ounce container nonfat
  ricotta
2 eggs
¾ cup orange juice frozen
  concentrate

¾ cup plus ⅓ cup sugar
1 teaspoon vanilla
1 16-ounce can unsweetened
  solid-packed pumpkin pie filling
1 egg white
1 teaspoon cinnamon
1 medium navel orange, thinly
  sliced (optional)
Several small fresh mint leaves
  (optional)

Preheat the oven to 325°F.

In a saucepan, heat 2 quarts water to boiling.

Meanwhile, completely line the outside of a 9-inch springform pan with heavy-duty foil (which is wider), making sure all the edges are sealed and the foil has no holes. Lightly spray the inside of the pan with oil. Add the gingersnap crumbs and flatten with the palm of your hand.

In a food processor or bowl of an electric mixer, beat together the cream cheeses, ricotta, eggs, orange juice concentrate, ¾ cup sugar, and vanilla until light and smooth. Measure 3½ cups cream cheese filling into the crust-lined pan. To the processor or bowl containing the remaining cheese mixture, add the pumpkin puree, ⅓ cup sugar, egg white, and cinnamon and pulse to mix well. Spoon the pumpkin mixture ¼ cup at a time onto the cream cheese mixture in the pan and, with a rubber spatula, cut through and swirl a few times to marble.

(continued)

Set the springform pan in a 14-inch by 9-inch by 3-inch pan and add enough boiling water to come halfway up the outside of the springform pan. Bake for 1 hour and 10 to 15 minutes, until firm but slightly jiggly. Turn the oven off and allow the cheesecake to cool in the oven for 1 hour. Remove to a wire rack to cool completely. Cover with foil or plastic wrap and refrigerate for 2 hours.

To serve, remove the cake to a serving platter, being careful that the cake doesn't crack. (Slide it off the pan bottom with both hands cupping the cake and get someone to help you if necessary.) If garnishing with the oranges, cut the slices in half and place around the edge of the cake, cut side down. Garnish in between orange slices with mint leaves.

PER SLICE: Saturated Fat: 3 gm   Total Fat: 6 gm
Cholesterol: 52 mg   Sodium: 328 mg   Calories: 261

Lemon-Amaretto Cheesecake
Serves 10

This is a smooth and creamy cake, spiked with irresistible Amaretto and the tang of fresh lemon. I save this for elegant meals and buffets (and when I want to treat myself for several days). You can substitute any fresh berry for the strawberries. This is one of the few recipes where egg yolks are used and they are necessary because egg substitutes don't work. Per slice, however, the overall cholesterol amount is very small.

Vegetable oil spray
1⅓ cups low-fat ground (processed) granola without raisins
1 cup nonfat yogurt cheese
2 cups nonfat cottage cheese
1 8-ounce package light cream cheese, room temperature

1 8-ounce package nonfat cream cheese, room temperature
¾ cup lemonade frozen concentrate
2 whole eggs and 2 egg whites
¼ cup sugar
¼ cup Amaretto
1½ cups marshmallow cream

1 tablespoon lemonade frozen
  concentrate
3 tablespoons Cassis (optional)
1 cup cranberry juice

3 cups sliced, fresh strawberries
  (about 1 pint), juice reserved
  (juice is optional), 3
  strawberries with leaves, for
  garnish
2 tablespoons arrowroot or
  cornstarch

Preheat the oven to 325°F.

In a medium saucepan, heat 3 cups water to boiling.

Meanwhile, completely line the outside of a 9-inch springform pan with heavy-duty foil (it is wider), making sure all the edges are sealed and the foil has no holes. Lightly spray the inside of the pan with oil. Sprinkle the granola over the bottom of the pan.

In a food processor, puree the yogurt and cottage cheese at least 3 minutes. Add the cream cheeses and process for 2 minutes. Add the lemonade concentrate, eggs, egg whites, sugar, and Amaretto and pulse to mix. Add the marshmallow cream and pulse 4 to 6 times to mix. Pour the mixture into the prepared pan.

Set the springform pan in a 14-inch by 9-inch by 3-inch pan and add enough boiling water to come halfway up the outside of the springform pan. Bake for 1 hour and 15 minutes. Turn the oven off and allow the cheesecake to cool in the oven for 1 hour. Remove to a wire rack to cool completely. Cover with foil or plastic wrap and refrigerate for at least 2 hours.

In a medium saucepan over medium heat, whisk together the lemonade concentrate, Cassis, cranberry juice, reserved strawberry juice, and cornstarch and cook about 3 minutes until thickened. Add the drained berries, stir lightly, and cook just until berries and sauce are thick. Refrigrate to chill; spoon over the cheesecake just before serving, garnish and serve cold.

■ PER SLICE: Saturated Fat: 3 gm   Total Fat: 6 gm   ■
Cholesterol: 62 mg   Sodium: 474 mg   Calories: 401

Apple Crisp

This is packed with tart and tender apples (I like Gravensteins) under a very crisp topping. Add ¼ cup raisins or toasted walnuts for texture and crunch, if you wish. For an extra touch, I serve it with a yogurt or low-fat ice cream topping, but this is also satisfying just as is. You can peel the apples for a less chewy crisp.

Vegetable oil spray
6 tart apples, cored and sliced
2 tablespoons fresh lemon juice
½ cup brown sugar
¼ teaspoon cinnamon
¼ cup oat bran
¼ cup rolled oats
¼ cup nonfat or low-fat granola
  (without raisins)

2 tablespoons flour
2 tablespoons brown sugar
4 tablespoons diet margarine
1 cup plain nonfat yogurt
3 to 4 tablespoons maple syrup or
  light corn syrup

Preheat the oven to 350°F.

Lightly spray an 8-inch by 8-inch baking dish with vegetable oil and arrange the apples in the dish. Sprinkle with the lemon juice, brown sugar, and cinnamon.

In a small nonstick saucepan over medium heat, cook the oat bran, rolled oats, granola, flour, brown sugar, and margarine for about 3 minutes, stirring well. Spoon the mixture over the apples and bake for 45 minutes. (Or cook in the microwave oven at high for 20 minutes with loosely covered plastic wrap (microwaving makes the topping less crisp.)

In a small bowl, whisk together the yogurt and maple syrup. To serve, drizzle the sauce around the edge of individual plates and spoon a serving of the crisp in the center.

PER SERVING: Saturated Fat: 1 gm   Total Fat: 5 gm
Cholesterol: 0 mg   Sodium: 82 mg   Calories: 298

Blueberry-Peach Buckle

Serves 12

Here is a home-style berry-filled cake that tastes best when blueberries and peaches are in the peak of season, but I have had great success using frozen fruit as well. It's my favorite breakfast cake, served plain, and it's a scrumptious dessert served with nonfat ice cream or No-Fat Whipped Topping (page 335).

CAKE:
2 cups sifted all-purpose flour
2 teaspoons baking powder
1 cup sugar
½ teaspoon salt (optional)
1 egg white
¼ cup egg substitute
¼ cup canola oil
½ cup nonfat milk
1 pint blueberries

½ teaspoon lemon zest (optional)
2 tablespoons flour

TOPPING:
¼ cup canola oil
½ cup brown sugar
½ teaspoon salt (optional)
⅓ cup all-purpose flour
2 medium ripe peaches, peeled,
    pitted, and chopped
½ teaspoon cinnamon

Preheat the oven to 350°F.

In a medium bowl, stir together the flour, baking powder, sugar, and salt, if using. In another bowl, beat the egg white until frothy; add the egg, oil, and milk and mix until well blended. Stir in the blueberries and lemon zest, sprinkle with 2 tablespoons flour, and fold carefully until just combined. Pour into a nonstick 8-inch or 9-inch deep-dish pie pan or a 9-inch by 5-inch by 3-inch nonstick loaf pan.

For the topping, in a small bowl, combine the oil, sugar, salt, if using, flour, peaches, and cinnamon and stir, mashing up the peaches until blended. Spoon the topping over the batter. Bake for 1 hour 45 minutes, until a cake tester or toothpick inserted in the center comes out clean. Bake an additional 10 minutes if necessary. Remove to a wire rack to cool slightly and serve warm or at room temperature.

PER SERVING: Saturated Fat: 1 gm   Total Fat: 9 gm
Cholesterol: 0 mg   Sodium: 103 mg   Calories: 299

Blackberry Cobbler

Serves 8

Fruit cobblers such as this one are so much better when prepared with peak of the season berries; however, feel free to substitute any fruit you have in abundance (even apples). This cobbler comes to table without the high-fat biscuit top crust but with a low-fat buttery crust.

Vegetable oil spray
2 pints blackberries
3 to 5 tablespoons fresh lemon
   juice
⅓ to ½ cup sugar
2½ tablespoons quick-cooking
   tapioca

¼ or ½ teaspoon cinnamon
1 recipe Buttery Lowered-Fat
   Piecrust (page 306)
1 teaspoon sugar

Preheat the oven to 375°F.

Lightly spray a 3-inch high-sided 6- to 8-inch square or round baking pan or dish with vegetable oil. In a large bowl, combine the blackberries, lemon juice, sugar, tapioca, and cinnamon to taste, and let sit for 15 minutes, tossing occasionally.

Using the technique in Buttery Lowered-Fat Piecrust (page 306), roll out the pie dough roughly 3 to 4 inches larger than the baking dish you are using and about ¼- to ⅛-inch thick. Put the dough in the baking dish, add the berry filling, and loosely fold the dough over the corners, creasing the edges (pleating if you want, or just gently wrapping it). The center will be open. Sprinkle the top of the dough with sugar, and bake uncovered for 50 to 60 minutes, until the mixture is juicy and the blackberries almost tender. Serve warm or at room temperature. If desired, top with No-Fat Whipped Topping (page 335), nonfat ice cream, vanilla yogurt, or frozen vanilla yogurt.

PER SERVING: Saturated Fat: 1 gm   Total Fat: 7 gm
        Cholesterol: 4 mg   Sodium: 18 mg   Calories: 234

Peach-Blueberry Layered Torte

Juicy peaches and blueberries are layered with cakelike sweetened bread crumbs to make this moist and dense tort. Substitute nectarines, black raspberries, or boysenberries if you wish. Spoon this luscious cake onto serving plates instead of slicing it.

6 slices fresh white bread, crust
   removed
Vegetable oil spray
½ cup sugar
2 teaspoons cinnamon
½ teaspoon ground ginger
1 cup diced dried peaches

1 6-ounce jar peach baby food
1 cup chunky applesauce
2 tablespoons peach or apricot
   brandy or liqueur (optional)
1½ cup fresh or frozen blueberries
   (not thawed)

Preheat the oven to 350°F.

In a food processor, process the bread a few slices at a time until crumbs. Line an 8-inch springform pan with foil and lightly spray the foil with vegetable oil.

Spray a large nonstick sauté pan with a vegetable oil and place over medium heat. Add the bread crumbs, sugar, cinnamon, and ginger and cook, tossing occasionally, for about 7 minutes, until the crumbs are brown and the sugar begins to melt. Remove from the heat and set aside.

In a medium bowl, stir together the dried peaches, peach baby food, applesauce, peach brandy, and blueberries.

Place one third of the crumbs on the bottom of the springform pan and top with half of the fruit mixture. Make another layer using one third of the crumbs and the remaining fruit mixture. Top with the last third of crumb mixture. Bake for 45 minutes. Remove to a wire rack to cool completely before serving.

PER SERVING: Saturated Fat: Trace   Total Fat: 1 gm
Cholesterol: 0 mg   Sodium: 121 mg   Calories: 282

Chocolaty Chocolate Brownies

Makes 36 1½-inch squares

These are chocolate rich and especially moist thanks to the addition of banana. If you are not a banana lover, fear not. You may omit it and the brownies are still rich winners. Just add ½ cup of baby prunes.

½ cup egg substitute or 8 egg
   whites
½ cup canola oil
1½ teaspoons vanilla
1 very ripe banana
1¼ cups sugar
½ cup plus 2 tablespoons
   unsweetened cocoa

1 cup sifted all-purpose flour
¼ cup oat bran
¼ teaspoon salt (optional)
½ cup chocolate chips
½ cup coarsely chopped walnuts
Baker's Joy
Confectioner's sugar

Preheat the oven to 350°F.

In a food processor, process the eggs until frothy. Add the oil, vanilla, and banana, and process until smooth. Add the sugar and cocoa and process until blended. Remove the bowl and blade, and stir in the flour, oat bran, and salt, if using, until well mixed. Stir in the chips and walnuts.

Spray a 9-inch by 9-inch baking pan with Baker's Joy, pour the batter into the pan, and bake for 30 to 35 minutes. Remove the pan to a wire rack to cool slightly. Sprinkle with confectioner's sugar and cut into 1-inch squares. Serve warm.

PER 3 1½-INCH SQUARES: Saturated Fat: 3 gm
Total Fat: 15 gm Cholesterol: 0 mg Sodium: 16 mg Calories: 295

Date-Apple Bars

This is an adaptation of a popular dessert from the fifties that we called matrimonial bars. In my updated version, a moist apple-date filling and two layers of oat pastry make the cookie dessert as irresistible as ever, without as much added fat.

Vegetable oil spray
8 ounces pitted chopped dates
½ cup granulated sugar
1 large Granny Smith or
    Greening apple, peeled, cored,
    and diced

½ cup walnuts, coarsely chopped
1¼ cups sifted all-purpose flour
1 teaspoon baking soda
2 cups quick-cooking or rolled oats
1 cup dark brown sugar, packed
½ cup canola oil

Preheat the oven to 325°F.

Lightly spray an 8-inch square nonstick baking pan with vegetable oil. In a medium nonstick saucepan over high heat, bring ½ cup water to boiling. Add the dates and sugar and cook for 10 to 12 minutes, until thick and smooth. Add the apple and cook, stirring, 2 minutes. Stir in the walnuts and remove from heat.

In a large bowl, stir together the flour, baking soda, oats, and brown sugar. With a spoon or fingers, work in the oil until the mixture is crumbly and moist. Set aside 1 cup of the mixture for topping. Press the remainder evenly in the bottom of the prepared pan.

Spread the date filling over the oat mixture and sprinkle evenly with reserved oat mixture; press the topping down with your hand or the back of a spoon. Bake 50 to 60 minutes, until firm and browned. Remove to a wire rack to cool. Cut into 1½- by 2-inch rectangles.

PER RECTANGLE: Saturated Fat: 0.5 gm   Total Fat: 7 gm
Cholesterol: 0 mg   Sodium: 57 mg   Calories: 188

Oatmeal Cookies

These old-fashioned cookies won't last the day in your house. The raisins and walnuts can be chopped in a processor.

½ cup canola oil

½ cup unsweetened applesauce

¾ cup brown sugar

½ cup light corn syrup

¼ cup egg substitute or 2 egg whites

¼ cup nonfat milk

2 cups sifted all-purpose flour

2 cups old-fashioned oatmeal

1 teaspoon baking powder

1½ teaspoons cinnamon

¼ teaspoon nutmeg

⅛ teaspoon allspice

1 cup chopped walnuts

1 cup whole or coarsely chopped raisins

Vegetable oil spray

Preheat the oven to 350°F.

In a large bowl, beat the oil, applesauce, sugar, syrup, eggs, and milk until light and creamy. In another bowl, stir together the flour, oatmeal, baking powder, cinnamon, nutmeg, allspice, walnuts and raisins. Add the creamed ingredients to the dry and blend well.

Lightly spray a baking sheet with vegetable oil, and drop the batter by the tablespoonful for larger cookies onto the prepared baking sheet 1 inch apart. Bake for 15 minutes and remove cookies to a wire rack to cool.

PER COOKIE: Saturated Fat: 0.5 gm   Total Fat: 8 gm
Cholesterol: 0 mg   Sodium: 36 mg   Calories: 196

Apricot-Grand Marnier Balls

These are quick to prepare——just thirty minutes from mixing bowl to serving platter. Slightly spirited fruity rounds with delightful tart and sweet flavors, I like to have them around for a snack or with tea or coffee, but they make a fine minidessert.

1 cup finely chopped dried apricots	1/4 cup marshmallow cream
2 tablespoons golden raisins	1 1/2 cups gingersnap crumbs
3 tablespoons Grand Marnier or other orange liqueur	

In a medium microwave-safe container, combine the apricots, raisins, and Grand Marnier. Cover with plastic wrap and cook at high 60 to 90 seconds; cool to room temperature. With a fork, stir in the marshmallow cream and 1 cup gingersnap crumbs. Form into 3/4-inch balls. Place the remaining crumbs on a plate or in a shallow bowl, and roll the balls in the crumbs to coat. Refrigerate overnight before serving. They'll keep for a week.

PER 2 BALLS: Saturated Fat: Trace Total Fat: 2 gm
Cholesterol: 0 mg Sodium: 146 mg Calories: 166

Almond Bananas with Pear Brandy

A light almond-flavored dessert, this makes perfect use of very ripe bananas (pears, too). Just make sure they have no major blemishes. It is easy and quick—taking 3 minutes to prepare and 15 minutes to cook unattended. I like to serve this with No-Fat Whipped Topping (page 335). Other sweet liqueurs, such as Grand Marnier, Drambouie, and Tia Maria, stand in well for the pear brandy. Nonfat or low-fat vanilla ice cream or frozen yogurt go with these too.

4 large, very ripe bananas, peeled	¼ teaspoon almond extract
½ cup sugar	¼ cup slivered almonds
¼ cup pear brandy	¼ cup blueberries

Cut the bananas in half lengthwise. In a large nonstick skillet over low heat, heat the bananas, sugar, brandy, almond extract, and slivered almonds; cover and simmer for 15 minutes. Add the blueberries during the last minute of cooking. Serve hot, warm, or cold.

PER SERVING: Saturated Fat: 0.5 gm Total Fat: 5 gm
Cholesterol: 0 mg Sodium: 2 mg Calories: 299

Rum Bananas

The easiest one-skillet dessert is also the richest. This simple mixture of rum, maple syrup (or brown sugar), and bananas is plenty satisfying as is. You may, however, want to serve them with nonfat vanilla yogurt or ice cream. Fresh blueberries or raspberries make excellent garnish and any sweet liqueur, such as Grand Marnier or Drambouie, can substitute for the rum.

4 large, very ripe bananas, peeled	*¼ cup dark or light rum*
½ cup maple syrup or brown	*1 teaspoon vanilla*
sugar	*¼ cup blueberries, for garnish*

Cut the bananas in half lengthwise. In a large nonstick skillet over low heat, heat the bananas, syrup, rum, and vanilla; cover and simmer for 15 minutes. Add the blueberries during the last minute of cooking. Serve hot.

PER SERVING: Saturated Fat: Trace Total Fat: 0.5 gm Cholesterol: 0 mg Sodium: 5 mg Calories: 276

Black Raspberry Sorbet

A quick and simple pure fruit dessert is wonderfully refreshing on a hot summer day. I've served this one for brunch as well as to the kids for afternoon snacks. Substitute almost any fruit you wish and it will work in this recipe. When you refreeze the sorbet and wish to serve it again, defrost slightly and repuree before serving.

½ cup finely granulated sugar (for unsweetened fruit) or 1½ teaspoons if sweetened
1 pound frozen black raspberries or boysenberries (with sugar), ¼ cup reserved, for garnish

¼ teaspoon lemon zest
¼ teaspoon lime or orange zest
Juice of one lemon
¼ cup nonfat vanilla yogurt
½ teaspoon cinnamon
4 mint leaves

In a food processor, process the sugar for 3 minutes until fine. Add the berries, zest, juice, yogurt, cinnamon and puree until smooth; check for sweetness, adding more sugar if necessary. Garnish with a mint leaf and fresh berries and serve immediately. For a more frozen sorbet, freeze the mixture in a plastic-lined 8-inch square pan. When frozen, remove, chop and process once again, and refreeze for 2 hours, or until just firm. Scoop into individual dessert cups, garnish, and serve immediately.

PER SERVING: Saturated Fat: 0 gm   Total Fat: Trace
Cholesterol: 0 mg   Sodium: 12 mg   Calories: 149

Chocolate Cookie Open-Face Ice Cream Sandwiches

Large and flat and nothing fancy, these dark semisoft cookies are perfect with 3-percent-fat ice cream and nonfat frozen yogurt toppings. For a make-ahead dessert for kids, spread the cookies with an inch of the ice cream in upward swirls, wrap in plastic wrap, and freeze.

Vegetable oil spray
¾ cup light brown sugar
½ cup sugar
¼ cup plus 1 tablespoon
   unsweetened cocoa
2 teaspoons instant coffee granules
1 cup rolled oats, toasted for 10
   minutes in a 350°F. oven
1½ cups all-purpose flour
¼ teaspoon baking soda

½ teaspoon baking powder
2 teaspoons cinnamon
⅓ cup either apricot or prune baby
   food
2 tablespoons canola oil
⅓ cup nonfat plain yogurt
1 pint 3-percent-fat coffee ice
   cream or nonfat frozen yogurt,
   softened

Preheat the oven to 350°F.

Lightly spray a nonstick baking sheet with vegetable oil.

In a large bowl, stir together the sugars, unsweetened cocoa, coffee granules, oats, flour, baking soda, baking powder, and cinnamon. Add each remaining ingredient one at a time, stirring well after each addition.

Drop the batter by the heaping tablespoonful onto the prepared baking sheet at least 2 inches apart. Spray the back of a spoon with vegetable oil and use it to flatten the cookies to ¼ inch to ½ inch in height. Bake for 12 to 15 minutes. Remove cookies to a wire rack to cool completely. Spread with ice cream or frozen yogurt and serve.

PER COOKIE: Saturated Fat: 0.5 gm   Total Fat: 3 gm
Cholesterol: Trace   Sodium: 79 mg   Calories: 238

Raspberry Sauce

Use this versatile dessert sauce on angel food cake, poached pears, rice or bread pudding, or as a topping on low-fat ice cream. Strain out the seeds if you like and if using frozen raspberries, don't add sugar.

1 pint raspberries, 12 berries
  reserved, for garnish
⅓ cup super-fine or regular
  granulated sugar

2 teaspoons fresh lemon juice
½ teaspoon lemon zest
Pinch of cinnamon

In a food processor or blender, combine the berries, sugar, lemon juice, zest, and cinnamon and process until blended for chunky. Serve warm or cold, topped with the reserved berries.

PER ¼ CUP: Saturated Fat: 0 gm   Total Fat: Trace
Cholesterol: 0 mg   Sodium: 0 mg   Calories: 63

No-Fat Whipped Topping

Serves 4

An excellent whipped topping can be made from nonfat (skim) milk if you have an immersion, or hand, blender. Use skim milk only, not 1 percent. Check the label; some nonfat milk is actually 1 percent. Some 100-percent nonfat milk won't whip up if it contains emulsifiers or stabilizers.

The milk must be very cold. Set it in the freezer for 10 minutes and it will usually whip up within 2 or 3 minutes. If it doesn't, the milk contains stabilizers or starches and will not whip. An immersion, or hand, blender is necessary. To change the flavor slightly, use almond extract instead of vanilla. I also add a stabilizer called Whip It. When added to the milk, it helps keep the fluff in the whip, but you don't have to.

Use this topping as soon as it is ready as it liquefies more rapidly than whipped cream.

½ cup nonfat milk, chilled in the freezer for 10 minutes

2 teaspoons sugar
1 teaspoon vanilla

Fill a large metal bowl with ice and water. In a smaller metal bowl, pour ¼ cup nonfat milk. With an up-and-down motion, whip the milk. Within a minute or two it will double in volume, then stiffen and quadruple. Add the sugar and vanilla, whip until incorporated, and serve immediately.

PER ¼ CUP: Saturated Fat: 0 gm Total Fat: 0 gm
Cholesterol: 0 mg Sodium: 16 mg Calories: 22

BREAKFASTS AND BRUNCHES

∷   ∷

I f you are just beginning to adapt your lifestyle to include healthful meals, begin with breakfast and brunch. They are the easiest meals to keep lush and indulgent and still be stripped of fat and calories. You can still jump-start your day with healthy and indulgent breakfasts and brunches without changing the quality or amount of most of the foods you like. This chapter is full of tips and recipes to help you get started. If you have already begun a healthful eating plan, you'll want to add these recipes to your repertoire.

∷ Healthy Choices for Breakfast ∷ and Brunch

There is a vast array of packaged healthful breakfast foods already available in supermarkets. There are so many good choices for a quick breakfast both at home or in restaurants that you never need rely on donuts (or bacon and fried eggs) again, which are one of the highest food sources causing weight gain, fat, and cholesterol in Americans.

AT HOME **Cereals** are made from grains such as wheat, corn, oats, rice, and others, including the bran, and provide complex carbohydrate energy, vitamins, minerals, and fiber. Choose hot cereals, such as grits, bulgur, wheat, oatmeal, or almost any of the cold varieties, such as corn flakes, shredded wheat, crisped rice, or wheat puffs. Read labels and select those with little fat. When eaten with skim milk or nonfat creamers instead of whole milk, hot or cold cereal is a nutrition bargain—low in fat and cholesterol yet satisfying.

Breads, such as bagels and 3-inch by ½-inch English muffins, have almost no fat at all. Pay attention to labels and don't pick one with high fat or more than 3 grams of fat. Select small bagels, those 2 to 2½ ounces or about the size of your fist. If larger, some are 5 or 6 ounces, eat only half. Other multigrain breads made without excess fats and oils are also fine choices for breakfast. Bran muffins are often high in fat and sugar.

Pancakes and waffles on their own can actually be low in fat. But when topped with a generous chunk of butter or heavy whipped cream, they compete with any other whipped cream and butter dish. Pancake mixes can have generous amounts of fat but most have very little. Again, look at the fat content on the label and select those with fewer than 3 grams of fat per serving. Use naturally nonfat toppings, including syrups, preserves, jams, conserves, jellies, and fresh fruits instead.

Eggs in the morning for many Americans are an important ritual, yet we know that lurking in every egg yolk, including those in lowered-cholesterol eggs, are high amounts of cholesterol. Substituting egg whites, which have no cholesterol, for whole eggs is very satisfying, especially when combined with steamed mushrooms or vegetables. There are many egg substitutes, too. They are all 99 percent real eggs and all are fat free, which taste excellent. I've discovered one or two brands that taste just like shell eggs.

Use egg whites or egg substitute for omelettes, scrambled eggs, pan-cakes, waffles, French toast, quiche, and other homemade goodies like coffee cakes and spoon breads, too.

> For 1 whole egg, substitute 2 egg whites
> or use 3 egg whites plus 1 teaspoon canola oil, if you aren't counting calories,
> or use ¼ cup fresh egg substitute
> or use ¼ cup frozen, thawed egg substitute.

Breakfast meats, such as sausage links and patties, fatty ham, bacon, and scrapple, are notorious for their high fat content. But low-fat choices are available that will satisfy a meat craving. Instead of using sausage, bacon, and regular ham, use Canadian bacon, soy sausages, vegetarian sausages, and Sausage Slims (page 361) as well as lean 3-percent ham or even lean bacon that's been stripped of its fat.

IN THE RESTAURANT Although the low-fat choices seem few when you look over a menu in a restaurant, ask the waiter what the chef might be able to offer "off the menu." Meanwhile, here are a few low-fat picks from almost any menu:

Cereals:
- Hot or cold with nonfat milk
- Nonfat or low-fat granola with nonfat milk
- Cornmeal grits or oatmeal with nonfat milk

Breads:
- Bagel, white or whole wheat toast, English muffin, or crumpet with half a patty of margarine
- Bagel with lox or smoked trout

Pancakes or waffles:
- Without extra butter or margarine
- With syrup or fruit

Fruit:
- Fresh fruit or fruit cup, canned fruit, fresh or canned fruit juice

Eggs:
- Scrambled egg whites or egg substitute omelette with lox, salmon, trout, Canadian bacon, or regular bacon (with the fat removed)

Breakfast Fat and Calorie Facts

Have this:

1 small bagel, 1 tablespoon jam: 235 calories, 1 gm fat

1 slice toast, 1 teaspoon jam: 109 calories, 1 gm fat

1 English muffin with ½ teaspoon margarine, 1 teaspoon honey or jelly: 173 calories, 3 gm fat

1 cup cereal with ½ cup nonfat milk: 140 calories, 0.5 gm fat

1 cup grits with ½ cup nonfat milk: 188 calories, 1 gm fat

1 waffle with ¼ cup syrup: 318 calories, 3 gm fat

2 pancakes with ¼ cup syrup: 348 calories, 5 gm fat

2 ounces lean Canadian bacon: 105 calories, 5 gm fat

3.5 ounces lox or salmon: 116 calories, 4 gm fat

3 egg whites or egg substitute omelette: 50 calories, 0 gm fat

Instead of:

1 bagel with 2 tablespoons cream cheese: 288 calories, 11 gm fat

1 slice toast with 1 pat butter and 1 teaspoon jam: 143 calories, 5 gm fat

1 English muffin with 1 pat butter and 2 tablespoons cream cheese: 271 calories, 15 gm fat

1 cup cereal with ½ cup half and half: 255 calories, 14 gm fat

1 cup grits with 1 pat butter: 181 calories, 5 gm fat

1 waffle with 1 pat butter and ¼ cup syrup: 354 calories, 7 gm fat

2 pancakes with 1 pat butter and ¼ cup syrup: 384 calories, 9 gm fat

2 ounces sausages: 209 calories, 18 gm fat

6 strips bacon: 219 calories, 19 gm fat

3 eggs and ⅓ cup cheese omelette: 374 calories, 27 gm fat

Asparagus and Brie Omelette

This omelette is unmatched by few brunch dishes in elegance, simplicity, and taste. If the asparagus are large and thick, use just 1 or 2 per serving. Use several if they are the small, slender variety.

Butter-flavored spray or
   ¼ teaspoon butter
1 cup egg substitute
2 tablespoons softened Brie
   (without skin), sliced

⅓ to ½ pound asparagus (8 or
   10 spears)
Salt (optional)
Freshly ground black pepper
2 tablespoons chopped parsley

Heat a 7-inch nonstick skillet over medium-high heat until hot and lightly spray with the butter-flavored spray (or add the butter and tip the pan to coat the bottom while melting). Reduce the heat to very low and pour in the eggs. Pull off several small pea-size bits of Brie and drop them over the surface of the eggs. Cover and cook for about 8 minutes, checking the bottom of the eggs with a rubber spatula to be sure they do not burn.

Meanwhile, in an asparagus steamer, nonstick saucepan, or large skillet, heat ½ inch water. Add the asparagus, cover, and steam for 2 to 3 minutes. Remove, drain, cover, and keep warm (they will keep on cooking).

When the eggs are firm, slice them in half, and arrange each half on an individual plate. Place several asparagus spears on the omelette and fold the omelette around the asparagus, with the ends of the asparagus sticking out. Add salt, if using, and pepper, sprinkle with parsley, and serve immediately.

PER SERVING: Saturated Fat: 2 gm   Total Fat: 3 gm
Cholesterol: 9 mg   Sodium: 227 mg   Calories: 99

Huevos Rancheros

Here is the Mexican ranch-style omelette that is a popular brunch dish all over the United States. Most supermarkets carry the soft flour tortillas that this dish requires.

Vegetable oil spray
4 6-inch flour tortillas
1 clove garlic, minced
1 large onion, coarsely chopped
1 green bell pepper, cut in ¾-inch squares, seeds reserved
1 cup low-sodium canned tomatoes or diced fresh tomatoes, juice reserved
2 teaspoons chili powder
½ teaspoon ground cumin

½ teaspoon dried oregano
Salt (optional)
Freshly ground black pepper
Several drops Tabasco or ⅛ teaspoon finely chopped and seeded jalapeños
4 egg whites
1 cup egg substitute
⅛ teaspoon turmeric (optional)
½ teaspoon chopped cilantro or parsley

Preheat the oven to 150°F.

Lightly spray a large nonstick skillet with vegetable oil and place over medium–high heat. Add the tortillas 1 at a time and lightly brown both sides. Fold each tortilla in half, and cut each half in two. Cover and keep warm in the oven.

In the same skillet over medium heat, add enough water to measure ¼ inch. Add the garlic, onion, and pepper, and cook, stirring occasionally, adding more water by the teaspoon if necessary, for about 5 minutes, until the vegetables are translucent and soft. Add the tomatoes, squeezing them through your fingers to break them up, ½ cup reserved tomato juice, pepper seeds, chili powder, cumin, oregano, salt, if using, pepper, and Tabasco; reduce the heat to medium low and cook for 8 to 10 minutes, stirring occasionally, until the sauce has thickened. Taste and adjust the seasonings if necessary, and set aside.

Meanwhile, in a small bowl, whisk the egg whites until frothy. Add the egg substitute and turmeric and whisk until frothy. Lightly spray a large nonstick skillet with vegetable oil and place over medium–high heat. Add the eggs and cook, scrambling them, stirring often.

To serve, place 2 folded tortilla pieces on individual plates. Top the tortillas with the eggs (tortillas protruding), then spoon the sauce on top of the eggs. Sprinkle with cilantro and serve immediately.

■■ PER SERVING: Saturated Fat: Trace Total Fat: 2 gm ■■
Cholesterol: 0 mg Sodium: 278 mg Calories: 162

Spicy Filled Tortilla Rolls
Serves 4

Another Tex-Mex flavor treat, these soft tortilla rolls can be made a day ahead, heated, and served to a hungry brunch bunch. These are pretty spicy but if you want more heat, add $1/4$ to $1/2$ teaspoon finely chopped seeded jalapeño.

Vegetable oil spray
1 small red onion, diced
1 medium red bell pepper, diced
2 cups egg substitute
1 cup whole kernel corn, fresh or
frozen and thawed
2 cups Yellow Salsa (page 280)
4 large corn or flour tortillas

1/3 cup shredded nonfat Cheddar
cheese
2 tablespoons shredded sharp
Cheddar cheese
1/2 cup chopped red or yellow
onion, for garnish
Several drops of Tabasco, for
garnish

Preheat the oven to 400°F.

Lightly spray a medium nonstick skillet with vegetable oil and place over medium-high heat. Add the onion and a few teaspoons water and cook, stirring, for 3 minutes. Add the bell pepper and cook 3 more minutes, adding more water by the teaspoon, if needed. Reduce the heat to medium and add the eggs; cook, stirring until the eggs are loosely set. Stir in the corn and ½ cup salsa and cook until well combined. Remove from the heat and set aside.

(continued)

Meanwhile, in a microwave-safe container, heat the remaining salsa at high for about 1 minute, and set aside. Lightly spray a 7-inch by 11-inch baking pan with vegetable oil. Place a tortilla on a cutting board and spoon one quarter of the egg mixture onto one edge; roll the tortilla up and place the roll in the baking pan edge side down. Repeat with the remaining 3 tortillas. Sprinkle the rolls with the cheese and bake 15 minutes, or until the cheese has melted.

To serve, place 1 tortilla on each individual plate, and spoon a tablespoon or two of the warmed salsa over the top. Sprinkle with onions and a few drops of Tabasco and serve immediately.

PER SERVING: Saturated Fat: 1 gm   Total Fat: 3 gm
Cholesterol: 4 mg   Sodium: 366 mg   Calories: 282

Curry-Chutney Omelette
Makes 4 omelettes

The tastes and textures of curry, chutney, and eggs always complement one another and this omelette is no exception. I like Hot Bengal, the spicy variety, a little better than Major Grey's chutney but both are good. They are both available in most supermarkets and in specialty food stores. I like to serve this omelette with a cool salad.

Vegetable oil spray

1 cup (4 ounces) sliced mushrooms

1 carrot, grated

¼ cup chopped onion

1 tablespoon curry powder

¼ teaspoon freshly ground black
pepper

¼ teaspoon ground cumin

1 cup nonfat milk

¼ cup apple juice

1 tablespoon cornstarch or
arrowroot

1 cup egg substitute

6 tablespoons prepared commercial
chutney, chopped if chunky

1 cup chopped Major Grey
chutney or Hot Bengal chutney

½ cup nonfat plain yogurt, for
garnish

¼ cup raisins or currants, for
garnish

Lightly spray a medium nonstick saucepan with vegetable oil and place over medium-high heat. Add a few tablespoons water, the mushrooms, carrot, onion, and curry powder and cook, stirring often, for about 4 minutes, until the onion is tender. Reduce the heat to low and stir in the pepper, cumin, and milk; simmer, stirring occasionally, for 3 minutes.

In a small nonstick saucepan over medium-high heat, whisk together the apple juice and cornstarch and cook, stirring constantly, about 1 minute, until just thickened. Pour the thickened mixture into the skillet, and mix well.

Meanwhile, lightly spray 12- to 14-inch nonstick skillet and place over medium heat. Add the eggs and 2 tablespoons water, and whisk until well blended. Reduce the heat to the lowest setting, tilting the pan occasionally so uncooked eggs flow to the bottom, making sure the omelette doesn't burn by occasionally lifting the bottom of the eggs with a rubber spatula. Cover and cook for 5 minutes, or until the eggs are firm.

To serve, divide the eggs into 4 wedges and place on individual plates. Top each omelette wedge with chutney, several spoonfuls curry sauce, and garnish with 2 tablespoons yogurt. Sprinkle with raisins and serve immediately.

■■ PER SERVING: Saturated Fat: Trace Total Fat: 1 gm ■■
Cholesterol: 2 mg Sodium: 353 mg Calories: 270

Egg-Filled Baked Tomato

Serves 6

Colorful, simple, and full of lively herbs, this dish is as tempting to look at as it is delicious to eat. The egg mixture puffs during baking.

4 ripe tomatoes sliced into 1¼-inch slices	¼ teaspoon basil
½ cup plus 1 tablespoon egg substitute	¼ teaspoon crushed red pepper
2 tablespoons dried herbed bread crumbs	Several drops Tabasco
2 ounces nonfat Cheddar or mozzarella, grated	Salt (optional)
¼ teaspoon oregano	Freshly ground black pepper
	Vegetable oil spray
	2 teaspoons grated nonfat Parmesan
	¼ teaspoon chopped parsley

Preheat the oven to 350°F.

With a grapefruit knife, scrape out a small ¼-inch deep by 2½-inch-wide well in the center of each tomato slice. In a small bowl, mix together the eggs, bread crumbs, cheese, oregano, basil, crushed red pepper, Tabasco, salt, if using, and pepper.

Lightly spray a large baking dish with vegetable oil. Arrange the tomato slices in the dish and spoon the egg mixture over the tomatoes. Sprinkle each with ½ teaspoon Parmesan and bake for 35 minutes. Sprinkle with parsley and serve immediately.

PER SERVING: Saturated Fat: 0 gm Total Fat: Trace
Cholesterol: 1 mg Sodium: 198 mg Calories: 54

Italian Garden Frittata

Frittata is the traditional Italian open-face omelette. With its colorful toppings, this is perfect for special occasion brunches. If you have some small, attractive, ovenproof, nonstick skillets, serve these frittatas right from the skillet at the table.

Vegetable oil spray
1 cup (4 ounces) sliced fresh
  mushrooms
1 cup sliced zucchini
½ sweet red bell pepper, julienned
½ green bell pepper, julienned
1 scallion, chopped
1 clove garlic, minced
1 cup egg substitute, lightly beaten

½ cup freshly grated nonfat
  Parmesan cheese
Freshly ground black pepper
¼ teaspoon basil
¼ teaspoon oregano
Paprika, for garnish
¼ cup sliced black or green olives,
  for garnish (optional)

In a large nonstick skillet lightly sprayed with vegetable oil, over medium-high heat, cook the mushrooms, zucchini, peppers, scallion, and garlic and several tablespoons water, stirring occasionally, about 5 minutes, until the vegetables are tender.

Meanwhile, in a medium bowl, combine the eggs with ¼ cup Parmesan and 3 tablespoons water. Add the pepper, basil, and oregano. Into individual 4-inch to 6-inch skillets, pour ¼ egg mixture (or pour into one large skillet). Spoon the vegetable mixture on top, and cook over low heat, about 4 minutes, being very careful not to burn the eggs, until they are set.

Serve from individual skillets or loosen around the edges with a rubber spatula, slide frittata onto a warmed serving plate, and cut into wedges. Sprinkle with remaining Parmesan, paprika, and olives and serve immediately.

PER SERVING: Saturated Fat: 0 gm   Total Fat: Trace
Cholesterol: 10 mg   Sodium: 316 mg   Calories: 98

Hash Browns

These spuds are simple, versatile, and quick—they're ready in 25 minutes. I like to shred them, but you can dice or julienne them as well. If you like lots of onions in your hash browns, this recipe will accommodate double the amount I call for. You can also add diced red, yellow, or green peppers.

2 large Spanish onions, shredded
  in a processor or large-hole
  grater
2 large russet potatoes, shredded in
  a processor or large-hole grater

1 teaspoon Old Bay seasoning
Salt (optional)
Freshly ground black pepper

In a large nonstick skillet in ¼ inch water, over medium heat, steam the onions, potatoes, and Old Bay seasoning, covered, for 15 minutes, stirring often (5 minutes uncovered), for about 20 minutes until the potatoes are tender and browned. Add more water if necessary. Add salt, if using, and pepper to taste and serve hot.

PER SERVING: Saturated Fat: 0 gm   Total Fat: 0 gm
Cholesterol: 0 mg   Sodium: 122 mg   Calories: 99

Potato Pancakes (Latkes)

Very crispy yet not greasy, these are a fine adaptation of the classic latke. Top with nonfat sour cream and homemade applesauce to serve in the traditional style, or serve with a crisp salad and Egg-Filled Baked Tomatoes (page 346).

4 large all-purpose potatoes (not
   baking)
1 onion, grated
2 to 3 egg whites, lightly beaten
¼ cup egg substitute

4 tablespoons all-purpose flour
Salt (optional)
Freshly ground black pepper
Butter-flavored cooking spray

Preheat the oven to 375°F.

Peel and grate the potatoes and onion, using the larger holes of a four-sided grater or a food processor. If the grated potato is not to be used immediately, immerse in a bowl of ice water; when ready to use (up to 2 hours), drain and squeeze out the excess moisture first with your hands, then again with a clean cloth or paper towel.

In a large bowl, mix together the grated potatoes, onions, egg whites, eggs, flour, salt, if using, and pepper. Spray a nonstick skillet with the butter-flavored spray and place over medium-low heat. When the pan is hot, spoon the potatoes into the skillet to form 4-inch pancakes. Cook about 5 minutes until brown; turn and brown the other side.

(Or you may make one large pancake by covering the pan and cooking over very low heat for 20 minutes, until brown. Turn and brown the other side.)

For crisper pancakes, transfer the cooked pancakes to a nonstick baking sheet and place in the oven for 10 to 15 minutes. Serve immediately.

PER SERVING: Saturated Fat: 0 gm   Total Fat: 0 gm
Cholesterol: 0 mg   Sodium: 59 mg   Calories: 198

Hearty Corned Beef Hash

This is a hearty and satisfying breakfast, brunch, or lunch, or dinner dish. Use corned beef from lean flank or top round rather than fattier brisket.

2 cooked (baked or boiled) potatoes, diced	1 cup diced cooked corned beef or lean roast beef
½ cup chopped yellow onion	Salt (optional)
1 scallion, finely chopped	Freshly ground black pepper

In a large nonstick skillet in ¼ inch water, over medium heat, steam the potatoes and onion for about 5 minutes, until the vegetables are tender. Add more water if necessary to prevent sticking. Add the scallion, corned beef, salt, if using, and pepper and cook until heated through. Serve immediately.

PER SERVING: Saturated Fat: 2 gm   Total Fat: 6 gm
Cholesterol: 30 mg   Sodium: 347 mg   Calories: 130

Calico Quilt Home Fries

These country-style potatoes are so hearty that I often serve them as the main dish accompanied by fresh fruit and Salt Biscuits (page 362).

Vegetable oil spray	2 tomatoes, diced
4 Idaho potatoes, scrubbed, diced, and patted dry with paper towel	1 teaspoon prepared mustard
	¼ teaspoon sugar
1 large onion, diced	Salt (optional)
2 cloves garlic, crushed	Freshly ground black pepper
1 6-ounce jar artichoke hearts, drained and sliced	⅓ cup grated nonfat Parmesan cheese
1 teaspoon fresh basil	½ cup nonfat sour cream

Preheat the oven to 425°F.

Lightly spray a large nonstick ovenproof skillet with vegetable oil and place over medium-high heat. Add the potatoes and lightly spray again; toss and lightly spray again. Cook, undisturbed for about 3 minutes, until a crunchy crust has formed on one side. Turn and cook until a crust forms on all the other sides so the potatoes look golden. Stir in the onion and continue cooking for about 10 minutes. Add the garlic, artichoke hearts, basil, tomatoes, mustard, sugar, salt, if using, and pepper and cook about 4 minutes, until all ingredients are heated through.

Sprinkle the mixture with Parmesan, place the skillet in the oven, and bake for 10 minutes. Remove to individual serving plates and top each with 2 tablespoons sour cream.

PER SERVING: Saturated Fat: 1 gm   Total Fat: 2 gm
Cholesterol: 4 mg   Sodium: 193 mg   Calories: 128

Triple-Decker French Toast

This showpiece of a brunch dish is baked rather than fried and, in spite of its rich texture and flavor, is surprisingly low in fat and calories. It is best assembled the night before as the ingredients meld and solidify slightly but can be prepared in 30 minutes on brunch day.

12 slices white bread
3 ounces nonfat cream cheese,
   room temperature
1 cup dried cherries or cranberries
½ to ⅓ cup brown sugar

4 slices (about 3 ounces total)
   lean, low-salt baked ham, ⅛-
   to ¼-inch thick, all visible fat
   removed
Vegetable oil spray
2 cups nonfat milk
1 cup egg substitute
1½ cups maple syrup

Preheat the oven to 450°F.

For each serving, spread a slice of bread with 1 tablespoon cream cheese, sprinkle with 1 tablespoon dried cherries and 1 teaspoon brown sugar, and top with a slice of ham. Spread a second slice of bread with 1 tablespoon cream cheese, 1 tablespoon cherries, and 1 teaspoon brown sugar. Place this layer, filling side up, on top of the first slice. Top the stack with a third bread slice. Repeat for the remaining 3 sandwiches. Reserve the leftover cherries and brown sugar. Lightly spray a 7-inch by 11-inch baking dish, and mix together the milk and eggs. Place the sandwiches in the milk mixture for 15 minutes, spooning the milk mixture over all the layers.

Top each sandwich with 1 tablespoon reserved brown sugar and tent with a piece of foil. Bake 15 to 20 minutes or until puffed and golden brown.

In a small microwave-safe container, heat the reserved cherries with the maple syrup at high for 60 to 90 seconds, just before serving (or heat in a small nonstick saucepan). Cut each stack into 4 triangles. Serve hot with the dried cherry syrup.

PER SERVING: Saturated Fat: 1 gm   Total Fat: 5 gm
   Cholesterol: 21 mg   Sodium: 861 mg   Calories: 802

Blueberry Pancakes

My favorite blueberry pancakes are made with so many berries that both the pan and pancakes are nearly purple. Add extra berries on top, and serve with pure maple or nutmeg syrup (which is a nutmeg-flavored corn syrup).

1 cup whole wheat or all-purpose
   flour
½ teaspoon baking powder
½ teaspoon baking soda
1 cup nonfat milk or low-fat
   buttermilk
¼ cup egg substitute
1 tablespoon canola, rapeseed, or
   safflower oil

1 teaspoon sugar
½ teaspoon vanilla
Vegetable oil spray
1 pint washed and drained fresh
   blueberries, laid out on a plate
   for ease
Warmed maple or nutmeg syrup

In a large bowl, mix together the flour, baking powder, and baking soda. In another bowl, mix together the milk, eggs, and oil. Add the liquid ingredients to the dry ingredients and stir until well blended.

Lightly spray a large nonstick skillet with vegetable oil and place over medium-high heat. When the pan is very hot, pour in enough batter to make 4 4-inch pancakes and immediately sprinkle with a large handful of berries, one at a time, enough to cover 80 to 90 percent of the pancake. Cook the pancakes until the batter stops bubbling; turn and cook a few minutes more. Serve immediately with warmed syrup.

PER SERVING: Saturated Fat: 0.5 gm   Total Fat: 4 gm
Cholesterol: 1 mg   Sodium: 276 mg   Calories: 206

Florida Sunshine Breakfast Rum Cake

A fruity, moist cake, this breakfast treat is soaked through with a sweet rum-and-orange-flavored glaze and then topped with chopped pecans. Plan to make this a day in advance since the cake must sit for at least 2 hours in order to absorb all the wonderful flavors.

Baker's Joy spray

2 cups plus 2 tablespoons sifted all-purpose flour

½ teaspoon baking powder

1 teaspoon baking soda

½ teaspoon salt (optional)

¼ teaspoon nutmeg

¼ teaspoon mace

½ teaspoon cinnamon

Pinch allspice

1 tablespoon orange zest

1 orange, peeled, seeded, and chopped

1 cup dried cranberries or tart cherries

¼ cup canola oil

⅓ cup unsweetened applesauce

¾ cup granulated sugar

¼ cup egg substitute

1 large egg white

1 cup fresh orange juice

½ cup coarsely chopped pecans (optional)

ORANGE GLAZE:

⅓ cup fresh orange juice

2 tablespoons fresh lemon juice

2 tablespoons granulated sugar

2 tablespoons dark rum

TOPPING:

¼ cup granulated sugar

½ teaspoon cinnamon

¼ cup finely chopped pecans

Preheat the oven to 350°F.

Lightly spray a 9-inch by 13-inch cake pan with Baker's Joy.

In a medium bowl, sift together 2 cups flour, baking powder, baking soda, salt, if using, nutmeg, mace, cinnamon, and allspice and set aside. In a food processor, combine the orange zest, orange sections, and cranberries; pulse to chop to ⅛-inch bits (being careful not to puree the mixture).

In a large bowl, whisk together the oil, applesauce, sugar, and eggs. Beginning and ending with the flour, alternately add the flour mixture and the orange juice to the applesauce mixture, beating well after each addition. Stir in the chopped orange-cranberry mixture and the nuts. The batter should be thin.

Spoon the batter into the prepared pan and bake on the center rack for 35 to 40 minutes, or until a cake tester or toothpick inserted in the center comes out clean. Remove to a wire rack to cool slightly.

Meanwhile, in a small nonstick saucepan over medium heat, combine the orange juice, lemon juice, sugar, and rum, and cook, stirring, until the sugar dissolves.

In a small bowl, stir together the sugar, cinnamon, and pecans and set aside.

Prick the cake top all over with a toothpick and pour the glaze over the cake. Sprinkle on the topping mixture and let the cake sit for at least 2 hours or overnight to absorb the glaze.

PER SERVING: Saturated Fat: 0.5 gm   Total Fat: 7 gm
Cholesterol: 0 mg   Sodium: 138 mg   Calories: 284

Pineapple Upside Down Coffee Cake

Serves 10

This is reminiscent of the dense and sweet pineapple upside down cake Grandmother Gracie used to make. If you can't find coconut flavoring extract, leave it out. The dessert thrives nicely without it. If you have a 12-inch iron skillet or a 10-inch square baking dish, use it for this cake.

1⅓ cups sifted all-purpose flour
⅔ cup sugar
2 teaspoons baking powder
⅔ cup low-fat buttermilk
¼ cup plus 1½ tablespoons liquid
   diet margarine
½ cup egg substitute
1½ teaspoons vanilla

¼ teaspoon coconut flavoring
1 16-ounce can pineapple slices,
   drained, reserving 2 tablespoons
   of the juice
12 to 20 pecan halves
1 cup dark brown sugar, loosely
   packed

Preheat the oven to 375°F.

Into a large bowl, sift the flour, sugar, and baking powder and stir with a rubber spatula until well mixed.

In another large bowl, stir together the buttermilk, ¼ cup liquid margarine, eggs, vanilla, and coconut flavoring. Stir the liquid ingredients into the dry ingredients and beat for 2 minutes, breaking up any lumps.

Lightly grease a 9-inch by 12-inch baking pan or 12-inch iron skillet with ½ tablespoon liquid margarine, rubbing the margarine with a paper towel over the bottom and sides of the pan.

Arrange the pineapple slices in the bottom of the pan (making any design you wish, such as whole rings around the outside and a ring in the center, or half rings, one next to another). In the center of each ring, in between the rings, and at the edges of the rings, place an unbroken pecan half, rounded side down.

Drizzle the remaining 1 tablespoon liquid margarine over the pineapple and nuts. Spoon over the pineapple and sprinkle with brown sugar. Carefully pour the batter into the pan, making sure all the nuts, brown sugar, and pineapple are covered.

Reduce the oven heat to 350°F. and bake for 40 to 50 minutes. When done, remove to a wire rack to cool for 15 to 20 minutes. Slide a flat rubber spatula around the edges of the cake, place a larger serving plate on top of the pan, and quickly invert the cake onto the plate, removing any pineapple rings, nuts, or brown sugar that has stuck to the cake pan and placing it back on the cake. Serve warm or cold.

■■ PER SERVING: Saturated Fat: I gm   Total Fat: 8 gm   ■■
Cholesterol: O mg   Sodium: 2OI mg   Calories: 3O2

Southern Oyster Sampler

■■ *Serves 4* ■■

Every southerner I know delights in this breakfast combo of oysters, scrambled eggs, grits, and country ham. As hearty as it sounds——and it is——this whole meal takes less than 30 minutes to prepare and serve.

Vegetable oil spray

1 cup regular (not instant) hominy
   grits

4 cups water, vegetable, or
   defatted chicken stock

Salt (optional)

Freshly ground black pepper

12 ounces fresh shucked medium
   oysters, blotted dry with paper
   towel (about 24 medium-size
   oysters)

Baker's Joy

2 cups crushed soda cracker crumbs

½ teaspoon butter

2 cups egg substitute

1 ounce cooked country ham,
   finely julienned (optional)

4 sprigs watercress

1 lemon, cut into 4 wedges

1 orange, cut into 4 wedges

Preheat the oven to 400°F.

Lightly spray a flat baking sheet with vegetable oil.

In a large microwave-safe container, stir together the grits, water, salt, if using, and pepper to taste and stir. Cook at high 10 to 14 minutes, stirring every 4 minutes, until creamy and thick. (Or in a large nonstick saucepan, cook over medium heat for 15 minutes.) Cover and set aside.

Arrange the oysters on a flat plate and spray lightly with Baker's Joy (or spray with vegetable oil spray and dust with flour). Place the cracker crumbs on a plate. Roll the oysters in the crumbs to coat and arrange on the prepared baking sheet about 1 inch apart; lightly spray again and bake, about 6 inches from the heat, 10 to 12 minutes, or until well browned (watching to be sure they don't burn).

Meanwhile, in a large nonstick skillet over medium–high heat, melt the butter and rub it around the bottom of the skillet with a rubber spatula. Add the eggs and salt, if using; reduce the heat and cook, occasionally stirring with a whisk to lift the eggs off the bottom, for about 4 minutes, or until the eggs are firm.

To serve, mound the grits on the side of individual plates; place one quarter of the julienned ham on the grits; line the oysters down the center; and arrange the eggs on the other side. Pepper liberally. Tuck a sprig of watercress under the grits; place a lemon wedge on the cress for the oysters, add an orange wedge for color, and serve immediately.

■■   PER SERVING: Saturated Fat: 2 gm   Total Fat: 8 gm   ■■
Cholesterol: 51 mg   Sodium: 998 mg   Calories: 422

Breakfast Pizza

■■   *Serves 6*   ■■

Kids love this low-fat breakfast. Have the ingredients ready to cook. It uses the cooked bread dough (Boboli, focaccia) available in most supermarkets.

Olive oil spray
1 medium onion, diced
1 red, green, or yellow bell
   pepper, diced, seeds reserved
1 cup egg substitute
1 tablespoon chopped fresh basil or
   1 teaspoon dried

2 medium zucchini, pricked
1 9-inch by 9-inch piece of
   focaccia (about 1 pound) or
   1 10-inch by 12-inch thin
   Boboli or pizza shell, prebaked
4 plum tomatoes, thinly sliced
Salt (optional)

Freshly ground black pepper

4 thin slices Canadian bacon
(about 2 ounces), julienned into
1/8-inch-wide strips

12 to 20 julienned red bell pepper
strips, for garnish

10 to 12 pitted chopped black
olives, for garnish

1/4 cup chopped cilantro or parsley,
for garnish

Preheat the oven to 400°F.

Lightly spray a baking sheet with olive oil and set aside.

Lightly spray a medium nonstick skillet with olive oil and place over medium-high heat. Add the onion, lightly spraying it, and sauté for 4 minutes, stirring frequently. Add the bell pepper and seeds and cook, adding a teaspoon water when needed, 3 minutes more. Stir in the eggs and basil, and cook, stirring, until the eggs are set.

In a microwave-safe container, soften the zucchini at high for 2 to 2½ minutes.

Place the focaccia on the prepared baking sheet and spoon the egg mixture on top. Thinly slice the softened zucchini into 1/4-inch-thick rounds. Place alternating rounds of zucchini and tomato on top of the egg mixture, with the vegetables overlapping slightly. Sprinkle the vegetables with salt, if using, and pepper and arrange the bacon strips evenly over all. Very lightly spray the top of the pizza with olive oil. (The pizza can be made up to a day ahead, wrapped in plastic, and refrigerated.) Bake 20 minutes if at room temperature or 25 to 30 minutes if chilled. Slice, add garnishes, and serve hot.

PER SLICE: Saturated Fat: 1 gm   Total Fat: 4 gm
Cholesterol: 9 mg   Sodium: 473 mg   Calories: 194

Stacked Breakfast

This tower of familiar breakfast foods couldn't be more fun to make for company or a special occasion. It takes about 35 to 40 minutes to prepare and can be made up to 2 days in advance. Waxed paper helps keep the omelettes flat, but foil also works.

Vegetable oil spray
1 cup egg substitute
8 ounces mushrooms, thinly sliced
8 ounces low-fat sausage (such as
  Sausage Slims, page 361),
  diced

1 cup nonfat cottage cheese
2 cloves garlic, minced
2 scallions, finely chopped
3 8-inch flour tortillas
½ cup low-fat mozzarella cheese,
  shredded

Preheat the oven to 400°F.

In a medium nonstick skillet lightly sprayed with vegetable oil over medium heat, pour ⅓ cup egg and swirl around the pan to evenly distribute. Reduce the heat to very low, cover, and cook about 30 seconds, or until firm but not dry. Remove and set aside between sheets of waxed paper. Repeat the process 2 more times to make a total of 3 flat omelettes. With a scissors, trim any dried or uneven egg on the edges. Lightly spray the skillet again, add the mushrooms and sausage and sauté over medium heat for 5 minutes, stirring; remove from the heat and drain.

Meanwhile, in a food processor or blender, process the cottage cheese about 3 minutes; add the garlic and scallions and pulse to mix, but don't puree.

Lightly spray a flat baking sheet with vegetable oil and heat the tortillas in the oven about 2 minutes. Remove, and place in each tortilla one of the egg omelettes, one third of the mushroom and sausage mixture, and one third of the cottage cheese mixture. Repeat layers, ending with the cottage cheese mixture. Sprinkle with mozzarella and bake 15 minutes or until the cheese has melted. Serve hot.

PER SERVING: Saturated Fat: 3 gm   Total Fat: 8 gm
Cholesterol: 32 mg   Sodium: 501 mg   Calories: 191

Sausage Slims

If you love pork sausage, you'll enjoy these homemade slims, especially when you serve them in a pool of maple syrup along with syrup-drenched waffles or pancakes. As with all sausages, they do better stored in the refrigerator for several hours or overnight to allow flavors to blend.

1 pound lean pork tenderloin, all exterior fat, gristle, and membrane removed, very coarsely chopped

½ teaspoon finely crumbled sage

½ teaspoon finely crumbled summer savory

¼ teaspoon finely crumbled marjoram

¼ teaspoon finely crumbled thyme

¼ teaspoon ground bay leaf

¼ teaspoon ground nutmeg

½ to 1 teaspoon brown sugar or maple syrup

½ teaspoon crushed red pepper

¼ teaspoon freshly ground black pepper

½ teaspoon salt (optional)

1 egg white

1 tablespoon canola oil

1 cup finely crushed corn flakes

6 tablespoons unsweetened applesauce

Vegetable oil spray

Preheat the oven to 375°F.

In a large bowl, mix together the pork, sage, savory, marjoram, thyme, bay leaf, nutmeg, sugar, crushed red pepper, black pepper, salt, if using, egg white, oil, corn flakes, and applesauce. (Mixing by hand works best; some suggest wearing plastic gloves when working with raw meat.) Refrigerate several hours or overnight. Form the meat into as many 1½-inch-round by ¼-inch-thick sausage patties as possible.

Lightly spray a large baking sheet with vegetable oil. Arrange patties on the sheet and bake 8 to 10 minutes until brown and crisp; turn and cook on both sides. Serve immediately.

PER PATTY: Saturated Fat: 1 gm   Total Fat: 4 gm
Cholesterol: 30 mg   Sodium: 61 mg   Calories: 100

Salt Biscuits

■■   ■■

There is nothing more comforting than a hot, tender homemade biscuit dripping with wild honey or slathered with mustard and topped with a sliver of country ham or topped with hot white sauce and diced poultry.

Baker's Joy
1 tablespoon all-purpose flour
2½ cups self-rising flour

¼ cup vegetable shortening or margarine
⅔ cup nonfat milk or buttermilk
¼ cup nonfat plain yogurt

Preheat the oven to 500°F.

Lightly spray a baking sheet or muffin tin with Baker's Joy. In a large bowl, combine the flours, shortening, milk, and yogurt, and stir with a whisk about 5 minutes until the flecks of shortening are small and evenly distributed. The dough should be sticky and be left on your fingers when touched. Swirl the dough around the bowl and, if too sticky, add a little more flour. With your fingers, shape dough into walnut-size pieces and place on the sheet, 3 across in 4 rows. The dough will be uneven looking. With the back or front of your fingers, press into the flour, then lightly press your flour-covered fingers on each muffin to flatten (and smooth), to ½-inch high. Bake for 10 minutes. Check the oven after 8 minutes and remove when golden.

■■   PER BISCUIT: Saturated Fat: 1 gm   Total Fat: 4 gm   ■■
Cholesterol: 0 mg   Sodium: 315 mg   Calories: 129

Oat Bran-Fruit Muffins

These muffins are slightly sweet, redolent of almond and packed with berries. Even better, they are quick and easy to make. If you substitute fresh cranberries for dried, add ¹/₃ cup sugar and 1 teaspoon grated lemon zest to the recipe. If you use fresh blueberries instead of dried, add ¹/₄ cup sugar and ¹/₄ teaspoon grated lemon zest to the recipe.

¼ cup all-purpose flour
¼ cup wheat bran flour
¼ cup oat bran
¾ cup quick-cooking oats
⅓ cup packed brown sugar
1 teaspoon baking soda
½ cup nonfat milk
¼ cup egg substitute

3 tablespoons canola oil
½ teaspoon almond extract
1 cup dried cranberries, blueberries, cherries, strawberries, or raisins
½ cup coarsely chopped walnuts or pecans (optional)
Vegetable oil spray

Preheat the oven to 375°F.

In a large bowl, combine the flours, oat bran, oats, sugar, and baking soda. In a small bowl, combine the milk, eggs, oil, and almond extract. Stir the milk mixture into the flour mixture until just moistened. Fold in the dried berries and nuts, if using.

Lightly spray muffin cups with vegetable oil and spoon the mixture into each cup, filling it ¾ full. Bake for 15 minutes or until light brown.

PER MUFFIN: Saturated Fat: Trace   Total Fat: 4 gm
Cholesterol: 0 mg   Sodium: 120 mg   Calories: 132

To order a catalog offering many of Lynn Fischer's favorite kitchen tools and specialty foods, call 1-800-835-2967, and ask for the *Healthy Indulgences* offer. Or write Healthy Indulgences, P.O. Box 4514, Decatur, IL 62525-4514.

Index

Bean(s) (*continued*)

garbanzo, hummus, 20

garbanzo, and pork sopa, Portuguese, 83

green, bundles, 138

green, southern-style, 137

and rice, 203

soup, French, 81

soup, Italian, 86

vegetarian chili, 206–7

white, grilled tuna with artichoke hearts and, 226–27

Beef:

and barley soup, 82

corned, hearty hash, 350

filet mignon au poivre, 262

gravy, 298–99

hamburgers with fixin's, 265

Marengo on toasted French bread, 264–65

old-fashioned meat loaf, 266

spaghetti and meatballs with marinara sauce, 168–69

stock, 53

stroganoff, 261

stuffed flank steak Kirov, 263

and vegetable stew, Tuscan, 84–85

Beet(s):

magenta soup, 61

with orange, gingered, 133

vinegar, 90–91

Berry:

pastry with yogurt cheese cream, 315–16

sauce, duck with, 256

Biscuits, salt, 362

Blackberry cobbler, 324

Black-eyed pea salsa, 284

Black raspberry sorbet, 332

Blueberry:

pancakes, 353

-peach buckle, 323

-peach layered torte, 325

vinegar, 91

Blue cheese or Roquefort dressing, 115

Bok choy, steamed, and oysters, 131

Bourbon beans, confetti, 205

Breakfasts and brunches, 337–63

fat and calories in, 340

healthy choices for, 337–39

in restaurants, 339

Brie and asparagus omelette, 341

Broccoli:

orzo with chicken and, 163

soup, cream of, 63

Brownies, chocolaty chocolate, 326

Bulgur:

soup, Italian, 72

tabbouleh, 195

Cabbage:

red, sweet and sour, 134

vegetable-stuffed, 132–33

Caesar salad, 94–95

Cakes:

coffee, pineapple upside down, 356–57

Florida sunshine breakfast rum, 354–55

gingerbread, 318

Grandma Ocean's chocolate, 316–17

Caper(s):

tomato, and olive sauce, vermicelli with, 180

and tricolor pepper salsa, 282

turkey fillets with raisins, pine nuts and, 251

vinegar, 91

Caponata:

hunky, 15

potato bouchées with, 37

Carrot(s):

chunky potatoes with turnips and, 149

ham, and asparagus sauté with honey-mustard sauce, 272

Catfish, poached, with lemon-rosemary mignonette, 213

Caviar:

eggplant, 16–17

red, and salmon dip, 21

Cheddar scalloped potatoes, 145

Cheese:

macaroni and, 162

onion soup with, 67

Cheesecakes:

lemon-Amaretto, 320–21

pumpkin and orange swirl, 319–20

Cherry, sour, pie, 310–11

Chicken, 234–35, 237

baked "fried," 242

Beth Mendelson's fricassee, 238

Caribbean rum with pineapple, 244–45

gravy, 296–97

Indonesian-style, in a parcel, 240–41

Key Largo salad, 108

lime-grilled, with mango-basil salsa, 247

mango-sauced, breast, 248

and noodles salad, sesame-peanut, 109

orzo with broccoli and, 163

roast, with rosemary and thyme, 239

soup, 57–58
stock, 52
Szechwan sweet and sour, 243–44
taco stack, 246
Chili:
and steak relish, spicy, 286
vegetarian, 206–7
Chive and onion vinegar, 91
Chocolate:
chocolaty brownies, 326
cookie open-face ice cream sandwiches, 333
Grandma Ocean's cake, 316–17
Cholesterol, 6, 210, 260
Chowders:
Grandma Gracie's corn, 60
New England, clam, 75
Chutney-curry omelette, 344–45
Cider or raspberry vinegar, 92
Clam(s):
dip, 17
New England, chowder, 75
sauce, linguine with, 165–66
Cocktail sauce, 290–91
Coffee cake, pineapple upside down, 356–57
Coleslaw with raisin vinaigrette, 103
Condiments, 277–78; *see also* Sauces
Cookie(s):
chocolate open-face ice cream sandwiches, 333
oatmeal, 328
Corn:
coins on shrimp, 32–33
Grandma Gracie's chowder, 60
and tomato salad, spicy, 95
Corned beef hash, hearty, 350
Cornish game hens, 236
Circassian, 253–54
Couscous:
lamb, with tomatoes, 270–71
saffron, with seven vegetables, 190
Crab:
and avocado gazpacho, 76
hot Maryland dip, 19
she-crab soup, 78
Cranberry:
-orange sauce, Lil Smith's, 294–95
-pear relish, pecan-crusted turkey fillets with, 249
Cream:
of broccoli soup, 63
of pumpkin or squash soup, 64–65

sauce, heavenly peas and onions in, 142
sour, dressing, 111–12, 120
-style mushroom-barley soup, 71
yogurt cheese, fresh berry pastry with, 315–16
Crookneck soup with croutons, curry, 66
Croutons, garlic, 94
Cucumber(s):
bull's-eye, 24–25
-horseradish sauce, creamy, 290
orange, fennel seed, and red onion salad, 101
Oriental salad, 99
-ribboned scallops, 31
Curry, curried:
apricot mayonnaise, 287
-chutney omelette, 344–45
crookneck soup with croutons, 66
dip, steamed artichokes with, 129

Dan dan noodles, 172
Date-apple bars, 327
Desserts, 303–35
ingredients in, 304–5
low-fat alternatives, 305–6
Deviled eggs à la Virginia Von Fremd, 27
Dijon mustard mayonnaise, 288
Dijon salad dressing, 110
Dill:
dressing, Lillian Smith's five-vinegar, 122
smoked salmon, and leek strudels, 45
vinegar, 91
Dips:
black bean, 14
clam, 17
curry, steamed artichokes with, 129
hot Maryland crab, 19
salmon and red caviar, 21
tofu-yogurt vegetable, 22
tonnato, 23
vegetable-onion, 25
Dressings, 87–93, 115–24
blue cheese or Roquefort, 115
classic vinaigrette, 116–17
cold duck sauce, 118
creamy herb, 104
five-vinegar dill, 122
green goddess, 121
herb or Italian, 116
oil in, 89–90, 93
orange-yogurt, 106
poppy-seed, 119

Olive oil, spinach with garlic and, 150–51
Olive(s):
    filling, phyllo tartlets with sun-dried tomatoes and, 35
    Kalamata, pasta with tomatoes, peppers, spinach and, 182–83
    tomato, and caper sauce, vermicelli with, 180
Omelettes:
    asparagus and Brie, 341
    curry-chutney, 344–45
Onion(s):
    caramelized, 141
    and chive vinegar, 91
    and peas in cream sauce, heavenly, 142
    red, cucumber, orange, and fennel seed salad, 101
    soup with cheese, 67
    -vegetable dip, 25
Orange:
    -cranberry sauce, Lil Smith's, 294–95
    cucumber, fennel seed, and red onion salad, 101
    gingered beets with, 133
    -Grand Marnier tart, 312–13
    and pumpkin swirl cheesecake, 319–20
    soy sauce, 296
    soy sauce and red grapes, tuna steaks with, 227
    -yogurt dressing, lentil salad with, 106
    zest, wild rice with quinoa, pecans and, 202–3
Orange roughy St. Tropez, 222
Oregano vinegar, 92
Orzo:
    with chicken and broccoli, 163
    reggae salad with pork, mango and, 114–15
Oyster(s):
    Rockefeller soup, 79
    southern, sampler, 357–58
    steamed bok choy and, 131

Pancakes, 338
    blueberry, 353
    potato (latkes), 349
Pappardelle with roasted red peppers, artichoke hearts, and cannellini beans, 164–65
Party food, 12, 13, 42–44
Pasta, 157–83
    basics, 158–59
    chicken soup with, 58
    dried, 158
    fresh, 158, 161
    sauces for, 171, 178
    sauce Siciliano, 301
    with tomatoes, olive, and caper sauce, 180
    see also specific pastas
Pastry, fresh berry, with yogurt cheese cream, 315–16
Peach:
    -blueberry buckle, 323
    -blueberry layered torte, 325
    salsa, 281
    tartlets, 314
Peach brandy and nectarine sauce, pork chops in, 274
Peanut-sesame chicken and noodles salad, 109
Pear brandy, almond bananas with, 330
Pear-cranberry relish, pecan-crusted turkey fillets with, 249
Peas:
    black-eyed, salsa, 284
    and onions in cream sauce, heavenly, 142
    Shanghai snow, 150
    snow, salmon and jicama salad with watercress and, 112–13
    sugar snap, and black bean salad, 107
Pecan(s):
    -crusted turkey fillets with pear-cranberry relish, 249
    flounder, 216
    wild rice with quinoa, orange zest and, 202–3
Penne, with sausage and roasted red bell pepper sauce, 166–67
Pepper(s), 3, 49
    filet mignon au poivre, 262
    hot, vinegar, 91
    jalapeño relish, 295
    pasta with tomatoes, spinach, and Kalamata olives, 182–83
    and polenta, 192–93
    roasted red, pappardelle with artichoke hearts, cannellini beans and, 164–65
    roasted red bell, and sausage sauce, penne with, 166–67
    tricolor, and caper salsa, 282
    wedges with Romesco filling, 29
Pesto:
    emerald, Asian lobster soup with, 77
    pita triangles, 33

Rice, 185, 187–88
  basmati, with shrimp and shiitake
    mushrooms, 196
  beans and, 203
  black beans and, 208
  chicken soup with, 58
  fried, 197
  Indonesian fried, 198
  pilaf, 199
  saffron, 200–201
  Spanish, 201
  with sun-dried tomatoes, 200
  wild see Wild rice
Risotto and summer vegetables, 198–99
Romano, marinara, 300
Romesco filling, pepper wedges with, 29
Root vegetables, scalloped, 156
Roquefort or blue cheese dressing, 115
Rosemary:
  -lemon mignonette, poached catfish
    with, 213
  roast chicken with thyme and, 239
Rum:
  bananas, 331
  Caribbean chicken with pineapple,
    244–45
  Florida sunshine breakfast cake, 354–55
Russian dressing, 117

Saffron:
  couscous with seven vegetables, 190
  rice, 200–201
Salad dressings, see Dressings
Salads, 87–115
Salmon:
  glazed grilled fillets, 223
  grilled, 225
  honeyed, on a bed of herbed zucchini,
    221
  and jicama salad with snow peas and
    watercress, 112–13
  mousse, 40
  poached steaks, 224
  and red caviar dip, 21
  smoked, leek, and dill strudels, 45
Salsas, 277–84
  black-eyed pea, 284
  cruda, 279
  mango-basil, lime-grilled chicken with,
    247
  peach, 281
  pineapple, sweet potato bundles with
    yogurt cheese and, 28–29

Rita Calvert's tropical mango,
  283
  tricolor pepper and caper, 282
  yellow, 280
Salt, 3, 6, 49, 304
Salt biscuits, 362
Sauces, 277–301
  applesauce, 294
  berry, duck with, 256
  bold barbecue, 291
  clam, linguine with, 165–66
  cocktail, 290–91
  cranberry-orange, Lil Smith's, 294–
    95
  cream, heavenly peas and onions in,
    142
  creamy horseradish-cucumber, 290
  curried apricot mayonnaise, 287
  Dijon mustard mayonnaise, 288
  fusilli mushroom marinara, 179
  Galveston salve and sopping, 275
  garlic, Chinese eggplant with, 136
  Hollandaise, 293
  honey-mustard, 272, 289
  mango chicken breast, 248
  marinara, spaghetti and meatballs with,
    168–69
  marinara Romano, 300
  mustard, monkfish with, 220
  nectarine and peach brandy, 274
  orange soy, 296
  Oriental hot mustard, 288
  for pasta, 171, 178
  pasta Siciliano, 301
  pepper wedges with Romesco filling,
    29
  raita, 285
  raspberry, 334
  sausage and roasted red bell pepper,
    166–67
  sherry, halibut with, 218
  tartar, 286–87
  tomato, olive, and caper, 180
  trout almandine, 229
  watercress, halibut with, 217
  white, 292
  see also Dips; Dressings; Gravy; Salsas
Sausage:
  Amalfi coast salad with fennel and, 96–
    97
  and roasted red bell pepper sauce,
    penne with, 166–67
  slims, 361